RUSSELL OF THE TIMES

War Despatches and Diaries

CAROLINE CHAPMAN

Bell & Hyman Limited

Published in 1984 by
BELL & HYMAN LIMITED
Denmark House
37-39 Queen Elizabeth Street
London SE1 2QB

ISBN: 0 7135 1439 6

Produced by Cameron Books
2a Roman Way, London N7 8XG
Designed by Ian Cameron
Managing editor: Jill Hollis
Editor: Janet Law

Printed and bound by R.J. Acford
Terminus Road Industrial Estate,
Chichester, Sussex.

I should like to thank the Archivist of *The
Times*, Mr Gordon Philips, for his friendly
advice and help in the early stages of this
book. Alan Hankinson's excellent and extensively researched biography of William Russell
provided me with a number of letter and anecdotes previously unknown to me, and I am
very grateful. I would also like to thank the
India Office Library, the National Army
Museum and Miss Frances Dimond of the
Royal Archives, Windsor.

To the two military men in my life.

Picture acknowledgements:

Reproduced by gracious of H.M. the Queen,
    Royal Archives, Windsor 61 left, 160, 166,
    172 right, 173, 177; Royal Library, Windsor
    161
Archives Départementales des Ardennes 145
    left
BBC Hulton Picture Library 11, 17 right, 20,
    36, 37, 39, 40 bottom, 42, 44, 48, 51 top, 52,
    53, 56, 68, 80, 84, 93, 96, 97, 111, 134 top,
    148, 150. 152, 154, 157, 158, 159, 164, 165
    right, 169, 172 left, 181
British Library, India Office Library &
Records 60 top, 65, 85, 87, 94, 175
British Museum 16
Detroit Public Library, Burton Historical
    Collection (photograph: Nemo Warr) 102
John Frost Historical Newspaper Service 129
    left
Imperial War Museum 46, 51 bottom, 54
Sir Bruce Ingram/Marlborough Fine Art
    (photograph: B.T. Batsford) 30
Library of Congress 107, 108, 120, 123, 129
    right
Mansell Collection jacket (front), 8, 19, 23,
    29, 32, 33, 34, 40 top, 47, 58, 60 bottom, 61
    right, 67, 83, 88, 145 right, 146, 151, 168 left
    and right, 183 left and right
Musée de l'Armée, Paris 139
Museum of City of New York 119
Museum of the Confederacy 103
National Archives 121, 126, 131
National Army Museum jacket (back), 24, 28,
    38, 41, 50, 64, 69, 70 right, 73, 74, 75, 77, 79
    bottom, 91, 180
National Portrait Gallery 17 left
Popperfoto 133, 134 left and right
Royal Photographic Society 43
Science Museum 45
Staatsbibliothek, Berlin 137
Süddeutscher Verlag 143
The Times 98, 186
Valentine Museum, Cook Collection 110
Victoria & Albert Museum frontispiece, 9, 57,
    149
Sam Wagstaff, New York 104, 109
Wehrgeschichtliches Museum, Rastatt 142
Western Reserve Historical Society 113

Endpapers:
'Publication of The Times—outside the office.'
From G.A. Sala's *Twice Around the Clock*,
1857.

Frontispiece:
William Russell dressed in an odd assortment
of clothes photographed in the Crimea by
Roger Fenton.

Contents

Introduction

In the mid nineteenth century when William Howard Russell made his first appearance in Fleet Street, newspapers bore little resemblance to those of today. All information, no matter what it was, appeared in identical sober columns with no banner headlines, only the occasional line drawing or map and, above all, no photographs.

Scholarly and conservative, *The Times* in the 1850s prided itself on its accuracy and lack of sensationalism. Read primarily by the upper classes, it was not only the undisputed king of the newspaper world, but had a circulation twice that of all its rivals together.

Until the Crimean War, although one or two isolated attempts had been made by the richer British newspapers to send a 'special' correspondent to the actual scene of a war, editors had relied mainly on official despatches from the commander in the field, extracts from soldiers' letters, or the services of part-time officers with a literary bent. Years later, during the Zulu War of 1879, Russell voiced his criticism of this system of gathering information:

> I hold a very strong opinion that the combination of staff employ and newspaper service is in no way advantageous to the public. There is no reason why half-pay officers should not act as correspondents with an army in the field, although it is obvious that if they intend to resume active service their criticisms on military operations, better guided and informed though they might be than those of unprofessional civilians, will be restrained or directed by personal considerations.

'How battle pictures are made'. Facsimile of a pencil sketch by Mr Melton Prior in *The Illustrated London News*, in the Zulu War, 1879.

The specially designed photographic van brought from England to the
Crimea by Roger Fenton in the spring of 1855.

The only visual record of events at that time was the work of amateur and professional
war artists. Many of the amateurs were serving soldiers who, unable to document what
was happening at the time, would later recreate from memory the particular action in
which they had taken part.

In 1842 the first issue of *The Illustrated London News* was published. It contained no
fewer than 30 line drawings, printed as wood block engravings. But it was a magazine,
not a newspaper. Although there was no shortage of photographers, it was to be many
years before newspapers mastered the technique of making the half-tone blocks
necessary to reproduce photographs.

In 1854, Roger Fenton, founder of the Royal Photographic Society, was sent out to
the Crimea (at the instigation of Prince Albert) in an attempt to redress the effect on
public morale engendered by the despatches of Russell and others. Fenton's photographs, however, show an altogether jollier and tidier war than that reported by
Russell. His subjects had to be carefully composed, then remain immobile for between
three and twenty seconds. Furthermore, he could take photographs only within a short
distance of his specially-equipped van as the plates had to be sensitised before exposure
and used before the emulsion dried.

During the American Civil War, photographers such as Matthew Brady (and his
staff) roamed the battlefields, taking thousands of superb pictures. These now con-
stitute a fascinating historical record of the war, but they were never seen by the

general public at the time. In 1880, an American newspaper printed the first photograph using the half-tone method (still in use today), but it was not until 1904 that the *Daily Mirror* became the first British newspaper to use photographs extensively.

When the Crimean War started, it was the first time that Britain had become engaged in a major conflict since the Battle of Waterloo in 1815. As the war gathered momentum, a deep sense of involvement gripped the nation and people longed for news. Where they could have expected dull official despatches, *The Times* brought them thrilling accounts which conjured up events of which they had previously had no conception. What was more, the anonymous writer—like all newspaper correspondents, Russell was not named—dared to criticise the way the war was being conducted.

A lesser man than Russell, backed by an unscrupulous newspaper, could have exploited the situation. But in Russell *The Times* had found the perfect correspondent, a man whose exceptional ability to write vivid prose was combined with energy, humanity and integrity. A friend said of him:

> You see, the man's eye was a lens: it afforded him microscopic aspects which had put on paper, and behold! the objects were there in all their minute veracity! And then the tone was so manly and just! No trace of party feeling or desire to chime in with the views of the man in the street. He knew the English public really wished for the plain truth, and that he endeavoured to give them, and only that.

When Russell first went to the Crimea, he was regarded by those in authority with both suspicion and contempt. Many were surprised that he had ever been given permission to accompany the army and they did all they could to make his life with them as difficult as possible, contriving to leave him behind whenever they could. But he refused either to be shaken off or to be silenced. Backed by the might of *The Times* his angry despatches ripped aside the veils of deception, exposing the horrifying consequences of the authorities' gross mismanagement of the war. It was said, not without cause, that he contributed to the collapse of Lord Aberdeen's government. There were those who even saw him, aided and abetted by John Thaddeus Delane, the highly influential Editor of *The Times*, as partly responsible for Lord Raglan's fall from grace and subsequent death. Never before had a mere journalist wielded such power.

But this power would not have been possible without the overwhelming support of Delane. It was he who urged Russell to: 'Continue as you have done, to tell the truth, and as much of it as you can, and leave such comment as may be dangerous to us, who are out of danger.' The force of Delane's personality was behind Russell, through the pages of the newspaper and through personal contact with those in authority.

Before the Crimean War, and for some years after it, the war correspondents' despatches to their newspapers were the only independent written accounts of such events. But to pretend that these accounts were entirely unbiased would be incorrect. Russell himself could be accused of a passion for things military which sometimes romanticised and coloured his view of war.

Senator Hiram Johnson said in 1917 that 'the first casualty when war comes is truth'. The American Civil War produced a new breed of journalist with scant regard for the truth. Accounts of battles frequently bore little relation to what had actually occurred. Each correspondent vied with his rivals to make his view the most dramatic; each tailored the facts to suit the politics of his newspaper. Significantly, it was Russell's objective and accurate reporting of the First Battle of Bull Run which brought the wrath of the American Press upon him and led to his departure from the country after only one year of the war. The North had been unable to stomach the truth (especially when told by a foreigner) that its army had cut and run.

From a late twentieth-century viewpoint, it seems incredible that a nineteenth-century battle was considered a spectacle which people would go and watch. Taking servants and hampers of food, they would select a strategic hilltop and settle down to enjoy all the 'pride and splendour of war.' But can one really blame them? Some of the battles must have been a memorable sight: the glittering officers mounted on matched thoroughbreds: the massed regiments wheeling and turning on the battlefield as though engaged in some surrealistic ballet. The spectators were shielded from the grim reality of it all by the intervening distance. When it was all over, they could pack up and go home.

Russell was a war correspondent for fifteen years before he used the telegraph, and it was his reluctance and inability to adapt his style to suit this medium that finally led to his eclipse. In 1876, when he was well into middle-age, a letter to Delane written from India shows that he was still unreconciled to it: 'I cannot describe to you the paralysing effect of sitting down to write a letter after you have sent off the bones of it by lightning.'

During the Franco-Prussian War of 1870-71 his despatches took up to ten days to reach *The Times*—well after those of many of his principal rivals. A reporter called Hands of the *New York Tribune* was reputedly the first to describe a battle over the telegraph wire. His account of the battle of Gravelotte was in his Editor's hands within three days.

Newspaper proprietors increasingly demanded up-to-the-minute reports and each wanted them first. Russell's detailed and literary despatches were already stale news by the time they reached the breakfast table. He often lost valuable time checking his facts and filling in what, to him, was essential detail. *The Times* pleaded with Russell to 'use the telegraph *freely*', but it was asking him to throw away all those qualities which had established him in his profession. He was now a man of fifty and it was asking too much.

The twentieth century has brought with it an ever-increasing avalanche of news. We have watched the President of the United States assassinated before our very eyes; the media's coverage of major wars is often so overwhelming that it begins to act as an

John Thaddeus Delane, Editor of *The Times* for 36 years, during which time the paper reached a peak of circulation and influence.

anaesthetic against the grim reality being presented. Russell's word pictures of the torment and squalor endured by soldiers in the Crimea represented the first chance the general public had been given to see the true face of war. A fellow correspondent, Edwin Godkin, commented that Russell's coverage of the Crimean War '...led to a real awakening of the official mind. It brought home to the War Office the fact that the public had something to say about the conduct of wars and that they are not the concern exclusively of sovereigns and statesmen.'

Unfortunately, the official mind also awoke to the realisation that it should exercise some control over what journalists were allowed to report, although it was not until the end of the Crimean War that any form of official censorship was introduced. By then it was too late to muzzle Russell and his fellow correspondents, but in subsequent campaigns censorship began to bite with increasing effect. 'Alas, the days of newspaper enterprise in war are over. What can one do with a censor, a 48-hour delay and a fifty word limit on the wire?'—the words of a young Winston Churchill during the war in South Africa.

Apart from his obvious ability to write, Russell had an astonishing gift for making friends, which opened doors that would have been firmly closed to anyone with a less irresistible personality. A.W. Kinglake, official historian of the Crimean War, gives this endearing picture of Russell as he knew him:

> His opportunity of gathering intelligence depended, of course, in a great measure upon communications which might be made to him by officers of their own free will: and it is evident that to draw full advantage from occasions formed in that way the enquirer must be so socially gifted, that by his own powers of conversation he can evoke the conversation of others. Russell was that and more: he was an Irish humorist whose very tones fetched a laugh... In those days when the army was moving after having disembarked at the Old Fort, he had not found the means to reorganize the needed campaigning arrangements which his voyage from Bulgaria had disturbed, and any small tribulation he suffered in consequence used to form the subject of his numerous plaintive laments... He always found sooner or later some blank leaves out of a pocket book and some stump of a pencil with which to write his letters—letters destined in the sheets of *The Times* to move the hearts and souls of our people at home and make them hang on his words... By the natural display of humour thus genial and taking he thawed a great deal of reserve, and men talked to him with much more openness than they would have been likely to show if approached by a solemn enquirer in evident search of dry facts. Russell also had abundant sagacity, and besides in his special calling was highly skilled, for what men told him he could seize with rare accuracy, and could convert at once into powerful narrative.

Russell made no secret of his love for the army, or of his passionate desire that Britain should succeed in its every endeavour. However, his patriotism did not blind him to the conduct of either the government or his fellow men; although it would have been easy for him to adopt the attitudes of the establishment—in Britain, he had many friends among the ruling classes—Russell displayed a remarkable ability to see the long-term effects of certain behaviour or policy and he never hesitated to criticise when he felt it was necessary. During the Indian Mutiny he was one of the first to realise that the indiscriminate revenge tactics of the British would only delay the reconciliation which had to come between the rulers and the ruled, if the Indian Empire was to survive at all. Similarly, in the Crimea, it was his genuine anger and indignation at the way the common soldiers were being treated that won their hearts and engendered the compassion of the British people for their plight.

Russell was born in March 1820, in Lily Vale, County Dublin, son of John Russell, whom he described affectionately as a 'large-limbed, solid, joyous man'. His mother was only seventeen when he was born and his father 24. Shortly after his birth his father's business collapsed and his parents left Ireland to settle in Liverpool, leaving their son in the care of his grandfather, Jack Kelly.

> All my early memories relate to hounds, horses and hunting; there were hounds all over the place, horses in the fields and men on horseback galloping, blowing horns, cracking of whips, tallyho-ing, yoicksing and general uproar. If the weather was fine on a hunting morning, Captain Jack was in fine spirits. His voice would be heard above the tumult outside the house, front and rear, as he sang... That voice has been silent for more than half a century, but I hear it still as though the singer were in the next room.

However, this happy-sounding state of affairs was not to last:

> My grandfather was a farmer, a grazier; there had been bad seasons and a fall in prices as well. There was trouble at Lily Vale. Men were stalking through the rooms with pencils and note-books, writing; men in the fields looking at the cattle, and writing; men in the stables examining horses and ponies, and writing; men measuring stacks in the farmyard, and writing. The hounds were taken from the kennels—I was told for the summer, but I never saw them again. The maids, too, began packing up my things. I was going up to Dublin, to my grandfather and grandmother Russell, and 'I would come back very soon'. But I never returned to see Lily Vale as I had known it.
> My grandfather William Russell in Dublin was very different from the tenant of Lily Vale. He was lame, but withal very active and alert; a short, stout, silver-haired, ruddy-cheeked man, clean shaven and bright-eyed, with a stentorian voice and quick temper which flamed out like gunpowder when the gout was in possession and his 'leg was bad'.

His first school of any importance was Dr Wall's in Hume Street, where he seems to have been flogged with distressing frequency. He then moved down the street to Dr Geoghegan's. He describes his time there:

> In that house I spent some of the happiest years of my life, and assuredly it was my own fault that I didn't turn to good account the teaching of one of the kindest of friends and most indulgent of masters. How deeply I am indebted to that just, considerate, and inflexible man perhaps I do not, with all my gratitude, understand.

He was attracted by military life from an early age and loved to watch the soldiers drilling at the local barracks. He even tried to enlist, but his grandfather prevented him. Instead, he and his friends joined battle with boys from other schools: 'Black eyes were as plentiful as blackberries, and I had my share.'

When Russell was seventeen his grandfather died and the family found itself severely short of money. There would not be a penny to spare for young Billy's further education. Much to his disgust, he was taken on by a distant relative as a tutor—a form of employment which seemed to fall far short of his ambitions. Judging from this description, he found ways of sugaring the pill:

> My pupils were docile and affectionate if not very hard-working or bright. We rode out with or without hounds; we fished in the streams near at hand, in the lochs a few miles distant; and I read for my entrance examination at Trinity with a proud feeling that I was working for myself and would ask no one for anything over and above my entrance fee.

Russell's academic life at Trinity College, Dublin, was unremarkable. His memories of his time there turn on more battles, this time with other undergraduates:

> There were glorious doings during election times, when the Trinity College

students—who were mostly Orangemen—met the Roman Catholics and engaged them in battle: but, alas! they were tyrannous and strong...the Dublin coal porters used to be called in to disperse us.

Happily, fate intervened. A cousin who worked for *The Times* arrived in Ireland to cover the elections. He engaged Russell as one of a team of young reporters, at a guinea a day plus expenses—unimaginable riches for an impecunious young man. The elections were a riotous business and Russell entered the maelstrom of Irish politics with relish. His life at this time seems to have been merely an extension of the battles he had fought in Hume Street and at Trinity. Quantities of whiskey were consumed, rhetoric flew and many heads were broken.

Concerned that it was impossible to appear at all the political meetings at once, Russell hit on the brilliant idea of stationing himself at the local hospital. With his personal knowledge of what Irish politics could do to the body corporate, he had a shrewd idea that many of the principal contestants would need medical attention at some point in the proceedings. He was right. His vivid and impassioned articles were singled out for special praise by *The Times*.

In 1842, John Delane offered Russell a post on the paper's reporting staff in the Press Gallery of the House of Commons. His immediate acceptance of the job marked the beginning of a long and very special relationship with the paper, and with its Editor in particular.

Russell must have been the obvious choice to go to Ireland in 1844 to report on the 'monster meetings' being held by Daniel O'Connell for the repeal of the Union. He was to say of O'Connell:

> I have never heard any orator who made so great an impression on me as O'Connell. It was not his argument, for it was often worthless, nor his language, which was frequently inelegant. It was his immense passion, his pathos, his fiery indignation ...As a speaker addressing a mob—a meeting of his own countrymen—I do not believe anyone equalled, or that anyone will equal, O'Connell.

But O'Connell was not to be allowed to weave his magic for long: he was arrested and tried for seditious conspiracy. Russell covered the trial for *The Times*. Even in those days there was sharp rivalry between the leading Fleet Street papers and on this occasion it manifested itself in a race to be first with the verdict of the trial. Russell takes up the story:

> Both the *Times*...and the *Morning Herald* had chartered special steamers to carry the news... It was very late on a Saturday night when the jury retired; the judge waited in court for some time, but went away after an hour's expectancy and the other newspaper correspondents left to get refreshments. I was sitting outside the court, wondering whether I should go to bed. Suddenly my boy rushed up to me. 'Jury just coming in,' he said.
>
> And they brought in a verdict of guilty. The moment I heard it I flew from the court, jumped on a car—drove to the station, where I had ordered a special train to be in readiness—got to Kingston—hailed the *Iron Duke*, the steamer chartered by the *Times*—got up steam in half an hour, and left with the consolation that the steamer of the *Morning Herald* was lying peacefully in harbour! Arrived at Holyhead—sped away—special to London—tried to sleep, couldn't—tight boots—took them off. Reached Euston, man waiting with cab, struggled to get on boots, only managed the left foot, and when I reached the *Times* office it was with one boot under my arm. As I got out of the cab in Printing House Square, a man in shirtsleeves—whom I took to be a printer—came up to me.
>
> 'So glad to see you safe over, sir!' he cried. 'So they've found him guilty?'
> 'Yes—guilty, my friend.' I replied.

The *Morning Herald* came out next day with the news of the fact, the bare fact

—as well as the *Times!* The gentleman in the shirt-sleeves was an emissary from their office!

It was a valuable lesson, learned the hard way.

While Russell was doing freelance work for *The Times*, he was also studying for the Bar. In 1846 he married an Irish girl, Mary Burroughs. Although he had enjoyed his Press Gallery work for *The Times*, he was paid only when the House was in session, and was thus always short of money. Marriage made Russell more concerned with his finances and when the *Morning Chronicle* offered him a regular job as a reporter on its staff, he accepted. Financial solvency was, however, to elude Russell all his life, and his monetary vagaries were to drive the poor manager of *The Times* to distraction throughout Russell's association with the paper.

His first major commission for the *Morning Chronicle* was to report the Irish famine:

> In all my subsequent career—breakfasting, dining and supping full of horrors in full tide of war—I never beheld sights so shocking as those which met my eyes in that famine tour of mine in the West. They were beyond not merely description, but imagination...the children digging up roots; the miserable crones and the scarecrow old men in the fields, the ghastly adults in the relief work—all were heartrending. One strange and fearful consequence was seen in the famished children: their faces, limbs and bodics became covered with fine long hair; their arms and legs dwindled, and their bellies became enormously swollen. They were bestial to behold.

In 1848 Russell was invited to work with *The Times* again—an unusual event as it was against the policy of the paper ever to re-employ anyone. For Russell the offer was heaven sent, as the *Morning Chronicle* was in financial trouble and his job with the paper had ceased to exist. Almost as soon as he rejoined *The Times* he found himself once more on his way to Ireland to cover the State Trials of the principal conspirators in 'the Rising'.

In June 1850 he was called to the Bar at the Middle Temple, but by July he had taken his first step towards the realisation of his true profession, although he appears to have been totally unaware of its significance at the time. *The Times* sent him as their special correspondent to cover the recent outbreak of hostilities in the Schleswig-Holstein dispute. He watched the Battle of Idstedt on 25th July, receiving a minor flesh wound in the process. Although his description of the battle gives little indication of the quality of writing he would later produce, he was correct in his assessment that the battle had been decisive.

The years that followed passed undramatically for Russell. He established himself as a regular writer of descriptive letters for *The Times*; one of his most moving contributions was an account of the funeral of the Duke of Wellington. He became a member and a constant habitué of the Garrick Club which was always to remain the hub of his extremely busy social life.

A remark in his retrospective book on the Crimean War, *The Great War with Russia,* shows how unprepared Russell was for the event which was to alter the course of his life so dramatically:

> When the year of grace 1854 opened on me I had no more idea of being what is now—absurdly, I think—called a 'war correspondent' than I had of becoming Lord Chancellor—nay, far less; for I confess I had at times visions of the Woolsack such as, I suppose, float in the air before the mind's eye of many sanguine barristers like myself.

But in the estimation of *The History of The Times*, summing up Russell's career almost 100 years later, he was on the threshold of becoming 'the most famous reporter who ever served *The Times*'.

The Crimean War

Although the Allies did not declare war on Russia until the end of March 1854, John Delane of *The Times* had already made the editorial decision which was to have such an effect on the life and career of William Russell by early February. He summoned Russell and informed him that:

> ...a very agreeable excursion to Malta with the Guards had been arranged...that my wife and family could join me—handsome pay and allowances would be given —in fact, everything was painted *couleur de rose*. When I made some objection on the score of losing my practice at the Bar, Mr Delane said, 'There is not the least chance of it, you'll be back by Easter, depend on it, and you will have a pleasant trip for a few weeks only.'

The origins of the Crimean War went back to the long-standing dispute over Russia's claims to the guardianship of the Holy Places in Palestine, then under the jurisdiction of the Turks. Tsar Nicholas I despised Turkey as the 'sick-man of Europe' and had been trying to engineer the collapse of the Ottoman Empire for some time. As the quarrel between the two nations deepened, a conference between Russia and the four other European powers involved in the dispute was held in Vienna. A solution was arrived at and communicated to the Turks, who rejected it. At this point, two of the signatories of the Vienna Note, Austria and Prussia, withdrew from the negotiations, leaving only France and Britain in the arena with Russia and Turkey.

France's involvement was due mainly to Napoleon III's need to secure his position on the throne of France, a position that he had occupied for barely two years. Exacting a final revenge over Russia for the French defeat of 1812 would confirm him as a power to be reckoned with, both at home and abroad. Sardinia also joined the alliance.

The involvement of Britain was heavily influenced by her suspicion of Russia's imperial ambitions. If Russia's intention was to expand her empire still further south and thus

The Battle of Sinope on 30th November 1853, during which the Russians destroyed the entire Turkish fleet. This act aroused great public anger and condemnation in Britain.

Left: Lord Raglan, Commander-in-Chief of the British Army, photo-graphed by Roger Fenton in Spring 1855. *Right:* The Earl of Cardigan, commander of the Light Brigade. His immediate superior was the Earl of Lucan, commander of the Cavalry Division. The two brothers-in-law loathed each other and were barely on speaking terms.

gain land access to the Eastern Mediterranean (thereby endangering Britain's overland route to India), then she must be stopped.

In June 1853 Russia confirmed British suspicions by occupying the Danubian prin-cipalities of Moldavia and Wallachia, which were joint protectorates of Russia and the Ottoman Empire. Secure in the knowledge that Britain and France would support her, Turkey declared war on Russia in October 1853. Six weeks later Russian ships sailed out of their naval base at Sebastopol and sank the antiquated Turkish fleet at Sinope on the Black Sea.

Although this was a perfectly legitimate act of war, anti-Russian feeling flared up in Britain. The nation clamoured for war. Diplomatically, there was nothing more that could be done, and Britain and France duly declared war in March 1854. It was a war that Britain was to fight with a tragically unprepared and mismanaged army that had not fought a battle since Waterloo, nearly 40 years previously. The War Office had changed little since the Napoleonic Wars and had become heavily enmeshed in its own outdated procedures. Lord Raglan, a man of 66 who had spent the previous 39 years behind a desk in Whitehall, was appointed Commander-in-Chief of the army.

As early as the first engagement in the Crimean War Russell gave this opinion of Raglan:

> That Lord Raglan was brave as a hero of antiquity, that he was kind to his friends and to his staff, that he was unmoved under fire, and unaffected by personal danger, that he was noble in manner, gracious in demeanour, of dignified bearing I am ready to admit; that he had many and great difficulties to contend with I believe; but that this brave and gallant nobleman had lost, if he ever possessed, the ability to conceive and execute large military plans—and that he had lost, if he ever possessed, the faculty of handling great bodies of men, I am firmly persuaded.

The British contingent consisted on one cavalry and five infantry divisions—about 30,000 men in all. Some of the generals commanding it were well over sixty, some had never seen active service and some had seen none since the Peninsular Wars. Raglan was not alone in expressing great contempt for what were called 'Indian Officers'—who were actually among the few British officers to have seen active service in the previous 40 years. One of the few Indian officers allowed a command of any significance was Sir Colin Campbell, who proved to be extremely able. The Commander-in-Chief was also handicapped by an inability to remember that the French were now Britain's allies.

On the political front, the government under Lord Aberdeen had complacently assumed that the arrival of the Guards and some French contingents in Malta would be enough to convince the Tsar that the Allies meant business, and that he would back down. He did no such thing, and, following declaration of war, the allied troops set sail for Gallipoli.

It had been intended that Russell should accompany the Guards when they left Southampton on 19th February, but the authorities, in spite of promises to Delane, prevented him doing so. It was the first indication of a hostility that was to complicate his life throughout the war. He eventually had to make his own way overland, rejoining the British contingent in Malta in time to set off with them for the east. From the landing at Gallipoli onwards, his despatches, and particularly his private letters to Delane, bristle with criticism of the British army's chaotic administration.

> On Saturday (April 8) the troops were landed and sent to their quarters. The force consisted of only some thousand and odd men, and, small as it was, it had to lie idle for two days and a half watching the seagulls, or with half-averted eye regarding the ceaseless activity of the French, the daily arrival of their steamers and the admirable completeness of all their arrangements in every detail—hospitals for the sick, bread and biscuit bakeries, wagon trains for carrying stores and baggage—every necessary and every comfort, indeed, at hand, the moment their ships came in.
>
> The camps in the neighbourhood of Gallipoli extended and increased in numbers every day, and with the augmentation of the allied forces, the privations to which the men were at first exposed became greater, the inefficiency of our arrangements more evident, and the excellence of the French commissariat administration more strikingly in contrast. Amid the multitude of complaints which met the ear from every side, the most prominent were charges against the commissariat; but the officers at Gallipoli were not to blame. The persons really culpable were those who sent them out without a proper staff and without the smallest foresight or consideration...
>
> The men suffered exceedingly from cold. Some of them, officers as well as privates, had no beds to lie upon. None of the soldiers had more than their single regulation blanket. They therefore reversed the order of things and dressed to go to bed, putting on all their spare clothing before they tried to sleep. The worst thing was the continued want of comforts for the sick. Many of the men labouring under diseases contracted at Malta were obliged to stay in camp in the cold, with only one blanket under them, as there was no provision for them at the temporary hospital.

Although absolving most of the officers and blaming 'those who sent them out', Russell had this to say of the commander of the Light Division, Sir George Brown:

> His hatred of hair amounted to almost a mania. 'Where there is hair there is dirt, and where there is dirt there will be disease.' That is an axiom on which was founded a vigorous war against all capillary adornments, and in vain engineers, exposed to all weathers, and staff officers, exhibit sore and bleedings lips; they must shave, no matter what the result is. The stocks [bands of leather bound

tightly around the throat] too, were ordered to be kept up, stiff as ever. On the march of the Rifles to their camp at least one man fell out of the ranks senseless; immediate recovery was effected by the simple process of opening the stock.

The day after this despatch appeared in *The Times*, the Secretary of War, the Duke of Newcastle, ordered a relaxation in 'the extreme formality of uniform, including the abolition of the stock'. Russell's despatches and private letters gave Delane the ammunition he needed to wield his influence, both publicly and behind the scenes, against the government. As details of the contents of Russell's reports began to filter back from England, his position with the army became still more precarious. In his own words, he had become a 'Gorgon and Hydra and Chimaera dire'.

While the army was still at Gallipoli, Russell went by ship through the Sea of Marmara to Constantinople; from there he crossed the Bosphorus to Scutari where the Guards were camped. His first impressions were unfavourable:

> In the stagnant water which ripples almost imperceptibly on the shore there floated all forms of nastiness and corruption which the prowling dogs, standing leg-deep as they wade about in search of offal, cannot destroy. The smell from the shore was noisome, but a few yards out from the fringe of buoyant cats, dogs, birds, straw, sticks—in fact, of all sorts of abominable flotsam and jetsam, which bob about on the pebbles unceasingly—the water became exquisitely clear and pure. The slaughter-house for the troops, erected by the sea-side, did not contribute, as may readily be imagined, to the cleanliness of this filthy beach, or the wholesomeness of the atmosphere.

The huge barracks, recently vacated by the Turks, were the temporary quarters for the British troops as they filtered up from Gallipoli. These too were in an appalling mess, 'inhabited in every nook and corner by legions of fleas and less active but more nauseous insects'. The barracks later became the main hospital in which the wounded returning from the Crimea were cared for by Florence Nightingale and her nurses.

Early in May it was announced that the Russian army had advanced into Bulgaria. The allied commanders, including the Turk Omar Pasha, met and made plans for the immediate departure of the French and British forces for the Bulgarian Black Sea port of Varna. It was hoped that this show of strength would contain the enemy forces on the east bank of the Danube.

The huge barracks at Scutari, some 350 miles from the Crimea, which later became the main hospital for the wounded, presided over by Florence Nightingale. Russell found it '…inhabited in every nook and corner by legions of fleas and less active but more nauseous insects.'

At the end of May the armies moved to Varna where they remained until the beginning of September, but by the end of July a serious cholera epidemic had broken out in the French and British camps.

The hospital was full, and numerous as our medical staff was and unremitting as were our medical officers in doing all that skill and humanity could suggest for the sufferers, there were painful cases in which the men did not procure the attention they required till it was too late.

The French losses from cholera were frightful. Convinced that there was something radically wrong in the air of the hospital at Varna, the French cleared out of the building altogether, and resolved to treat their cases in the field. The hospital had been formerly used as a Turkish barrack...

Although not very old, the building was far from being in thorough repair. The windows were broken, the walls in parts were cracked and shaky, and the floors were mouldering and rotten. Like all places which have been inhabited by Turkish soldiers for any time, the smell of the buildings was abominable. Men sent in there with fevers and other disorders were frequently attacked with the cholera in its worst form and died with unusual rapidity, in spite of all that could be done to save them. I visited the hospital and observed that a long train of carts filled with sick soldiers were drawn up by the walls. There were thirty-five carts, with three or four men in each. These were sick French soldiers sent in from the camps and waiting till room could be found for them in the hospital. A number of soldiers were sitting down by the roadside and here and there the moonbeams flashed brightly off their piled arms. The men were silent; not a song, not a laugh. A gloom, seldom seen among French troops, reigned amid these groups of grey-coated men and the quiet that prevailed was only broken now and then by the moans and cries of the poor sufferers in the carts...

On the night of August 10th, a great fire broke out at Varna, which utterly destroyed more than a quarter of the town. The sailors of the ships, and the French and English soldiery stationed near the town, worked for the ten hours during which the fire lasted with the greatest energy; but as a brisk wind prevailed, which fanned the flames as they leapt along the wooden streets, their efforts were not as successful as they deserved... The howling of the inhabitants,

Varna Bay: the allied expedition fleet getting under way for the Crimea.

the yells of the Turks, the clamour of women, children, dogs, and horses, were appalling... The French lost great quantities of provisions, and we had many thousand rations of biscuit utterly consumed. In addition, immense quantities of stores were destroyed—10,000 pairs of soldiers' shoes and an immense quantity of cavalry sabres, which were found amid the ruins fused into the most fantastic shapes. To add to our misfortunes the cholera broke out in the fleet in Varna Bay and at Baltschik with extraordinary virulence...

After the great fire...the cholera seemed to diminish in the town itself and the reports from the various camps were much more favourable than before. It was found, indeed, that the plan of wide open encampments answered in checking disease. The British army was scattered broad-cast all over the country, from Monastir to Varna, a distance of twenty-six or twenty-seven miles. The Duke of Cambridge's division had marched in from Aladyn and was encamped towards the south-western side of the bay. It appeared that notwithstanding the exquisite beauty of the country around Aladyn, it was a hot-bed of fever and dysentery. The same was true of Devno, which was called by the Turks 'the Valley of Death'; and had we consulted the natives ere we pitched our camps, we assuredly should never have gone either to Aladyn or Devno, notwithstanding the charms of their position and the temptations offered by the abundant supply of water and by the adjacent woods.

Horrors occurred here every day which were shocking to think of. Walking by the beach one might see some straw sticking up through the sand, and on scraping it away with his stick, be horrified at bringing to light the face of a corpse which had been deposited there with a wisp of straw around it, a prey to dogs and vultures. Dead bodies rose up from the bottom in the harbour and bobbed grimly around in the water or floated in from sea and drifted past the sickened gazers on board the ships—all buoyant, bolt upright, and hideous in the sun.

On 24th August a Council of War decided that the allied forces should proceed to the Crimea where it was hoped they would finally come face to face with the Russian army. On 7th September 50,000 men in 600 ships set sail.

It was a vast armada. No pen could describe its effect upon the eye. Ere an hour had elapsed it had extended itself over half the circumference of the horizon. Possibly no expedition so complex and so terrible in its means of destruction, with such enormous power in engines of war and such capabilities of locomotion, was ever yet sent forth by any worldly power. The fleet, in five irregular and straggling lines, flanked by men-of-war and war steamers, advanced slowly, filling the atmosphere with innumerable columns of smoke, which gradually flattened out into streaks and joined the clouds, adding to the sombre appearance of this well-named 'Black' Sea. The land was lost to view very speedily beneath the coal clouds and the steam clouds of the fleet, and as we advanced not an object was visible in the half of the great circle which lay before us, save the dark waves and the cold sky.

On the 10th, Raglan (who had set sail with no clear idea of where they would land) reconnoitred as far as Sebastopol. He observed that the fortifications 'appeared to bristle with guns', so on the 14th they landed at Calamita Bay 35 miles north of Sebastopol. As before, the French were first ashore, their camps quickly established. The British eventually disembarked with their horses which had suffered dreadfully en route. Once again there was chaos:

Few of those who were with the expedition will forget the night of the 14th September. Seldom or never were 27,000 Englishmen more miserable. No tents had been sent on shore, partly because there had been no time to land them, partly because there was no certainty of our being able to find carriage for them in case of a move. Towards night the sky looked very black and lowering; the wind rose, and the rain fell in torrents. The showers increased about midnight, and early in the morning fell in drenching sheets which pierced through the blankets and great-coats of the houseless and tentless soldiers. Let the reader imagine some of these old generals and young lords and gentlemen exposed hour after hour to the violence of pitiless storms, with no bed but the reeking puddle under the saturated blankets, or bits of useless waterproof wrappers, and the twenty-odd thousand poor fellows who could not get 'dry bits' of ground, and had to sleep, or try to sleep, in little lochs and water courses—no fire to cheer them, no hot grog, and the prospect of no breakfast.

The tents were unloaded during the day only to be returned to the ships before nightfall, so the second night was a repeat of the first.

The soldiers now had their first glimpse of the enemy: small bands of Cossacks could be seen on the surrounding hills reconnoitring the allied positions: 'They were rough-looking fellows, mounted on sturdy little horses; but the regularity of their order and the celerity of their movements showed that they were regulars and by no means despicable foes.'

After four days at Calamita Bay the allied commanders decided to march south towards Sebastopol, although they were still not sure of the whereabouts of the Russian army. The march began in blazing sunshine, with Russell firmly in attendance.

The troops presented a splendid appearance. The effect of these grand masses of soldiery descending the ridges of the hills, rank after rank, with the sun playing over the forests of glittering steel, can never be forgotten by those who witnessed it. At last, the smoke of burning villages and farm-houses announced that the enemy in front were aware of our march... Many sick men fell out and were carried to the rear. It was a painful sight—a sad contrast to the magnificent appearance of the army in front, to behold litter after litter borne past to the carts with the poor sufferers who had dropped from illness and fatigue.

The exhausted allied armies bivouacked that night with the glow of the Russian camp fires clearly visible across the intervening plain. They had found the enemy. Daylight would reveal the strength of the Russian position: 50,000 men were drawn up on the heights above the river Alma in what their commander, Prince Mentschikoff, understandably considered to be an impregnable position.

The allied battle plan was simple enough and dictated largely by the course of the river which separated the opposing armies. The British divisions would attack south across the river with the French on their right: the French right was to be covered by the fleet which would steam along parallel to the shore with a firing range of two miles inland. Russell wrote that, apart from a brief look round by one of the French generals,

...no other reconnaissance was made of the Russian position by the other generals. They did not reconnoitre the Alma, nor did they procure any information respecting the strength of the enemy or of the ground they occupied. They even concerted their plan before they had seen the enemy at all, relying on the bravery of the troops not only to force the Russians from their lines, but, if necessary, to swim or to ford a stream of unknown depth, with steep rotten banks, the bridges across which might, for all they knew, have been destroyed by the enemy.

September 20th was another insufferably hot day. The British troops were supposed to be ready by 6 a.m. but they were disorganised and late, keeping the French waiting. It was about ten o'clock before they moved towards the Alma.

At the distance of two miles we halted to obtain a little time to gather up our rear, and then the troops steadily advanced in grand lines, like the waves of the

The Battle of the Alma, as seen by the French from the right of the battle front, showing the struggle to drag the guns up to the Heights. In the foreground are Zouaves, originally native troops from Algeria.

ocean. The bright scarlet and red with the white-slashings of the breast of the coat and the cross belts, though rendering a man conspicuous enough, give him an appearance of size which other uniforms do not produce. The dark French columns on our right looked very small compared to our battalions, though we knew they were quite as strong; but the marching of our allies, laden as they were with all their packs, etc., was wonderful—the pace at which they went was really 'killing'. It was observable, too, that our staff was showy and more numerous than that of the French. Nothing in the shape of head-dress strikes the eye so much as a cocked hat and bunch of white cock's feathers, and several of our best officers very wisely doffed the latter adornment, thinking that they were quite conspicuous enough by their advanced positions on horseback and by the number of their staff around them. At this time I was riding in front, and when the regiments halted I went through the Light Division, part of the 2nd Division, the Guards and the Highlanders. I found all my friends, save one or two, in high spirits. Some had received letters from wives and children by the mail, which made them look grave and think seriously on the struggle to come. Others were joking and laughing in the best possible spirits. Many a laugh did I hear from lips which in two hours more were closed for ever. The officers and men made the most of this delay and ate whatever they had with them; but there was a great want of water, and the salt pork made them so thirsty that in the subsequent passage of the Alma, under the heaviest fire, the men stopped to drink and to fill their water canteens...

As we advanced, we could see the enemy very distinctly—their great-coated masses resembling patches of wood on the hill sides. The line of the river below the heights they occupied was indicated by patches of the richest verdure and by belts of fine fruit trees and vineyards.

Meanwhile, the French had somehow managed to haul their guns on to the heights on the Russian left and proceeded to enfilade the enemy artillery. At about 1.30 p.m. the allies came under heavy fire from the Russian centre, and Lord Raglan ordered them to lie down.

The Rifles in advance of our left were sharply engaged with the enemy in the vineyard, and anxious to see what was going on, I rode over in that direction and arrived at the place where were stationed the staff of the Light Division. Sir George Brown was just at the time giving some orders to one of his Aides relative to the 'Russian cavalry on our left front'. I looked across the stream, and saw, indeed, some cavalry and guns slowly moving down towards the stream from the elevated ground over its banks; but my eye at the same time caught a most formidable-looking mass of burnished helmets, tipped with brass, just above the top of the hill on our left, at the other side of the river. One could see plainly through the glass that they were Russian infantry, but I believe the gallant old General thought at the time that they were cavalry. Sir George looked full of fight, clean-shaven, neat and compact; I could not help thinking, however, there was a little pleasant malice in his salutation to me. As he rode past, he said, in a very jaunty, Hyde Park manner, 'It's a very fine day, Mr Russell'. At this moment the whole of our right was almost obscured by the clouds of black smoke from the burning village on our right, and the front of the Russian line above us had burst into a volcano of flame and white smoke—the roar of the artillery became terrible —we could hear the heavy rush of the shot, those terrible dumps into the ground and the crash of the trees, through which it tore with resistless fury and force; splinters and masses of stone flew out of the walls. It was rather provoking to be told so coolly it was a very fine day amid such circumstances; but at that very moment the men near us were ordered to advance... As I had no desire to lead my old friends of the Light Division into action, I rode towards the right to rejoin Sir de Lacy Evans, if possible; and as I got on the road, I saw Lord Raglan's staff riding towards the river, and the shot came flinging close to me, one, indeed, killing one of two bandsmen who were carrying a litter close to my side, after passing over the head of my horse. It knocked away the side of his face, and he fell dead—a horrible sight. The batteries of the Second Division were unlimbered

The Battle of the Alma, 20th September 1854, sketched by Henry Clifford, V.C. As an officer in the Rifle Brigade, he would have seen the attack from slightly to the left of centre of the battle front.

in front, and were firing with great steadiness on the Russians; and now and then a rocket, with a fiery tail and a huge waving mane of white smoke, rushed with a shrill shout against the enemy's massive batteries. Before me all was smoke—our men were lying down still; but the Rifles…were driving back the enemy's sharp-shooters with signal gallantry, and clearing the orchards and vineyards in our front by a searching fire.

My position was becoming awkward. Far away in the rear was the baggage, from which one could see nothing; but where I was placed was very much ex-posed. A shell burst over my head, and one of the fragments tore past my face with an angry whir-r-r, and knocked up the earth at my poor pony's feet. Close at hand, and before me, was a tolerably good stone-house, one storey high, with a large court-yard, in which were several stacks of hay that had not yet caught fire. I rode into this yard, fastened up my pony to the rope binding one of the ricks, and entered the house…and established myself at the window, from which I could see the Russian artillerymen serving their guns, their figures, now distinctly re-vealed against the hill side, and again lost in a spurting whirl of smoke. I was thinking what a terrible sort of field-day this was, and combating an uneasy longing to get to the front, when a tremendous crash, as though a thunderclap had burst over my head, took place right above me, and in the same instant I was struck and covered with pieces of broken tiles, mortar and stones, the window out of which I was looking flew into pieces, parts of the roof fell down, and the room was filled with smoke.

There was no mistaking this warning to quit. A shell had burst in the ceiling. As I ran out into the yard I found my pony had broken loose, but I easily caught him, and scarcely had I mounted when I heard a tremendous roll of musketry on my left front, and looking in the direction, I saw the lines of our red jackets in the stream, and swarming over the wooden bridge. A mass of Russians were at the other side of the stream, firing down on them from the high banks, but the ad vance of the men across the bridge forced these battalions to retire; and I saw, with feelings which I cannot express, the Light Division, scrambling, rushing, foaming like a bloody surge up the ascent, and in a storm of fire, bright steel, and whirling smoke, charge towards the deadly epaulement, from which came roar and flash incessantly… The rush of shot was appalling and I recollect that I was particularly annoyed by the birds, which were flying about distractedly in the smoke, as I thought they were fragments of shell

All this time the roar of the battle was increasing. I went back to my old spot; in doing so I had to ride gently, for wounded men came along in all directions. One was cut in two by a round shot as he approached… Just at this moment I saw the Guards advancing in the most majestic and stately order up the hill, while through the intervals and at their flanks poured the broken masses of the Light Division, which their officers were busy in re-forming. The Highlanders who were beyond them I could not see; but I never will forget the awful fury, the powerful detonation of the tremendous volleys which Guards and Highlanders poured in upon the Russian battalions, which in vain tried to defend their batteries and to check the onward march of that tide of victory.

The approach of the Light Division—why should I not dwell fondly on every act of that gallant body, the first 'put at' everything throughout the campaign? —was in double columns of brigades. Their course was marked by killed and wounded, for the Russians poured down a heavy vertical fire on our straggling lines. They were straggling, but not weak; the whole Brigade, at a word from their officers, made a simultaneous rush up the bank and as they crowned it, met their enemies with a furious and close fire of their deadly rifles. The dense bat-talions were smitten deeply and as the Light Division advanced to meet them, they rapidly fell back to the left, leaving many dead and wounded men close to

the river's banks. After a momentary delay, these gallant regiments, led by Brigadier Codrington and Sir George Brown, advanced up the slope which was swept
by the guns of the entrenched battery.

Grape, canister, round and shell tore through their ranks, and the infantry on
the flanks of the battery advancing at an angle to it, poured in a steady fire upon
them from point-blank distance. It must be confessed that this advance was very
disorderly—the men had not only got into confusion in the river from stopping to
drink, but had disordered their ranks by attacks on the grapes in the vineyards on
their way. Every foot they advanced was marked by lines of slain or wounded
men. The 7th Fusileers, smitten by a storm of grape, reeling to and fro like some
brave ship battling with a tempest, but which still holds on its desperate way,
within a few seconds lost a third of its men... The 23rd Regiment was, however,
exposed more, if that were possible, to that lethal hail. In less than two minutes
from the time they crowned the bank till they neared the battery, the storm had
smitten down twelve of their officers, of whom eight never rose again. The 19th
marched right up towards the mouths of the roaring cannon which swept down
their ranks; the 33rd, which had moved up with the greatest audacity over broken,
ground towards the flank of the epaulement, was for the moment checked by the
pitiless pelting of this iron rain.

...When Sir George Brown went down, a rifleman assisted him on his horse
again, and with the greatest coolness, as they stood under a murderous fire,
saluted the General as he got once more into his seat, and said, 'Are your stirrups
the right length, sir?'

At last it became apparent to Russell that the Russians were gradually beginning to
withdraw some of their artillery.

But the enemy had not yet abandoned their position. An enormous division of
infantry...marched straight upon the Brigade of Guards, which it exceeded in
numbers by three to one. The Guards advanced to meet them in perfect order.
Some round shot struck the rear of the Russian columns, and immediately they
began to melt away from the rear, and wavered for an instant; still they came on
slowly, and began file-firing from their fronts instead of charging as their officers
evidently intended them to do. The distance between them was rapidly dimin-
ishing, when suddenly the whole Brigade poured in on their dense masses a fire so
destructive that it annihilated the whole of their front ranks in an instant, and left
a ridge of killed and wounded men on the ground. The enemy, after a vain attempt
to shake off the panic and disorder occasioned by that rain of death, renewed
their fire very feebly for a few seconds, and then without waiting for a repetition
of our reply, turned as our men advanced with bayonets at the charge, retreated
over the brow of the hill, and marched off to join the mass of the Russian army,
who were retreating with all possible speed. Our cavalry rode up to the crest of
the hill and looked after the enemy... It was near five o'clock; the Battle of the
Alma was won. The men halted on the battlefield, and as the Commander-in-
Chief, the Duke of Cambridge, Sir de Lacy Evans, and the other popular generals
rode in front of the line, the soldiers shouted, and when Lord Raglan was in front
of the Guards, the whole army burst into a tremendous cheer, which made one's
heart leap—the effect of that cheer can never be forgotten by those who heard it.

Then the clearing up began:

The Russian dead were all buried together in pits, and were carried down to their
graves as they lay. Our parties buried 1,200 men. The British soldiers who fell
were buried in pits in the same way. Their firelocks and the useful portions of
their military equipment were alone preserved. It was a sad sight to see the litters

borne in from all quarters hour after hour—to watch the working parties as they wandered about the plain turning down the blankets which had been stretched over the wounded, to behold if they were yet alive, or were food for the worms, and then adding many a habitant to the yawning pits which lay with insatiable mouths gaping on the hill side—or covering up the poor sufferers destined to pass another night of indescribable agony. The thirst of the wounded seemed intolerable, and our men—all honour to the noble fellows—went about relieving the wants of the miserable creatures as far as they could.

With the Russian army in retreat, the allies relaxed for a moment. Not so Russell who, even in the thick of the battle, had begun to forsee the difficulties of writing his despatch. In *The Great War with Russia* (1895) he wrote:

How was I to describe what I had not seen? Where learn the facts for which they were waiting at home? My eyes swam as I tried to make notes of what I heard. I was worn out with excitement, fatigue, and want of food. I had been more than ten hours in the saddle; my wretched horse, bleeding badly from a cut in the leg, was unable to carry me. My head throbbed, my heart beat as though it would burst. I suppose I was unnerved by want of food and rest, but I was so much overcome by what I saw that I could not remain where the fight had been closest and deadliest. I longed to get away from it—from the exultation of others in which thought for the dead was forgotten or unexpressed. It was now that the weight of the task I had accepted fell on my soul like lead.

He thought also of Lord Raglan, faced with the same problem:

Every line he wrote was charged with fate and fortune. I was only scribbling. I did not grasp the fact that I had it in my power to give a halo of glory to some unknown warrior by putting his name in type. Indeed for many a month I never understood that particular attribute of my unfortunate position though it had been appreciated by my friends, and I may say now in all sincerity and truth I never knowingly made use of it.

It has been said that the Crimean War could have ended with the Battle of the Alma had the Russians not been allowed to retreat to the safety of Sebastopol. Raglan wanted to pursue them but St Arnaud (the French Commander) insisted on time to reorganise his troops. Thus the Russians were given precious time in which to strengthen Sebastopol's inadequate defences, while the allied armies executed an extraordinary flank march round the city and set up their camps to the south of it. Russell spent most of the march in the bottom of a cart in the grip of a high fever, but roused himself in time to get his first view of the harbour at Balaclava.

I never was more astonished in my life than when on the morning of Tuesday September 26th I halted on the top of one of the numerous hills of which this portion of the Crimea is composed, and looking down saw under my feet a little pond, closely compressed by the sides of high rocky mountains; on it floated some six or seven English ships, for which exit seemed quite hopeless. The bay is like a highland tarn, some half mile in length from the sea, and varies from 250 to 120 yards in breadth. The shores are so steep and precipitous that they shut out as it were the expanse of the harbour, and made it appear much smaller than it really is. Towards the sea the cliffs close up and completely overlap the narrow channel which leads to the haven, so that it is quite invisible.

This 'highland tarn' was the British army's only lifeline to the outside world. The previously picturesque little town of Balaclava rapidly became a muddy hell. Cholera and dysentery continued unabated and the movement of stores from the harbour to the encampment on the heights above was a constant nightmare.

The harbour at Balaclava which reminded Russell of a 'highland tarn'
but was the British army's only lifeline to the outside world.

A siege of Sebastopol was now inevitable. On 17th October, after three weeks of
consolidating their positions before the city, the allies commenced a bombardment
which continued for nearly a week. As it was at no time followed up by an assault, the
Russians, guided by the engineering genius of Colonel Franz Todleben, merely rebuilt
the defences as fast as they were destroyed.

Rumours that the enemy was planning something reached a climax on 24th October
when Lord Raglan received definite information that an attack would be made on
Balaclava. However, no special precautions were taken, and it was not until dawn the
next day, when some of the Turkish redoubts on the Causeway Heights were attacked,
that the British sprang into action.

Awakened by the gunfire, Russell hurried to the edge of the plateau where he took
up a position near Lord Raglan and his staff, looking down on the plain of Balaclava.

> Never did the painter's eye rest on a more beautiful scene than I beheld from the
> ridge... The fleecy vapours still hung around the mountain tops, and mingled with
> the ascending volumes of smoke; the patch of sea sparkled freshly in the rays of
> the morning sun, but its light was eclipsed by the flashes which gleamed from the
> masses of armed men below.
>
> Looking to the left towards the gorge, we beheld six compact masses of Russian
> infantry, which had just debouched from the mountain passes near the Tchernaya,
> and were slowly advancing with solemn stateliness up the valley. Immediately in
> their front was a regular line of artillery at least twenty pieces strong. Two bat-
> teries of light guns were already a mile in advance of them and were playing with

energy on the redoubts... Behind these guns, in front of the infantry, were enormous bodies of cavalry. They were in six compact squares, three on each flank, moving down *en echelon* towards us, and the valley was lit up with the blaze of their sabres and lance points and gay accoutrements... Just as I came up the Russians had carried No.1 redoubt... and their horsemen were chasing the Turks across the interval which lay between it and redoubt No.2.

At that moment the cavalry, under Lord Lucan, were formed in glittering masses—the Light Brigade, under Lord Cardigan, in advance; the Heavy Brigade, under Brigadier General Scarlett, in reserve. They were drawn up just in front of their encampment, and were concealed from the view of the enemy by a slight 'wave' in the plain. Considerably to the rear of their right the 93rd Highlanders were drawn up in line, in front of the approach to Balaclava.

No.2 redoubt fell, the Turks fleeing towards Balaclava and the waiting 93rd. The Russian cavalry took No.3 redoubt in its stride and, 'as it advanced they gathered up their skirmishers with great speed and in excellent order—the shifting trails of men, which played all over the valley like moonlight on the water, contracted, gathered up, and the little *peloton* in a few moments became a solid column. When the Russians reached the brow of the ridge of the Causeway Heights,

...they perceived the Highlanders drawn up at the distance of some half mile, calmly waiting their approach. They halted, and squadron after squadron came up from the rear, till they had a body of some 3,500 men along the ridge... The silence was oppressive; between the cannon bursts one could hear the champing of bits and the clink of sabres in the valley below. The Russians on their left drew breath for a moment, and then in one grand line charged in towards Balaclava. The ground flew beneath their horses' feet; gathering speed at every stride, they dashed on towards that thin red streak tipped with a line of steel. The Turks fired

The 'thin red streak' of the 93rd Highlanders, commanded by Sir Colin Campbell, standing firm in the path of the Russian cavalry on 25th October 1854. Russell's phrase was later amended to the now famous 'thin red line'.

British Cavalry, probably Dragoon Guards, drawn up in readiness before Balaclava on 25th October 1854. Sketch by Constantin Guys.

a volley at eight hundred yards and ran. As the Russians came within six hundred yards, down went that line of steel in front, and out rang a rolling volley of Minié musketry. The distance was too great; the Russians were not checked, but still swept onwards through the smoke, with the whole force of horse and man, here and there knocked over by the shot of our batteries above. With breathless suspense every one awaited the bursting of the wave upon the line of Gaelic rock; but ere they came within two hundred and fifty yards, another deadly volley flashed from the levelled rifle and carried terror among the Russians. They wheeled about, opened files right and left and fled faster than they came. 'Bravo, Highlanders! well done!' shouted the excited spectators.

Next, the Heavy Brigade, under the command of Brigadier General Scarlett, performed what has been called 'one of the great feats of cavalry against cavalry in the history of Europe'. On orders from Lord Raglan, Scarlett was going to the aid of the 93rd when the main force of the Russian cavalry suddenly appeared over the brow of the Causeway Heights to his left. He immediately wheeled his 500 men to face directly uphill towards the three to four thousand strong cavalry.

The instant they came in sight, the trumpets of our cavalry gave out the warning blast which told us all that in another moment we should see the shock of battle beneath our very eyes. Lord Raglan, all his staff and escort...French generals and officers...on the height, were spectators of the scene as though they were looking on the stage from the boxes of a theatre. Nearly everyone dismounted and sat down, and not a word was said. The Russians advanced down the hill at a slow canter, which they changed into a trot, and at last nearly halted. Their first line was at least double the length of ours—it was three times as deep. Behind them was a similar line, equally strong and compact.

The trumpets rang out again through the valley, and the Greys and Enniskilleners went right at the centre of the Russian cavalry. The space between them was only a few hundred yards; it was scarce enough to let the horses 'gather way', nor had the men quite space sufficient for the full play of their sword arms. The Russian line brought forward each wing as our cavalry advanced, and threatened to annihilate them as they passed on. Turning a little to their left, so as to meet the Russian right, the Greys rushed on with a cheer that thrilled to every heart

—the wild shout of the Enniskilleners rose through the air at the same instant. As lightning flashed through cloud, the Greys and Enniskilleners pierced through the dark masses of Russians. The shock was but for a moment. There was a clash of steel and a light play of sword-blades in the air, and then the Greys and the red-coats disappeared in the midst of the shaken and quivering columns. In another moment we saw them emerging with diminished numbers and in broken order, charging against the second line. It was a terrible moment. The first line of Russians, which had been utterly smashed by our charge, and had fled off at one flank and towards the centre, were coming back to swallow up our handful of men. By sheer steel and sheer courage Enniskillener and Scot were winning their desperate way right through the enemy's squadrons, and already grey horses and red coats had appeared right at the rear of the second mass, when, with irresistible force, like one bolt from a bow, the 4th Dragoon Guards, riding straight at the right flank of the Russians, and the 5th Dragoon Guards, following close after the Enniskilleners, rushed at the remnants of the first line of the enemy, went through it as though it were made of pasteboard and put them to utter rout...a cheer burst from every lip...officers and men took off their caps and shouted with delight.

Meanwhile, the Light Brigade was in a frenzy. Why had it not been allowed to pursue the fleeing Russian cavalry? It was at this moment that Raglan, remote on his hilltop, decided the time had come to recover the redoubts, the Causeway Heights and the Woronzoff Road. His position, some 600 feet above the floor of the valley, afforded him a panoramic view of the battle, whereas the cavalry commander, Lord Lucan, could see nothing owing to the undulations of the plain. Raglan's last order to him had been to advance and recapture the redoubts immediately, without waiting for infantry support which had been ordered and would arrive later. It being a maxim of war that 'cavalry never act without a support', Lucan had interpreted the order as meaning that he should not advance until the infantry support arrived. Three-quarters of an hour passed while the watchers on the hill waited for action from Lucan and he waited for the infantry.

Suddenly, it was observed with consternation that the Russians were beginning to remove the British naval guns from the redoubts. As captured guns were considered a proof of victory, Raglan now issued the fatal and ambiguous order which precipitated the charge of the Light Brigade: 'Lord Raglan wishes the cavalry to advance rapidly to the front—follow the enemy and try to prevent the enemy carrying away the guns. Troop Horse Artillery may accompany. French cavalry is on your left. Immediate.'

It was at this point that a young cavalry officer called Captain Lewis Nolan played a decisive role. In Russell's words: 'A braver soldier than Captain Nolan the army did not possess. A matchless horseman and a first-rate swordsman.' He had constantly raged against Raglan for keeping the cavalry 'in a bandbox' and now, desperate to see his beloved Light Brigade employed at last, he snatched the order from Raglan's aide-de-camp and spurred his horse over the edge of the heights to where Lucan waited. Lucan could still see nothing and he did not understand the order. 'Attack, sir? Attack what? What guns, sir?' Nolan flung out his arm, pointing not at the redoubts on the Heights but down the North Valley to the Russian guns which had regrouped and were now aimed straight up the valley at the Light Brigade. 'There, my lord, is your enemy, there are your guns.'

Lucan had no alternative but to pass on the order to Lord Cardigan. There was still no sign of support of any kind and 'there was a plain to charge over before the enemy's guns could be reached, of a mile and a half in length'. With the immortal remark, 'Well, here goes the last of the Brundenells' (his family name), Cardigan gave the order: 'The Brigade will advance. Walk, march, trot.'

At ten minutes past eleven, our Light Cavalry Brigade advanced... They swept proudly past, glittering in the morning sun in all the pride and splendour of war.

We could scarcely believe the evidence of our senses. Surely that handful of men were not going to charge an army in position?

...They advanced in two lines, quickening their pace as they closed towards the enemy. A more fearful spectacle was never witnessed than by those who, without the power to aid, beheld their heroic countrymen rushing to the arms of death. At the distance of 1,200 yards the whole line of the enemy belched forth, from thirty iron mouths, a flood of smoke and flame, through which hissed the deadly balls. Their flight was marked by instant gaps in our ranks, by dead men and horses, by steeds flying wounded or riderless across the plain. The first line was broken—it was joined by the second, they never halted or checked their speed an instant. With diminished ranks, thinned by those thirty guns, which the Russians had laid with the most deadly accuracy, with a halo of flashing steel above their heads, and with a cheer which was many a noble fellow's death-cry, they flew into the smoke of the batteries; but ere they were lost from view, the plain was strewed with their bodies and with the carcasses of horses...

Through the clouds of smoke we could see their sabres flashing as they rode up to the guns and dashed between them, cutting down the gunners as they stood. To our delight we saw them returning, after breaking through a column of Russian infantry and scattering them like chaff, when the flank fire of the battery on the hill swept them down, scattered and broken as they were. At the very moment when they were about to retreat a regiment of Lancers was hurled upon their flank. Colonel Shewell, of the 8th Hussars, saw the danger, and rode his few men straight at them, cutting his way through with fearful loss. The other regiments turned and engaged in a deperate encounter. With courage too great almost for credence they were breaking their way through the columns which enveloped them, when there took place an act of atrocity without parallel in the modern warfare of civilized nations. The Russian gunners, when the storm of cavalry passed, returned to their guns, and poured murderous volleys of grape and can-on the mass of struggling men and horses. It was as much as our Heavy Cavalry Brigade could do to cover the retreat of the miserable remnants of that band of heroes as they returned to the place they had so lately quitted in all the pride of life. At thirty-five minutes past eleven not a British soldier, except the dead and dying, was left in front of those bloody Muscovite guns.

The Light Brigade, with Lord Cardigan at its head, just about to reach the Russian guns.

The Charge of the Light Brigade at the moment when the leading riders
reached the Russian guns. The central figure in this picture could well be
Lord Cardigan.

Captain Nolan, as he rode in advance of the first line, cheering them on, was
killed by the first shot fired. Lord Lucan was slightly wounded. Lord Cardigan
received a lance thrust through his clothes.

It is now thought possible that Nolan was not cheering them on but had realised to his
horror that the Light Brigade was going the wrong way and was desperately trying to
turn the cavalry. The fatal charge took less than half an hour. Of the 'gallant 600'
(historians have estimated that there were nearly 700) 195 men and 200 horses survived.

The rest of the day achieved little for either side. The Russians retained control of
the redoubts on the Causeway Heights and the mouth of the gorge of the River Tchernaya.
The most devastating strategic loss of the day, not fully comprehended at the time, was
the control of the Woronzoff Road. This was the only route connecting Balaclava with
the British encampment on the heights above and, as Russell says in a retrospective
view of the war: 'The sufferings of the winter would have been immensely alleviated—
indeed, the relief to us would have been incalculable—by the retention of the Woronzoff
Road.'

For the next ten days very little happened apart from a certain amount of harassment
on both sides. There appears to have been scant preparation made for any further offensive
by the enemy and the weather had worsened considerably. But on 5th November: 'No
one suspected for a moment that enormous masses of Russians were creeping up the
ragged sides of the heights over the Valley of Inkerman, on the undefended flank of
the Second Division.' Within minutes the outlying pickets were overwhelmed and the
general alarm given.

Russell staggered out of bed to the rattle of musketry and, taking 'all the biscuit I
could lay my hands on, a lump of cheese in one holster, a revolver and a flask of rum
and water in the other', leapt on to his horse and set off in the drizzling dawn for the
ridge overlooking Inkerman. He arrived in time to witness the charge of the Guards,
led by the Duke of Cambridge, against the grey-coated masses of the enemy, surging
out of Sebastopol in a desperate attempt to break the siege.

Second charge of the Guards at the Battle of Inkerman, 5th November 1854, a battle which was fought in swirling fog and drizzle.

Then commenced the bloodiest struggle ever witnessed since war cursed the earth. The bayonet was often the only weapon employed in conflicts of the most obstinate and deadly character. We had been prone to believe that no foe could withstand the British soldier wielding his favourite weapon, but at Inkerman not only did we charge in vain—not only were desperate encounters between masses of men maintained with the bayonet alone—but we were obliged to resist bayonet to bayonet again and again, as they charged us with incredible fury and determination.

The Battle of Inkerman admits of no description. It was a series of dreadful deeds of daring, of sanguinary hand-to-hand fights, of despairing rallies, of desperate assaults—in glens and valleys, in brushwood glades and remote dells, and from which the conquerors, Russian or British, issued only to engage fresh foes, till our old supremacy, so rudely assailed, was triumphantly asserted, and the battalions of the Czar gave way before our steady courage and the chivalrous fire of France. No one, however placed, could have witnessed even a small portion of the doings of this eventful day, for the vapours, fog, and drizzling mist obscured the ground where the struggle took place to such an extent as to render it impossible to see what was going on at the distance of a few yards. Besides this, the irregular nature of the ground, the rapid fall of the hill towards Inkerman, where the deadliest fight took place, would have prevented anyone under the most favourable circumstances from seeing more than a very insignificant and detailed piece of the terrible work below.

Our generals could not see where to go. They could not tell where the enemy were—from what side they were coming, nor where they were coming to. In darkness, gloom, and rain they had to lead our lines through thick scrubby bushes and thorny brakes, which broke our ranks and irritated the men, while every pace was marked by a corpse or man wounded by an enemy whose position was only indicated by the rattle of musketry and the rush of ball and shell...

A shell came right among the staff—it exploded in Captain Somerset's horse, ripping him open; it then struck down Captain Gordon's horse and killed him at once, and then blew away General Strangway's leg, so that it hung by a shred of flesh and bit of cloth from the skin. The poor old General never moved a muscle of his face. He said merely, in a gentle voice, 'Will anyone be kind enough to lift me off my horse?' He was taken down and laid on the ground, while his life-blood ebbed fast, and at last he was carried to the rear.

Matters were becoming desperate—by sheer weight of numbers the Russians were beginning to force the British line back.

...but at last came help. About ten o'clock a body of French infantry appeared on our right—a joyful sight to our struggling regiments... Their trumpets sounded above the din of battle, and when we watched their eager advance right on the flank of the enemy we knew the day was won...the Russians began to retire, and at twelve o'clock they were driven pell-mell down the hill towards the valley.

The battle was won, but the cost was appalling: Russell made a tour of the battlefield two days later.

The British and the French, many of whom had been murdered by the Russians as they lay wounded, wore terrible frowns on their faces, with which the agonies of death had clad them. Some in their last throes had torn up the earth in their hands, and held the grass between their fingers up towards heaven. All the men who exhibited such signs of pain had been bayoneted; the dead men who lay with an eternal smile on their lips had been shot. But the wounded—for two days they had lain where the hand and the ball had felled them...

The Russians, groaning and palpitating as they lay around, were far more numerous. Some were placed together in heaps, that they might be the more readily removed. Others glared upon you from the bushes with the ferocity of wild beasts, as they hugged their wounds. Some implored, in an unknown tongue, but in accents not to be mistaken, water, or succour; holding out their mutilated and shattered limbs, or pointing to the track of the lacerating ball. The sullen, angry scowl of some of these men was fearful. Fanaticism and immortal hate spake through their angry eyeballs, and he who gazed on them with pity and compassion could at last (unwillingly) understand how these men would in their savage passion kill the wounded, and fire on the conqueror who, in his generous humanity, had aided them as he passed.

In a letter to Delane, four days after the battle, Russell wrote: 'A heavy responsibility rests on those whose neglect enabled the enemy to attack us where we were least prepared for it, and whose indifference led them to despise precautions which taken in time might have saved as many valuable lives, and have trebled the loss of the enemy, had they been bold enough to have assaulted us behind intrenchments. We have nothing to rejoice over, and almost everything to deplore, in the battle of Inkerman.' Of his own part in the proceedings Russell wrote:

Here was I in a raging battle... And let me say, it is—for a man who has no orders to obey, no orders to give, to find himself under fire, a strange position—very uncomfortable to say the least of it. He cannot if he cares for his own good opinion, or for those around him, gallop off *ventre à terre*. If a bullet finds its billet in his body corporate, he knows that the general verdict will be 'Serve him right' what business had he to get in the way? If a correspondent is involved in the thick of a battle, he has to consider whether he ought to trust to his imagination for his facts, or whether he will run the chance of dying without emolument or glory, present or posthumous, and depriving his editor of 'any account of the proceedings'.

It was now realised that there was no hope of taking Sebastopol before Christmas and preparations must be made for the army to winter in the Crimea. Russell wrote to Delane: 'The prospect of wintering here is appalling.' The circumstances under which the men were living were already hopelessly inadequate and the officers were no better off, as Russell describes in a despatch published in *The Times*.

> The oldest soldiers never witnessed nor heard of a campaign in which general officers were obliged to live out in tents on the open field, for the want of a roof to cover them, and generals who passed their youth in the Peninsular war, and who had witnessed a good deal of fighting since that time in various parts of the world, were unanimous in declaring that they never knew or read of a war in which the officers were exposed to such hardships. They landed without anything but what they could carry, and they marched beside their men, slept by them, fought by them, and died by them, undistinguished from them in any respect, except by the deadly epaulet and swordbelt, which have cost so many lives. The survivors were often unable to get their things from on board ship. They laid down at night in the clothes which they wore during the day; many delicately-nurtured youths never changed shirt or shoes for weeks together, and they were deprived of the use of water for ablution, except to a very limited extent...
>
> On the 14th of November came a new calamity—the camp was visited by a hurricane. It commenced shortly after six o'clock a.m. and was preceded by rain and squalls.
>
> For about an hour I had been in a listless state between waking and sleeping, listening to the pelting of the rain against the fluttering canvas of the tent, or dodging the streams of water which flowed underneath it, saturating our blankets and collecting on the mackintosh sheets in pools. The sound of the rain, its heavy

A contemporary map showing the siege works and disposition of the allied camps before Sebastopol in February 1855.

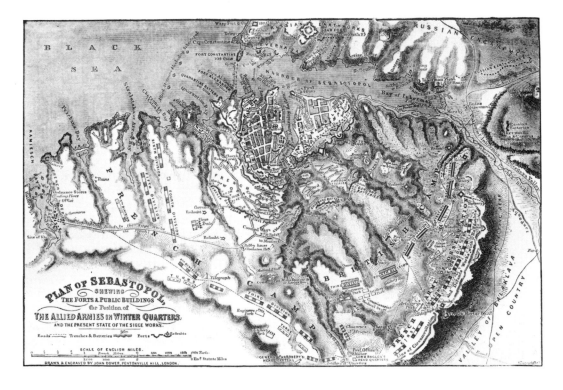

Russell writing in his tent during the winter of 1854-55. The castle stands
at the mouth of the harbour at Balaclava, which is just visible on the far
right of the picture.

beating on the earth, had become gradually swallowed up by the noise of the
rushing of the wind over the common, and by the flapping of the tents as they
rocked more violently beneath its force. Gradually the sides of the canvas, which
were tucked in under big stones to secure them, began to rise and flutter,
permitting the wind to enter playfully and drive before it sheets of rain right into
one's face; the pegs began to indicate painful indecision and want of firmness of
purpose.

...a harsh screaming sound, increasing in vehemence as it approached, struck us
with horror. As it passed along we heard the snapping of tent-poles and the sharp
crack of timber and canvas. On it came, 'a mighty and a strong wind'; the pole
broke off short in the middle, as if it were glass, and in an instant we were pressed
down and half stifled by the heavy folds of the wet canvas, which beat us about
the head with the greatest fury. Half breathless and blind, I struggled for the
door. Such a sight met the eye! The whole headquarters' camp was beaten flat to
the earth, and the unhappy occupants were rushing through the mud in all
directions in chase of their effects and clothes, as they strove to make their way to
the roofless and windowless barns and stables for shelter...

The air was filled with blankets, hats, greatcoats, little coats, and even tables
and chairs. Mackintoshes, quilts, india-rubber tubs, bed-clothes, sheets of tent-
canvas went whirling like leaves in the gale towards Sebastopol. The shingle roofs
of the outhouses were torn away and scattered over the camp, and a portion of
the roof of Lord Raglan's house was carried off to join them. The barns and
commissariat-sheds were laid bare at once, large arabas, or wagons, which stood
close to us, were overturned; men and horses were knocked down and rolled over
and over; the ambulance wagons were turned topsy-turvy.

The hurricane continued all that day and night but the next day dawned bright and
cold. Concerned about rumours of the state of Balaclava, Russell rode down to assess
the damage.

The Sentry before Sebastopol, November 1854, by H.J. Wilkinson from the 9th Regiment.

On approaching the town, signs of the tempest increased at every step. At the narrow neck of the harbour two or three large boats were lying, driven inland several yards from the water; the shores were lined with trusses of hay which had floated out of the wrecks outside the harbour, and masts and spars of all sizes were stranded on the beach or floated about among the shipping.

Sentinel of the Zouaves at Sebastopol; painting by W. Simpson, 1855.

The condition of Balaclava at that time is utterly indescribable. The narrow main street was a channel of mud, through which horses, wagons, camels, mules, and soldiers and sailors, and men of all nations scrambled and plunged, and jostled.

But the long-term effects of the hurricane were no less deadly. The loss from the wrecked ships of so many precious supplies, particularly the warm clothing, was a disaster throughout that terrible winter. Moreover, the investment of Sebastopol had to be maintained, in spite of a severe shortage of ammunition. A comment from Russell, part grim and part humorous, must have summed up the general feeling:

The siege drags its slow length along day after day till one is out of patience with it. The sensation of weariness produced by this slow cannonade is indescribable. It must be something like that which would be experienced by a man who lived in a house where an amateur played on the big drum in the drawing-room, morning, noon, and night.

As the months dragged on he continued with his self-appointed task of making known the true state of the British army and of laying the blame unhesitatingly with the authorities.

...In the tents the water was sometimes a foot deep—our men had neither warm nor waterproof clothing—they were out for twelve hours at a time in the trenches—they were plunged into the inevitable miseries of a winter campaign —and not a soul seemed to care for their comfort, or even for their lives. These were hard truths, which sooner or later must have come to the ears of the people of England. It was right they should know that the wretched beggar who wandered about the streets of London in the rain led the life of a prince compared with the British soldiers who were fighting for their country, and who, we were complacently assured by the home authorities, were the best appointed army in Europe.

Camp of the 1st Division with the heights of Inkerman in the distance.

The catalogue of failure went on: why the ludicrous adherence to 'regulations' which delayed the landing of stores from the ships? Why were the wooden huts still on board? Why had no proper roads from Balaclava been constructed during the dry weather to replace the loss of the Woronzoff Road? He described the daily ritual of transporting supplies, now further complicated by frequent heavy falls of snow. The sick and wounded had to be carried in the opposite direction, from the heights to the harbour, where they were loaded on ships for Scutari.

> They formed one of the most ghastly processions that ever poet imagined. Many of these men were all but dead. With closed eyes, open mouths, and ghastly attenuated faces, they were borne along two and two, the thin stream of breath visible in the frosty air alone showing they were still alive. One figure was a horror—a corpse, stone dead, strapped upright in its seat, its legs hanging stiffly down, the eyes staring wide open, the teeth set on the protruding tongue, the head and body nodding with frightful mockery of life at each stride of the mule over the broken road...

Embarkation of the sick and wounded at Balaclava en route to the hospital at Scutari.

It would have astonished a stranger riding out from Balaclava to the front to have seen the multitudes of dead horses all along the road. In every gully were piles of the remains of these wretched animals, torn to pieces by wild dogs and vultures, and many of the equine survivors of the desperate charge at Balaclava lay rotting away by the side of the cavalry camp. The attitudes of some of the skeletons were curious. Some had dropped down dead and were frozen stiff as they fell; others were struggling, as it were, to rise from their miry graves. Nearly all of the carcasses had been skinned by the Turks and French, who used the hides to cover their huts, and many suspicious-looking gaps, too, suggestive of horse-steak, had been cut out in their flanks.

The standard of the army was also deteriorating. Many of the original officers were either dead or too sick to remain in the Crimea. By early 1855 the number of sick had risen to 23,076, the majority of whom were experienced soldiers, and the army before Sebastopol was made up of raw recruits led by officers who were mere novices. During that winter, the loss of men through sickness was eight times the casualty rate on the battlefield.

In fact, the Russian army was in a similar state. Although constant reinforcements were arriving in Sebastopol from the north, what was not realised at the time was that two thirds of them were dying from sickness and hunger as a result of the long winter journey through Russia. Russell wrote:

Hundreds of men had to go into the trenches at night with no covering but their greatcoats, and no protection for their feet but their regimental shoes. The trenches were two and three feet deep with mud, snow, and half-frozen slush.

As to the town itself [Balaclava], words could not describe its filth, its horrors, its hospitals, its burials, its dead and dying Turks, its crowded lanes, its noisome sheds, its beastly purlieus, or its decay. The dead, laid out as they died, were lying side by side with the living, and the latter presented a spectacle beyond all imagination. The commonest accessories of a hospital were wanting; there was not the least attention paid to decency or cleanliness—the stench was appalling —the foetid air could barely struggle out to taint the atmosphere, save through the chinks in the walls and roofs, and, for all I could observe, these men died without the least effort to save them. There they laid just as they were let gently

The return of one of the working parties from the trenches, December 1854. A drawing by a soldier from the 9th Regiment.

down upon the ground by the poor fellows, their comrades, who brought them on their backs from the camp with the greatest tenderness, but who were not allowed to remain with them. The sick appeared to be tended by the sick, and the dying by the dying.

Russell was constantly 'honoured by a good deal of abuse' in the London newspapers for 'telling the truth'. There were those too who maintained that his detailed despatches had given valuable information to the enemy:

> But I could not tell lies to 'make things pleasant'. There was not a single man in the camp who could put his hand upon his heart and declare he believed that one single casualty had been caused to us by information communicated to the enemy by me or any other newspaper correspondent. The only things the partisans of misrule could allege was, that I did not 'make things pleasant' to the authorities, and that, amid the filth and starvation, and deadly stagnation of the camp, I did not go about 'babbling of green fields', of present abundance, and of prospects of victory.

It was this persistent refusal to 'make things pleasant' which aroused public opinion at home against the ineptitude of the Aberdeen government, and it was forced to resign in February. When the Duke of Newcastle, the Secretary of War, came out to the Crimea he said to Russell one day: 'It was you who turned out the government, Mr Russell'.

Since the Battle of Inkerman the position of both armies had hardly altered: fortifications and trenches had been strengthened and extended, and the sporadic bombardments continued. At last the weather began to improve and with it new hope flowed into the allied armies. Better roads and even a railway were built from Balaclava, and the town itself was cleaned up. The health of both men and horses improved and food and warm clothing were plentiful. But Russell was not going to let anyone forget the past:

> From hunger, unwholesome food and comparative nakedness, the camp was plunged into a sea of abundance, filled with sheep and sheepskins, wooden huts, furs, comforters, mufflers, flannel shirts, tracts, soups, preserved meats, potted game and spirits; but it was, unfortunately, just in proportion as they did not want them that comforts and even luxuries were showered upon them. In such weather a tent was as good—some say better than—a hut. Where were the huts when the snow was on the ground, and where was the warm clothing when cold rains and bitter winds racked the joints? Just where our fresh meat and vegetables were when scurvy and scorbutic dysentery were raging in the canvas cantonment before Sebastopol?

> Zouaves slinking along the trenches at Sebastopol. In the words of a Captain in the Light Dragoons they were '...certainly the finest troops for courage after the English.'

Supplies from England piling up on the Ordnance Wharf, Balaclava, in the spring of 1855. Photograph by Roger Fenton.

Spring had come. Flowers carpeted the battlefield; birds suddenly reappeared and '...it was strange to hear them piping and twittering about the bushes in the intervals of the booming of the cannon'. Some of the officers went duck shooting on the River Tchernaya, and there were even race meetings, to the complete mystification of the Cossack pickets.

Several burial truces were arranged so that the no-man's-land which separated the two front lines could be cleared of the dead and dying. Russell describes one such occasion:

> The sight was strange beyond description. French, English, and Russian officers were walking about saluting each other courteously as they passed, and occasionally entering into conversation, and a constant interchange of little civilities, such as offering and receiving cigar-lights, was going on in each little group. Some of the Russian officers were evidently men of high rank and breeding. Their polished manners contrasted remarkably with their plain and rather coarse clothing...
>
> But while all this civility was going on, we were walking among the dead, over blood-stained ground, covered with evidence of recent fight. Broken muskets, bayonets, cartouch-boxes, caps, fragments of clothing, straps and belts, pieces of shell, little pools of clotted blood, shot—round and grape—shattered gabions and sandbags, were visible around us on every side, and through the midst of the

crowd stalked a solemn procession of soldiers bearing their departed comrades to their long home. I counted 77 litters borne past me in 15 minutes—each filled with a dead enemy.

In the second week in April the allies began a colossal bombardment in the hope that it would soften up Sebastopol's defences and reduce its fire power. The British wanted to follow this up with an attack but were overruled by the French. A second bombardment followed a few days later but still no assault was made. At the beginning of May, 5,000 Sardinians, 'excellent and soldier-like troops', arrived.

On May 23rd an allied force set sail to capture the Russian port of Kertch 150 miles to the east of Balaclava. If the allies could control this port, they would also control the Sea of Azov and thus endanger the Russian lines of supply and communication. Russell managed to evade the authorities, who were again trying to thwart him, and accompanied the expedition. Although he wrote that 'the success of the expedition by land and sea was complete, rapid and glorious', he also created a great deal of controversy by his angry criticism of the looting and destruction carried out by small sections of the allied troops while ashore.

At last, on 7th June, the allies agreed to attack the main defences of Sebastopol: two massive earthworks, the Redan and the Mamelon, and the immensely strong stone-built Malakoff tower. The French were to capture the Mamelon while the British mounted a diversionary assault on the Quarries, a small defensive position which the Russians had constructed in front of the Redan. The attack was left until the evening when the British took the minor objective of the Quarries with no difficulty, but it was the French action which attracted all the attention.

Detail from the map on page 36 showing the main Russian defences—the Redan in the centre and the Malakoff and Mamelon (not named) to the right.

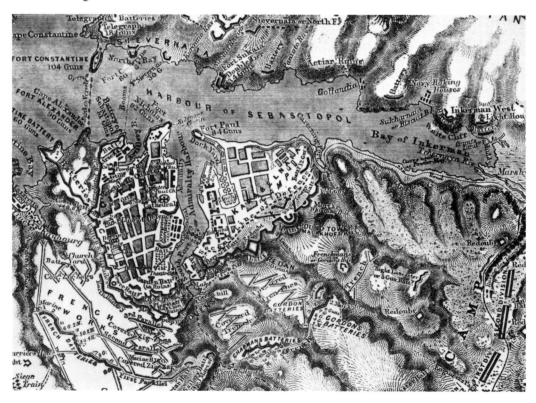

Council of War, showing the three allied commanders, Lord Raglan,
Omar Pasha and General Pélissier, photographed by Roger Fenton at 5
a.m. on 6th June 1855 - the morning of the assault on the Mamelon.

The French went up the steep to the Mamelon in most beautiful style and in loose
order, and every straining eye was upon their movements, which the declining
daylight did not throw out into bold relief. Still their figures, like light shadows
flitting across the dun barrier of earthworks, were seen to mount up unfailingly
—running, climbing, scrambling like skirmishers up the slopes on to the body of
the work, amid a plunging fire from the guns, which, owing to their loose form-
ation, did them as yet little damage. As an officer, who saw Bosquet wave them
on, said at the moment, 'They went in like a clever pack of hounds.'

It had been hoped that the allies would then continue the offensive by capturing the
Malakoff and the Redan but the French, wisely as it turned out, counselled caution and
time to consolidate. The next attempt was to be on 18th June, a significant date for
many, particularly Lord Raglan, as it was the anniversary of the Battle of Waterloo.

This whole attack was a complete failure. Many allied lives were lost and about 3,000
men wounded. Russell once again was quite clear in his own mind as to what had gone
wrong and did not hesitate to say so:

Our officers were outwitted by the subtlety of the Russians, who had for some
time masked their guns, or withdrawn them from the embrasures, as if they were
overpowered and silenced by our fire. No more decisive proof of the inefficiency
of our force could be afforded than this fact—that in no case did the troops
destined to assault and carry the Redan reach the outer part of the work; that no
ladders were placed in the ditch; and that a very small portion indeed of the

Kamiesch harbour, the French army's Balaclava, considered by those
who visited it to be far better organised.

storming party reached the abattis, which was placed many yards in front of the
ditch of the Redan. It cannot be said that on this occasion our men exhibited any
want of courage; but so abortive and so weak was the attack, that the Russians
actually got outside the parapet of the Redan, jeered and laughed at our soldiers
as they fired upon them at the abattis, and mockingly invited the 'Inglisky' to
come nearer.

Another burial truce was agreed upon but for some unknown reason, not allowed to
take effect until the afternoon of the following day.

It was agonizing to see the wounded men who were lying there under a broiling
sun, parched with excruciating thirst, racked with fever, and agonized with
pain—to behold them waving their caps faintly, or making signals towards our
lines, over which they could see the white flag waving. They lay where they fell,
or had scrambled into the holes formed by shells; and there they had been for
thirty hours.

It must have been with a sense of deliverance that Russell left the gloom and depression of the British camp for a month's leave in Therapia where his wife met him.
Almost immediately came news of Lord Raglan's death, after a short fever. Although
saddened by the news, Russell later wrote:

I have never seen any reason to alter the opinion that Lord Raglan was an
accomplished gentleman, as brave a soldier as ever drew a sword, an amiable,
honourable, kindly man, animated by zeal for the public service, of the most
unswerving fidelity to truth, devoted to his duty and to his profession...but he
appears to have been a man of strong prejudices and weak resolution, possessed
of limited information, offensively cold to those whom, like Omar Pasha, he
considered vulgar or obtrusive, coerced without difficulty by the influence of a
stronger will, and too apt to depend upon those around him when he should have
used his own eyes. Still, there was a simplicity about his manner, something of the
old heroic type in his character, which would have compensated for even graver
defects, if their results had not been, in many instances, so unfortunate for our
arms!

General Simpson was appointed to succeed Raglan. According to Russell, 'he was
destitute of those acquirements and personal characteristics which in Lord Raglan

compensated for a certain apathy and marble calmness which his admirers extolled as virtues'.

A month of boredom, sickness and inaction followed the abortive attack on 18th June. Eventually, it was the Russians who broke the monotony by attacking in force across the River Tchernaya. It was the Alma over again but in reverse, with the French occupying the Fedukhine Heights and the Russians having to cross the river and then charge up the steep slopes, raked from above by the French guns and from their left flank by the Sardinian batteries.

The first enemy attack was fended off, but only just, and they soon came on again. In spite of the immense bravery and tenacity of the Russian soldiers they were unable to scale the Heights and were continuously decimated by the murderous cross-fire of the French and Sardinian artillery. 'They were soon fleeing in all directions, pursued by the French.'

After the battle, the armies sank back into the dreary routine of the siege, still aware that the enemy could attack at any time. There was a universal dread among the allied troops of another winter in the Crimea. Everyone hoped that the Russians would try another attack across the Tchernaya. With their armies in surprisingly good shape and their defences greatly strengthened since the previous engagement, the allies were confident that the next attack would be Russia's last. However, on 5th September, it was the allies who took the initiative:

Suddenly, close to the Bastion du Mât three jets of flame sprang up into the air... The French had exploded three fougasses to blow in the counterscarp and to serve as a signal to their men. In a moment, from the sea to the Dockyard Creek, a stream of fire three miles in length seemed to run like a train from battery to battery, and fleecy, curling, rich white smoke ascended, as though the earth had suddenly been rent in the throes of an earthquake and was vomiting forth the material of her volcanoes.

The lines of the French trenches were at once covered as though the very clouds of Heaven had settled down upon them and were whirled about in spiral jets, in festoons, in clustering bunches, in columns and in sheets, all commingled, and uniting as it were by the vehement flames beneath. The crash of such a tremendous fire must have been appalling... The iron storm tore over the Russian

Battle of Tchernaya, 16th August 1855. The Russian attack was defeated by French and Sardinian forces with the British taking no part except for providing some artillery support.

An extraordinary photograph showing victorious Zouaves perched on the captured Malakoff. The weird, statuesque figure superimposed on the picture presumably represents *'la gloire'* of France.

lines, tossing up, as if in sport, jets of earth and dust, rending asunder gabions, and 'squelching' the parapets, or dashing in amongst the houses and ruins in their rear. The terrible files of this flying army extending about four miles in front, rushed across the plain, carrying death and terror in their train, swept with heavy and irresistible wings the Russian flanks, and searched their centre to the core. A volley so startling, simultaneous, and tremendously powerful, was probably never before discharged since cannon were introduced. The Russians seemed for a while utterly paralysed.

But they soon began to return the fire and the cannonade continued all day, punctuated by occasional pauses. When darkness fell the French started afresh with mortars and heavy guns. 'There was not one instant in which the shells did not whistle through the air; not a moment in which the sky was not seamed by their fiery curves or illuminated by their explosion.' The bombardment continued throughout the night of the 6th September. At dawn on the 7th 'the whole of the batteries from Quarantine to Inkerman began their fire with a grand crash,' and continued all day except for three short lulls. Russell wrote:

The contest on which the eyes of Europe had been turned so long—the event on which the hopes of so many mighty empires depended—was all but determined. A dull, strange silence, broken at distant intervals by the crash of citadels and palaces as they were blown into dust, succeeded to the incessant dialogue of the cannon which had spoken so loudly and so angrily throughout an entire year. Tired armies, separated from each other by a sea of fires, rested on their arms, and gazed with various emotions on all that remained of the object of their conflicts.

On the third day, 8th September, the bombardment stopped. The weather changed abruptly and became bitterly cold. A biting wind blew a harsh dust into the faces of the allied troops as they crouched expectantly in their trenches.

At five minutes before twelve o'clock, the French, like a swarm of bees, issued forth from their trenches close to the Malakoff, scrambled up its face, and were through the embrasures in the twinkling of an eye. They crossed the seven metres of ground which separated them from the enemy at a few bounds—they drifted as lightly and quickly as autumn leaves before the wind, battalion after battalion, into the embrasures, and in a minute or two after the head of their column issued from the ditch the tricolour was floating over the Bastion.

This was the signal for the British to attack the Redan, a formidable earthwork which had proved too tough for the 1,200 men that had been thrown against it in June. Learning nothing from this previous mistake, General Simpson again sent in only 1,380 soldiers —compared with the French who pitted 36,000, with a further 10,000 in reserve, against the Malakoff.

The Light Division, closely followed by the Second Division, attacked with energy and managed to reach the salient. Here they became hopelessly trapped within its narrow confines; officers fell like ninepins, the regiments became confused and inter-mingled and the Russians poured a rapid fire into the struggling masses. After an hour of this slaughter, the British soldiers broke and began leaping back into the fifteen foot ditch and trying to escape up the other side.

Bleeding, panting, and exhausted, our men lay in heaps in the ditch beneath the parapet, sheltered themselves behind stones and in bomb craters in the external slope of the work, or tried to pass back to our advanced parallel and sap, having to run the gauntlet of a tremendous fire. Many of them lost their lives or were seriously wounded in this attempt...the dead, the dying, the wounded, and the uninjured, were all lying in piles together.

The assault on the Redan was a disaster. The fact that the French had taken and held the Malakoff in such fine style made the humiliation of the British attack all the more painful. There was 'deep depression in camp' that night.

When the allied armies awoke next day, it was to find to their incredulity that Sebastopol was theirs. The Russians had abandoned the southern part of the city during the night. Soon after midnight,

...wandering fires gleamed through the streets and outskirts of the town—point after point became alight—the flames shone out of the windows of the houses —rows of mansions caught and burned up, and before daybreak the town of Sebastopol—that fine and stately mistress of the Euxine, on which we had so often turned a longing eye—was on fire from the sea to the Dockyard Creek. Fort Alexander was blown up early in the night, with a stupendous crash that made the very earth reel. At sunrise, four large explosions on the left followed in quick succession, and announced the destruction of the Quarantine Fort, and of the magazines of the batteries of the Central Bastion and Flagstaff Fort. In a moment afterwards the Redan was the scene of a very heavy explosion, which must have destroyed a number of wounded men on both sides. The Flagstaff and Garden Batteries blew up, one after another, at 4.45. At 5.30 there were two of the largest and grandest explosions on the left that ever shook the earth—most probably from Fort Alexander and the Grand Magazine. The rush of black smoke, grey and white vapour, masses of stone, beams of timber, and masonry into the air was appalling, and then followed the roar of a great bombardment; it was a magazine of shells blown up into the air, and exploding like some gigantic pyrotechnic display in the sky—innumerable flashes of fire twittering high up in the column of dark smoke over the town and then changing rapidly into as many balls of white smoke, like little clouds.

Under cover of this destruction, the Russian commander with 'masterly skill' transferred all his men, artillery and supplies across the bridge of boats in Dockyard Creek which connected the southern and northern halves of Sebastopol. The allies made no move to prevent this retreat but merely stood and watched.

This was followed by a rush to look round the ruined city and in particular the great defences over which so much blood had been shed. Russell describes the scene within the Malakoff as 'too terrible to dwell upon'.

The Russians lay inside the work in heaps, like carcasses in a butcher's cart; and the wounds—the blood—the sight exceeded all I had hitherto witnessed.

Descending from the Malakoff, we came upon a suburb of ruined houses open to the sea—it was filled with dead. The Russians had crept away into holes and corners in every house, to die like poisoned rats; artillery horses, with their entrails torn open by shot, were stretched all over the space at the back of the Malakoff, marking the place where the Russians moved up their last column to re-take it under the cover of a heavy field battery. Every house, the church, some public buildings, sentry-boxes—all alike were broken and riddled by cannon and mortar.

Of all the pictures of the horrors of war which have ever been presented to the world, the hospital of Sebastopol offered the most heartrending and revolting.

The carnage that resulted from the British attempt to cross the ditch of the Redan on the 8th September 1855. Sketch by Henry Clifford, V.C.

One of the hospitals in Sebastopol—the conditions bear out Russell's horrifying descriptions of what the allies found when they entered the city.

The building used as an hospital was inside the dockyard wall and was peculiarly
exposed to the action of shot and shell bounding over the Redan; it bore in sides,
roof, windows, and doors, frequent and distinctive proofs of the severity of the
cannonade.

Entering one of these doors, I beheld such a sight as few men, thank God, have
ever witnessed. In a long, low room, supported by square pillars arched at the
top, and dimly lighted through shattered and unglazed window-frames, lay the
wounded Russians. The wounded, did I say? No, but the dead—the rotten and

A panorama of the ruins of Sebastopol, photographed from the Malakoff
after the siege.

Cavalry camp in July 1855.

festering corpses of the soldiers, who were left to die in their extreme agony, untended, uncared for, packed as close as they could be stowed, some on the floor, others on wretched trestles and bedsteads or pallets of straw, sopped and saturated with blood which oozed and trickled through upon the floor, mingling with the droppings of corruption. With the roar of exploding fortresses in their ears—with shells and shot pouring through the roof and sides of the rooms in which they lay—with the crackling and hissing of fire around them, these poor fellows, who had served their loving friend and master the Czar but too well, were consigned to their terrible fate. Many might have been saved by ordinary care. Many lay, yet alive, with maggots crawling about in their wounds. Many, nearly mad by the scene around them, or seeking escape from it in their extremest agony, had rolled away under the beds and glared out on the heart-stricken spectator. Many, with legs and arms broken and twisted, the jagged splinters sticking through the raw flesh, implored air, water, food, or pity, or, deprived of speech by the approach of death or by dreadful injuries in the head or trunk, pointed to the lethal spot. Many seemed bent alone on making their peace with Heaven. The attitudes of some were so hideously fantastic as to root one to the ground by a sort of dreadful fascination. The bodies of numbers of men were swollen and bloated to an incredible degree; and the features, distended to a gigantic size, with eyes protruding from the sockets and the blackened tongue lolling out of the mouth, compressed tightly by the teeth which had set upon it in the death-rattle, made one shudder and reel round...

Climbing up to the Redan, which was fearfully cumbered with the dead, we witnessed the scene of the desperate attack and defence which cost both sides so much blood. The ditch outside made one sick—it was piled up with English dead, some of them scorched and blackened by the explosion, and others lacerated beyond recognition...

The Russian commander's next move was to scuttle his entire fleet which he did with silent efficiency during the night:

The work of destruction sped rapidly. The vessels were soon nothing but huge arks of blinding light, which hissed and crackled fiercely and threw up clouds of sparks and embers; and the guns, as they became hot, exploded, and shook the crazy hulls to atoms. One after another they went down into the seething waters...

The Russians, so far from flying in discomfort over boundless wastes, calmly strengthened their position on the north side. The face of the country bristled with their cannon and their batteries. Day and night the roar of their guns sounded through our camp, and occasionally equalled the noise of the old cannonades, which we hoped had died into silence for ever. There was no sign of any intention on their part to abandon a position on which they had lavished so much care and labour. In their new position they had placed between themselves and us a deep arm of the sea, a river, and the sides of a plateau as steep as a wall. We permitted them to get off at their leisure, and looked on, while the Russian battalions filed over the narrow bridge, emerging in unbroken order out of that frightful sea of raging fire and smoke which was tossed up into billows of flame by the frequent explosion of great fortresses and magazines.

Once again, the allies had thrown away their chance of a complete victory. 'Why did not the English move?' asked Russell in bewilderment. And in *The Times* he reminded his readers of an anniversary:

It is just one year to this day since we landed at Calamita Bay. In that time we have stormed the heights of the Alma, sustained the glorious disaster of Balaclava, fought the great fight of Inkerman, swept the Sea of Azov and its seaboard, wasted Kertch, and seized upon Ycnikale—have witnessed the battle of the Tchernaya—have opened seven bombardments upon Sebastopol—have held in check every general and every soldier that Russia could spare; and now, after the endurance of every ill that an enemy at home and abroad could inflict upon us—after passing through the summer's heat and winter's frost—after being purged in the fire of sickness and death, repulse and disaster, and above all in the fiery glow of victory, the British standard floats above Sebastopol. But our army is not the same... some regiments have been thrice renewed, others have been changed twice over.

The unreal situation continued. Tons of supplies were still coming in to Balaclava, transported to the army camps on roads which were being constantly improved. But for

Cooking house of the 8th Hussars. Photograph by Roger Fenton.

what? No one seemed to know. Finally, five months after the fall of Sebastopol and almost two years to the day since the British advance contingents had sailed for Gallipoli, news of an armistice reached the stagnating armies. It was followed at the end of March 1856 by the signature of a peace treaty which guaranteed the integrity of the Turkish Empire, scheduled the independence of Moldavia and Wallachia, declared the Black Sea a neutral zone, but did not mention the Holy Places.

Russell returned to an England which saluted him as a hero, called him 'Balaclava Russell' and heaped acclaim on him. Two years of reporting the horror and indeed, the 'glory and splendour' of the war had secured him a place in history.

Politically and territorially, the Crimean War was not fought in vain. For one thing, it drove Russia out of Central European politics for many years. But it was the British soldier who benefited most in the long run, although at the expense of so much blood and misery. Russell's devastating disclosures of the incompetence of the authorities, powerfully supported by Delane and *The Times*, had finally shaken the army administrators out of their lethargy of 40 years. Sweeping changes were made throughout the army.

Perhaps the most enduring effect of the war was the transformation brought about in the care of the sick and wounded both on the battlefield and at home. Russell had set the train of events in motion with his descriptions of the state of the wounded after the Battle of Alma, but it was the vehemence of attacks on the authorities by Thomas Chenery, *The Times's* correspondent at Constantinople (who had witnessed the arrival of the wounded at Scutari with mounting horror) that finally made an impact on public opinion. Delane backed him to the hilt and launched an appeal in *The Times* which raised £20,000. It was this money which funded the sending of Florence Nightingale with her staff of 38 nurses to Scutari.

Of Russell's involvement in the Crimea, Field Marshall Sir Evelyn Wood wrote in the *Fortnightly Review*:

> He incurred much enmity, but few unprejudiced men who were in the Crimea will now attempt to call in question the fact that by awakening the conscience of the British nation to the sufferings of its troops, he saved the remnant of those grand battalions we landed in September.

Crimean War casualties who were visited by Queen Victoria in Chatham Hospital in 1856.

The Indian Mutiny

'Not one year home from the Crimea and I am once more on my way to the East—another and a farther East.' Thus opens Russell's *Diary of the Indian Mutiny*. He continues:

> Hideous massacres of men, women and children...were reported to us with such seasoning of horrors, made by skilful masters in that sort of cookery, as the imagination had never before devised. I had been deeply impressed by those awful scenes. I was moved to the inner soul by the narratives which came to us by every mail, and I felt that our struggle against those monsters of cruelty and lust must be crowned by Heaven with success. But after a time I began, mail after mail, to seek for evidence of the truth of those disgusting anecdotes glossed with still more revolting insinuations. I never doubted them, but I wanted proof, and none was forthcoming. All the stories we heard emanated from Calcutta, and the people of Calcutta were far from the districts where, no doubt, most treacherous and wholesale murder had been perpetrated. At last I was going out to the very country which had acquired such fearful interest in our eyes, and I hoped to join my countrymen ere their vengeance was consummated, and India was once more restored, at least, to the tranquility of conquest.

The Mutiny was already seven months old by the time Russell, once more as correspondent for *The Times*, found himself 'plunging through head seas like a cormorant in a tide-way', on his way to India. The causes of this imperial upheaval were complex and manifold. Unrest and resentment against the British, particularly the East India Company, had been smouldering for years, gathering momentum as the rulers beame increasingly estranged from the ruled, preferring the company of their families and friends and living separate lives, walled up in their clubs and cantonments. Gone was the old camaraderie between the officers and their Indian soldiers, and, with it, their link with the mainstream of opinion in the barracks and bazaars.

During the early part of the nineteenth century a wave of liberal reform and evangelicalism had swept out from England, bringing with it missionaries bent on converting India to Christianity. Everywhere the people saw real or imagined signs of their religion being threatened. The forbidding of the practice of *suttee* (the voluntary immolation of a Hindu widow on her husband's funeral pyre) was taken as one such sign. There were many others. But it was the affair of the greased cartridges which provided the catalyst.

When the new Enfield rifle was introduced into India the troops were issued with greased cartridges, the ends of which had to be bitten off to release the gunpowder. A rumour began that the grease was made either from the fat of cows or pigs, which made using the cartridges an act of degradation for Muslims (who consider the pig to be unclean) and an act of sacrilege for Hindus (for whom the cow is sacred).

This rumour had already caused one incident in March 1857 when a young soldier went berserk and shot at his commanding officer. He was tried and hanged, and his name, Pandy, lived on as the British army's nickname for a mutineer. Finally, in May, at Meerut (one of the main military stations), some soldiers of the Indian Cavalry refused to handle the cartridges, although they were identical to those that they had been using for years. They were court-martialled, publicly degraded in front of the entire garrison and gaoled for ten years. The next day the town erupted. Many British officers and their families were killed or wounded. Leaving the town ablaze, the mutineers galloped off to Delhi, where the old King of Delhi, Bahadur Shah Zafar, reluctantly agreed to become the nominal leader of the Mutiny. Bahadur, the last of the Moghul monarchs, had been pensioned off by the British government and it was understood that when he died, his imperial title would die with him.

It must be remembered that the Mutiny never spread to the rest of India: it was confined to the valley of the Ganges and to the Bengal army only. When it is considered how thinly the British army was spread, this was very fortunate for them. For a population of 150 million people, India had an army of approximately 300,000: of these only about 40,000 were Europeans. It should also be remembered that the British were fighting soldiers whom they had trained and armed. Once the disaster at Meerut became known, the British officers were all faced with the same dilemma—should they continue to trust the native troops under their command, or should they disarm them, thereby displaying a distrust which might turn otherwise loyal troops against them? It was an awesome choice and many, with hindsight, made the wrong decision.

The 'hideous massacres' to which Russell referred were principally those at Cawnpore and Lucknow. Cawnpore was of strategic importance as it commanded one of the main crossings over the river Ganges. The man considered to be the instigator of the uprising was the Nana Sahib; and although there was never any proof, there were many who felt that he was the *éminence grise* behind the entire Mutiny. The British residents of Cawnpore were besieged for eighteen days in two hospital barracks on the edge of the cantonment. When the aged Major-General Wheeler surrendered it was on the understanding that the survivors would receive a safe passage to Allahabad, 100 miles down river. But no sooner were they safely (as they thought) in the boats, than they were fired upon from all sides. The pathetic remnant which survived this massacre—upwards of 200 women and children—were taken to the House of Women in the town. Just over two weeks later every single one was murdered, their bodies dismembered

The bridge of boats over the Jumna River, crossed in May 1857 by the rebels on their way from Meerut (where the Mutiny started) to Delhi to persuade the reluctant King of Delhi to assume symbolic leadership of the Indian Mutiny.

Ruins of the Lucknow Residency where Sir Henry Lawrence was one of
the first to be killed during the siege in July 1857.

and thrown down a well in the courtyard, filling the 50-foot shaft almost to capacity.
The revenge taken in Cawnpore by the British was no less appalling, carried out in a
vindictive frenzy by one man in particular, a Brigadier General James Neill, who firmly
believed he was doing God's work.

At Lucknow, the capital city of Oudh (now Uttar Pradesh), another longer and more
terrible siege took place within the grounds of the Residency. From the beginning of
July a force of 1,720 men, about 700 of whom were loyal Indian troops, defended the
Residency and its civilian inmates. They were led by the much-loved Sir Henry Lawrence
who was one of the first to die. Eighty-seven days later those who remained had somehow survived the ceaseless artillery fire, shortage of food, sickness and the heat. On
25th September, an army of 3,000 under Brigadier General Henry Havelock and Sir
James Outram managed to bring in some reinforcements, but they did not have enough
men to break the siege entirely, and it dragged on for a further 50 days. On 17th
November Sir Colin Campbell's force raised the siege sufficiently to enable the
survivors to be helped to safety. But the town itself remained in rebel hands.

At this point we should return to Russell, now sweating his way across the Red Sea,
being regaled by his fellow passengers with their views on the Mutiny—and what they
considered the British should do about it.

> Do they agree upon any one point connected with the mutinies, or with the char-
> acter of the people? Not one! There was much talk of 'rascally Mohammedans'
> and 'slimy, treacherous Hindus'. 'By Jove! sir,' exclaims the major, who has by
> this time got to the walnut stage of argument, to which he has arrived by grad-
> ations of sherry, port, ale, and Madeira,—'By Jove!' he exclaims, thickly and
> fiercely, with every vein in his forehead swoln like whipcord, 'those niggers are
> such a confounded sensual lazy set, cramming themselves with ghee and sweet-
> meats, and smoking their cursed chillimjees all day and all night, that you might
> as well think to train pigs. Ho you! punkah chordo, or I'll knock—Suppose we go
> up and have a cigar!' The fact is, I fear that the favourites of heaven—the civi-
> lizers of the world...are naturally the most intolerant in the world.

The interior of the Secundra Bagh after the slaughter of 2,000 sepoy rebels by Sir Colin Campbell's troops during the second attempt to relieve Lucknow in November 1857. Russell was with the third and final relief four months later.

On 19th January 1858, Russell arrived in Calcutta, parts of which seemed to remind him, curiously enough, of Moscow (which he had visited on behalf of *The Times* to report on the coronation of Tsar Alexander II in 1856). His first important meeting was with the Governor General of India, Lord Canning, who was about to leave for Allahabad. He found him 'worn-looking, and anxious, and heavy with care' and surrounded on all sides by despatch boxes. He made a number of other visits and seemed to find friends everywhere from his Crimean days. He was also busy making arrangements for his 700-mile journey up-country to join Sir Colin Campbell and his forces at Cawnpore. This included arming himself with pistols and a rifle. To look after all his belongings, he had engaged an Eurasian servant called Simon who was to serve him well in the months that followed.

Russell set off by train on 4th February, later transferring to a gharry—a sort of box on wheels pulled by horses—in which it was possible to both eat and sleep. When not sleeping in this contraption, he spent the night at one of the government *dâk* bungalows along the way. He observed that although they were intended for Indians and British alike, none of the Indians would dare to stay in them. Russell seemed to be painfully aware of the antagonism around him and wrote in his diary:

> In no instance is a friendly glance directed to the white man's carriage. Oh, that language of the eye! Who can doubt? Who can misinterpret it? It is by it alone that I have learned our race is not even feared at times by many, and that by all it is disliked. Pray God I have read it falsely.

At Allahabad he met up with Lord Canning and his entourage and visited him in his splendid tented camp:

> After a short delay, I was told his Excellency would receive me, and I was introduced to one of those grand tents which would be a palace in the eyes of any field-marshal in Europe. A few servants, in the red and gold of the Viceroy's

livery, were sitting under one of the spacious canvas eaves, where, indeed, the shade, even now, was not ungrateful. There were purdahs of fine matting, and doors, and flaps to pass, ere one could get inside. There soft Persian carpets received the feet in beds of flowers; the partitions of the tent, which was as large as a London saloon, were fitted with glass doors; but I was told afterwards, that Lord Canning had by no means carried tent-luxury to its fullest extent, and that, in fact, as Governor-General, he had rather curtailed the usual establishment.

Russell continued on his way, following in the wake of the force under Brigadier General Neill which had been sent to avenge the massacre at Cawnpore. Hung on trees by the wayside were the bodies of natives suspected of being mutineers. 'I hear many stories, the truth of which I would doubt if I could. Our first spring was terrible; I fear our claws were indiscriminating.'

It was natural that Russell should visit the House of the Women when he reached Cawnpore and he admitted that he found a fascination in places 'where great crimes have been perpetrated'. Typically, he was aware that there were two sides to the story and he was obviously alive to the anomalies of Victorian morality, as the following remarks from his diary show:

In fact, the peculiar aggravation of the Cawnpore massacres was this, that the deed was done by a subject race—by black men who dared to shed the blood of their masters, and that of poor helpless ladies and children. Here we had not only a servile war and a sort of Jacquerie combined, but we had a war of religion, a war of race, and a war of revenge, of hope, of some national promptings to shake off the yoke of a stranger, and to re-establish the full power of native chiefs, and the full sway of native religions.

He made every effort to establish the truth behind each facet of the story of the massacre. At no time did he find any proof that any of the women had been raped. He pointed out that the pathetic writings on the walls of the 'slaughter-house' had not been

Russell's gharry—one of the vehicles he used for his 700-mile expedition to Cawnpore to join Sir Colin Campbell for the relief of Lucknow.

Satichaura or Massacre Ghat, Cawnpore in a remarkable photograph
taken just after the Mutiny. It was visited by Russell on his way from
Calcutta to join the army for the relief of Lucknow.

there when Havelock had first seen the place and so could not have been done by the
prisoners, as had been alleged. Therefore, they must have been added after the
recapture of Cawnpore and used as propaganda to inflame the British soldiers further.

It was essential that Russell should meet Sir Colin Campbell, Commander-in-Chief
of the army which was to attempt to retake the town of Lucknow. Without Campbell's

The courtyard in the House of Women, Cawnpore, where the survivors
of the massacre at the boats were imprisoned and subsequently murdered.

active co-operation he would be unable to accompany the expedition. He need not have worried. They had known each other in the Crimea and Sir Colin was 'frank and cordial'.

'Now, Mr. Russell, I'll be candid with you. We shall make a compact. You shall know everything that is going on. You shall see all my reports, and get every information that I have myself, on the condition that you do not mention it in camp, or let it be known in any way, except in your letter to England.' 'I accept the condition, sir; and I promise you it shall be faithfully observed.'

Both men were to be as good as their word. And Russell found to his delight that a tent had been put up for him just opposite the Commander-in-Chief's.

But what a tent it was! True, only a simple pole; but then it was on the Indian establishment. I thought of the miserable little shell of rotten calico, under which I braved the Bulgarian sun, or the ill-shaped, tottering tent in which Collingwood, Dickson, and I had suffered from insects, robbers, and ghosts, not to mention hunger, in the onion bed at Gallipoli; of the poor fabric that went to the winds on the 14th November before Sebastopol...and then I turned round and round in my new edifice in ever-renewed admiration. The pole is a veritable pillar, varnished or painted yellow, with a fine brass socket in the centre; from the top spreads out the sloping roof to the square side walls. The inside is curiously lined with buff calico with a dark pattern, and beneath one's feet a carpet of striped blue and buff laid over the soft sand, is truly Persian in its yielding softness.

Next Russell had another pilgrimage to make: the site of the siege of Cawnpore. His diary contains the following description:

Left: Sir Colin Campbell, Commander-in-Chief of the Army, whom Russell had known and respected in the Crimea and with whom he travelled on the final relief of Lucknow in March, 1858. *Right:* Nana Sahib, the man considered by many to be the instigator of the Indian Mutiny.

It was a horrible spot! Inside the shattered rooms, which had been the scene of such devotion and suffering, are heaps of rubbish and filth. The entrenchment is used as a *cloaca maxima* by the natives, camp-followers, coolies, and others who bivouac in the sandy plains around it. The smells are revolting. Rows of gorged vultures sit with outspread wings on the mouldering parapets, or perch in clusters on the two or three leafless trees at the angle of the works by which we enter. I shot one with my revolver; and as the revolting creature disgorged its meal, twisting its bare black snake-like neck to and fro, I made a vow I would never incur such a disgusting sight again.

Another extract from Russell's diary, written while still at Cawnpore, gives an emotional but enlightened view of the British way of life in nineteenth-century India: it is a sad indictment of British rule.

Among those heaps of dust and ashes, those arid mounds of bricks, those new-made trenches, I try in vain to realise what was once this station of Cawnpore. The solemn etiquette, the visits to the Brigadier and the General *en grande tenue*, the invitations to dinner, the white kid-gloves, the balls, the liveries, the affectation of the *plus haut ton des hauts tons*, the millinery anxieties of the ladies, the ices, and Champagne, and supper, the golden-robed Nana Sahib moving about amid haughty stares and ill-concealed dislike. 'What the deuce does the General ask that nigger here for?' The little and big flirtations, the drives on the road—a dull, ceremonious pleasure—the faded fun of the private theatricals, the exotic absurdities of the masonic revels, the marryings and givings in marriage, the little bills done by the rich merchants, the small and great pecuniary relations between the station and the bazaar, the sense of security—and then on all this exaggerated relief of an English garrison-town and watering-place, the deep gloom of apprehension—at first 'a shave of old Smith's,' then a well-authenticated report, then a certainty of disaffection—rolling like thunder-clouds, and darkening the glassy surface of the gay society till it burst on it in stormy and cruel reality. But I cannot.

'Ah! you should have seen Cawnpore in its palmy days, when there were two cavalry regiments here, a lot of artillery, and three regiments of infantry in the cantonments. Chock full of pretty women! The private theatricals every week; balls, and picnics, and dinners every evening. By Jove! it's too horrible to look at it now!' And so, indeed, it was. But one is tempted to ask if there is not some lesson and some warning given to our race in reference to India by the tremendous catastrophe of Cawnpore?

How are we to prevent its recurrence? I am deeply impressed by the difficulty of ruling India, as it is now governed by force, exercised by a few who are obliged to employ natives as the instruments of coercion. That force is the base of our rule I have no doubt; for I see nothing else but force employed in our relations with the governed. The efforts to improve the condition of the people are made by bodies or individuals who have no connection with the Government. The action of the Government in matters of improvement is only excited by consideration of revenue. Does it, as the great instructor of the people, the exponent of our superior morality and civilisation—does it observe treaties, show itself moderate, and just, and regardless of gain? Are not our courts of law condemned by ourselves? Are they not admitted to be a curse and a blight upon the country? In effect, the grave, unhappy doubt which settles on my mind is, whether India is the better for our rule, so far as regards the social condition of the great mass of the people. We have put down widow-burning, we have sought to check infanticide; but I have travelled hundreds of miles through a country peopled with beggars and covered with wigwam villages.

By now Russell was longing to be off on the march to recapture Lucknow, besieged since July of the previous year; he describes, in anticipation, the army's departure the next day:

> To-night, the great mess-tent, which will be borne by four camels and an elephant, will be packed up, with our apparatus of tables, plate, crockery, bitter beer, and provisions, and the army of servants which belong to it; and we take the field, very much as his majesty Louis the Great would depart from Versailles, for the theatre of war. As for myself, I am delighted at the prospect of escaping from this monotonous dreary dusty Cawnpore, and the very hum and no drum sort of life I have been leading. Oudh is, they say, the garden of India; here everything is blighted, burnt, and ruined.

Before dawn on 27th February, the army had crossed the Ganges and begun the 40-mile journey to Lucknow.

> We got out on the road; where, in silence and order, the Rifle Brigade was plunging with steady tramp through the dust. As the moon sank in the heavens, the line of our march became more and more like some dream of the other world, or some recollections of a great scene at a theatre than anything else. The horizontal rays just touched the gleaming arms and the heads of the men, lighted up the upper portions of the camels and the elephants, which resembled islands in an opaque sea, whilst the plain looked like an inky waste, dotted with star-like fires.

The army now consisted of about 20,000 men and a large number of guns and mortars. When it is considered that for 10,000 soldiers, about 30,000 camp followers were required, it is understandable why a baggage train of this sort could stretch for up to ten miles, every mile of which had to be safeguarded against possible enemy attack. A description in Russell's diary of breakfast that day illustrates the use made of many of these camp followers:

> The sun was just beginning to make himself disagreeable, when, after several halts, we caught sight of some tents partly hidden in trees. 'Thank goodness! there's our camp. Canter over, and get some breakfast.' And there, sure enough, was our mess-tent pitched; the tables covered with snow-white cloths, our plates, chairs, knives and forks, all ready—the curries smoking, and the array of servants standing with folded arms waiting for their masters.

One of the acknowledged heroes of the Mutiny was Thomas Kavanagh, who had been in the Residency during the siege of Lucknow. When it was learned that Sir Colin Campbell was on his way to relieve them in November, he had volunteered to escape from the city in Indian disguise, find Sir Colin and guide him in. This was a singularly brave thing to do, particularly as Kavanagh was tall and blond. Russell met him and was impressed. He made the observation that if ever a man should get the Victoria Cross it should be Kavanagh, although at that time civilians were never awarded them. (In fact, the rules were subsequently changed to include civilians, and Kavanagh received his V.C. from Queen Victoria in 1860.)

When Sir Colin's force had relieved the Residency in November, he had left Sir James Outram and 4,000 men to hold the Alambagh, a large building which lay four miles to the south of Lucknow on the road from Cawnpore. As Sir Colin now approached the city the two forces joined and camp was made '...in a series of magnificently-wooded parks, attached to several palaces, or country houses, of the royal family of Oudh, south of the Dilkusha [Park]. The trees were of great age and extreme beauty, affording us a fine shade and cover to innumerable langurs, or black-faced long-tailed monkeys with white hair and whiskers.'

Thomas Kavanagh who, although a tall, blond Irishman, disguised himself as an Indian and escaped from the besieged city of Lucknow to make
contact with Sir Colin Campbell and then guided the army in.

Russell described one of the park's most remarkable features, the Martinière, at that
time in the hands of the rebels:

> At first glance one exclaims, 'How beautiful! what a splendid building!' at the
> second, 'why it must have been built by a madman!' At the distance of more than
> half a mile we can make out the eccentric array of statues, the huge lions' heads,
> the incongruous columns, arches, pillars, windows, and flights of stairs leading to
> nothing, which are the distinguishing features of the Martinière. The centre of the
> building is the most grotesque; the wide sweep of the wings and their curve
> inwards from the triad stairs leading to the entrance has a fine effect. But the
> statues! they are perched on every angle, drawn up as close as they can stand all
> along the roof, fixed on the pinnacles, and corners, and pillars, in all directions.

Having made a tour of the park, he was standing talking with a group of officers under
a tree. He noticed that the rebels in the Martinière were carefully aiming a large gun in
their direction.

> 'I think,' said I, modestly, 'they are going to fire at us.' As I spoke, pluff came a
> spurt of smoke with a red tongue in it—a second of suspense, and whi-s-s-sh, right
> for us came the round-shot within a foot of our heads, plumped into the ground,
> with a storm of dust and small stones, beyond us, and then rising rushed over the

wall into the Chief's camp. It is not etiquette, strictly speaking, to bow to a round-shot on duty; but we were not on duty, and we all 'bobbed', gently, pleasantly, and unconcernedly, as it were. Each man smiled as he looked at his neighbour. 'Begad, that was a near shave for some of us; we'd better get from this tree—we're only drawing fire.' A sensible remark, and each man stalked away, very savage with the enemy, and affecting a great indifference. Just some twelve inches lower, and where had been the brains of some of us, or the subtler part?

After this dignified retreat, Russell entered the Dilkusha building itself, 'nothing more nor less than a good specimen of a French chateau', and went up through the ruins to the flat roof. From there he could see the city of Lucknow:

A vision of palaces, minars, domes azure and golden, cupolas, colonnade, long façades of fair perspective in pillar and column, terraced roofs—all rising up amid a calm still ocean of the brightest verdure. Look for miles and miles away, and still the ocean spreads, and the towers of the fairy-city gleam in its midst. Spires of gold glitter in the sun. Turrets and gilded spires shine like constellations. There is nothing mean or squalid to be seen. There is a city more vast than Paris, as it seems, and more brilliant, lying before us. Is this a city in Oudh? Is this the capital of a semi-barbarous race, erected by a corrupt, effete, and degraded dynasty? I confess I felt inclined to rub my eyes again and again.

The flat roof of the Dilkusha became the principal vantage point for Sir Colin, his staff and for Russell, who spent many hours there during the next few days, employing his telescope to good effect. Having been given a pass which allowed him the freedom to go about as he pleased, he conscientiously visited all the outposts and spent some time watching the bridge which was being built across the River Gumti.

The Martinière, a college in Lucknow for European and Eurasian children, photographed in the early 1850s before it was destroyed in the fighting.

Sir Colin's plan of attack entailed splitting the army into two: one half, under the command of General Sir James Outram, was to cross the river by this bridge, execute a wide flanking movement and attack the city from the north. Sir Colin's force would attack from the east.

Russell described a typical evening meal during this period of suspense before the attack was launched:

> Dinner passed just the same as usual. We were all talking of heavy guns, battering, and storming, for half an hour, and then dropped into our usual quasi controversial conversation. Our condensation increases the number of our visitors and guests, and the mess has as many as five or six-and-twenty covers laid; plates of all patterns, flanked by fifty or more little salt and pepper turrets; a silver Lucknow on a waste of table cloth. To-night some guns are to be sent up to the ridge, behind the wall, on the right front of the Dilkusha, to open on the angle of the Martinière to-morrow morning. Sir Colin and the chief of staff are in constant intercourse. Bruce is busy with spies; Napier with plans. We have no politicals in camp.

On 9th March, Outram's force attacked and secured the Chakar Kothi, the Badshahbagh (a large walled garden) and the Iron Bridge over the Gumti. There was hard fighting and some shameful examples of wanton cruelty carried out by the British forces against the rebels. Russell was told this story by a shocked acquaintance who had witnessed the appalling death of a sepoy:

> ...he was pulled by the legs to a convenient place, where he was held down, pricked in the face and body by the bayonets of some soldiery, whilst others collected fuel for a small pyre, and when all was ready—the man was roasted alive! There were Englishmen looking on, more than one officer saw it. No one offered to interfere! The horror of this infernal cruelty was aggravated by an attempt of the miserable wretch to escape when half-burned to death. By a sudden effort he leaped away, and with the flesh hanging from his bones, ran for a few yards ere he was caught, brought back, put on the fire again, and held there by bayonets till his remains were consumed. 'And his cries, and the dreadful scene,' said my friend, 'will haunt me to my dying hour.' 'Why didn't you interfere?' 'I dared not, the Sikhs were furious. They had lost Anderson, our own men encouraged them, and I could do nothing.'

Sir Colin's forces took the Martinière with comparative ease and Russell made a brief tour of the deserted rebel trenches:

> The ground is covered with their tulas, or cooking places, and with little other remnants—no beef-bones and beer-bottles as in the case of the British, or tin cases as in that of the French, or rags and cabbage-stalks as in that of the Russian, are strewed over their camping-ground.

The Commander-in-Chief had been delaying his main attack until a force of Gurkhas arrived which he had been promised by the Maharajah Jung Bahadur, the *de facto* ruler of Nepal. This contingent would swell the size of the British army to 30,000 and since the rebel forces were reputed to number 100,000, every extra man was welcome.

Sir Colin had ordered his state tent to be erected and all those present had been ordered to turn out in full uniform for the arrival of the Maharajah.

> Four o'clock came, no signs of Jung Bahadur. A quarter of an hour passed by; the Chief walked up and down with one hand behind his back, and the other working nervously... At half-past four the regular cannonading close at hand ceased, and

Maharajah Jung Bahadur.

up rose a startling heavy rolling fire of musketry. We all knew what it meant. The assault on the Begum Kothie was being delivered. Sir Colin listened as a hunter does to the distant cry of the hounds. Louder and louder rang the musketry. Come quickly, Sir Jung, or you will find an empty tent! Just at this moment, however, the agitation among the crowd of camp followers, and the 'Stand to your arms,' warned us that the Maharajah was at hand, and, in a minute or so, he made his appearance at the end of the lane formed by the guard of honour, and walked up towards the tent in a very slow and dignified sort of strut, followed by a staff of Gurkhas... Our eyes were fixed on him, but our ears were listening to the raging of the fight. Sir Colin walked to the door of the tent, met the Maharajah, took him by the hand, and led him inside... The durbar was open. It consisted of fine speeches, interpreted by Captain Metcalfe, whilst the English and the Nepalese were examining each other. Stout, Calmuck-faced, high-shouldered, bow-legged men these latter, very richly attired in a kind of compromise between European and Asiatic uniform. As to Jung himself, he blazed like a peacock's tail in the sun... But brighter than any gem the Maharajah wore is his eye, which shines with a cold light, resembling a ball of phosphorus. What a tiger-like, cruel, crafty, subtle eye! How it glanced, and glittered, and rolled, piercing the recesses of the tent... In the midst of the durbar an officer of Mansfield's staff comes in to announce to Sir Colin that 'the Begum Kothie is taken. Very little loss on our side. About five hundred of the enemy killed!' As we could not cheer aloud, every man did so mentally. Jung tried to look pleased when he heard the news, which Sir Colin announced with great vivacity. The

A panorama of Lucknow photographed by Felice Beato from the roof of the Kaiserbagh after the siege in 1858. When Russell first saw the city he described it thus: 'A vision of palaces...there is a city more vast than Paris and more brilliant...'

A gateway leading into the Kaiserbagh, Lucknow. Photograph by Felice
Beato, 1858.

durbar had all along been stupid enough, but when the bagpipes outside were set
loose affairs became desperate, and yet no one dared leave. [Russell frequently
expressed a loathing for bagpipes.]

His Highness eventually left on his richly encrusted elephant, but it was too late by
then to see the assault on the Begum Kothie. The next day Russell walked round the
shattered Begum's palace, through 'chambers of horrors ineffable'. On 14th March,

An orderly came up the avenue at full speed, with a small piece of folded paper in
his hand. He delivered it at one of the tents. In a second or two, I saw Norman, at
his usual canter, hurrying across the street. 'What is it, Norman? Have we got the
Imambarra?' 'The Imambarra! Why, man, we're in the Kaiserbagh!' Here, indeed, was news. The camp was in commotion. Syces running to and fro, the Chief
and all his staff calling for their horses. What a scamper to the Begum Kothie...
Listen to the cheering behind us. Sir Colin is riding up the street. Now he has
dismounted, and is marching up the steps of the Imambarra amidst the shouts of
the troops. What a scene of destruction meets the eye as we enter the great hall.
It is no exaggeration to say the marble pavement is covered two or three inches
deep with fragments of broken mirrors and of the chandeliers which once hung
from the ceilings; and the men are busy smashing still. This mischief is rude,
senseless, and brutal, but no one cares to stop it... The heat was sweltering, and I
pitied our men as they stood under its rays, many of them unprovided with proper

protection against the sun, and retaining their old European outfit. And these poor fellows might be exposed for hours, not only to this terrible heat, but to a hard struggle and severe fighting.

Russell continued through the ruins of the Imambarra and found himself in a court of the Kaiserbagh. Bullets were flying in all directions and everywhere 'discord and chaos reigned'.

It was one of the strangest and most distressing sights that could be seen; but it was also most exciting. Discipline may hold soldiers together till the fight is won; but it assuredly does not exist for a moment after an assault has been delivered, or a storm has taken place. Imagine courts as large as the Temple Gardens, surrounded with ranges of palaces... In the body of the court are statues, lines of lamp-posts, fountains, orange-groves, aqueducts, and kiosks with burnished domes of metal. Through all these, hither and thither, with loud cries, dart European and native soldiery, firing at the windows, from which come now and then dropping shots or hisses a musket-ball. At every door there is an eager crowd, smashing the panels with the stocks of their firelocks, or breaking the fastenings by discharge of their weapons... Here and there the invaders have forced their way into the long corridors, and you hear the musketry rattling inside; the crash of glass, the shouts and yells of the combatants, and little jets of smoke curl out of the closed lattices. Lying amid the orange-groves are dead and dying sepoys; and the white statues are reddened with blood. Leaning against a smiling Venus is a British soldier shot through the neck, gasping and at every gasp bleeding to death! Here and there officers are running to and fro after their men, persuading or threatening in vain. From the broken portals issue soldiers laden with loot or plunder. Shawls, rich tapestry, gold and silver brocade, caskets of jewels, arms, splendid dresses. The men are wild with fury and lust for gold— literally drunk with plunder.

Court after court the scene is still the same. These courts open one to the other by lofty gateways, ornamented with the double fish of the royal family of Oudh, or by arched passages, in which lie the dead sepoys, their clothes smouldering on their flesh...

Oh, the toil of that day! Never had I felt such exhaustion. It was horrid enough to have to stumble through endless courts which were like vapour baths, amid dead bodies, through sights worthy of the Inferno, by blazing walls which might

Left: The plundering of the Kaiserbagh, which took place after the building had been wrested from the mutineers and filled Russell with disgust. *Right:* A rebel trooper or sowar.

be pregnant with mines over breaches, in and out smouldering embrasures, across frail ladders, suffocated by deadly smells of rotting corpses, of rotten ghee, or vile native scents; but the seething crowd of camp followers into which we emerged in Hazrutgunj was something worse. As ravenous, and almost as foul as vultures, they were packed in a dense mass in the street, afraid or unable to go into the palaces, and like the birds they resembled, waiting till the fight was done to prey on their plunder.

With the Kaiserbagh now in British hands, they pressed on to secure the Residency. Then began the task of infiltrating the main city in order to flush out the rebels from its narrow streets.

It was necessary to proceed with great caution in this street-fighting, and our advance was gradual but sure. On every side were sights which I would fain have shut my eyes on, sounds which I would not readily listen to again, as well as scenes of wonderful novelty and interest. The dust, the heat, the excitement were overpowering.

Russell and his friend Lieutenant Patrick Stewart (Deputy Superintendent of the Indian Telegraphs) climbed a lofty, tapering minaret and looked out over the city.

Alas, words! words! how poor you are to depict the scene which met the eye of the infidel from the quiet retreat of the muezzin! Lucknow, in its broad expanse of palaces, its groves and gardens, its courts and squares, its mosques and temples, its wide-spreading, squalid quarters of mean, close houses, amid which are kiosks and mansions of rich citizens, surrounded by trees, all lay at our feet, with the Dilkusha, and Martinière, and distant Alumbagh plainly visible, and the umbrageous plains clothed in the richest vegetation, and covered with woodland, which encompasses the city. In the midst winds the Gumti, placid and silvery, though its waters are heavy with the dead. Across the Stone bridge, in wild confusion, are pouring the rebels, the sepoys, badmashes, matchlockmen, and inhabitants of the place, and from the Iron bridge our guns are opening on them incessantly, and the showers of our Enfield bullets cut the surface of the waters like rain.

Later accounts accused Sir Colin of allowing many of the rebels to escape. They were thus able to re-form under their *zemindars* (chiefs) and continue a resistance which prolonged the Mutiny for another year. Even at the time Russell wrote in his diary:

To-day's work has not been very successful in causing loss to the enemy. It is evident most of them have escaped. The philanthropists who were cheering each other with the thought that there was sure 'to be a good bag at Lucknow,' will be disappointed. It must be admitted that it is unfortunate we could not inflict on the rebels such a severe punishment as would ensure their complete discomfiture and prevent them assembling in other strongholds to renew their opposition to our rule.

For the British forces in Lucknow all that now remained was the fortification of the city against the return of the rebels. Russell makes this tart entry in his diary: 'Napier is engaged in drawing up a report on the alterations and defences of Lucknow, of a *grandiose* and very elevated character. It is imperial in conception; but where is the money to come from?' There were other matters that he felt unhappy about:

March 22nd. Today I procured a copy of Lord Canning's Proclamation, which I sent to London, where no doubt it will excite as much disapprobation as it does here. I have not heard one voice raised in its defence; and even those who are habitually silent, now open their mouths to condemn the policy which must perpetuate the rebellion in Oudh.

Lord Canning, 100 miles away at Allahabad, was mistakenly under the impression that the fall of Lucknow had been followed by the complete submission of the rest of Oudh. His proclamation declared that the British government would confiscate all the lands of Oudh as a reprisal against those who had co-operated with the mutineers. Outram, as Commissioner of the Province, felt quite unable to carry out this vengeful policy and left for Calcutta to try to persuade Canning to modify his harsh ruling. Russell was sad to see him go as he had developed a deep respect and liking for the man.

There now seemed no alternative but to pursue the rebel chiefs and their followers throughout Oudh and Rohilkhand and force them to surrender one by one. Sir Colin's force therefore left Lucknow for Cawnpore, marching by night when it was slightly cooler. Russell had fallen prey to dysentery. Fortunately he was able to convalesce for two days at Cawnpore in the house of his friend John Sherer, who was the Magistrate there.

> April 20th.—Chowbeypore to Poorwah.—Oh, Sir Colin, this is very severe! At 2.15 this morning we were on our way to Poorwah, thirteen miles. The fatigue and monotony of these slow, long marches in the dark, are indescribable. You can see nothing. Unrefreshed by sleep, only half-awake, every moment you catch yourself just going over the horse's shoulder. You must look out lest you ride over soldiers or camp-followers who throng the road, mingled with flocks of goats, sheep, tats or ponies, camels, bullocks, begum-carts, all shrouded in dusk and darkness. At last dawn comes, very slowly, no glory in it, no clouds—on the horizon there is a dim fog of dust, a haze which hides the sun. There is no colour, no atmosphere. The moment the sun shows above the haze, he burns you like fire. As you pass through the villages, ghost-like figures clad in white rise from their charpoys, which are laid out in the street, stare at you for a moment, and sink to sleep again. Early marches, how I hate you! and yet you must be, for the men must be got under cover ere the sun is long out... The great object is to get the men under the shade of the trees, the Commander-in-Chief of course getting the best place... I fasten up my horse if the syce is not up, and take a sleep with one eye open for the mess-camels. One by one the staff come in. Sir Colin and the chief of the staff are generally some time behind us. Then comes their escort, a handful of cavalry; next the interminable line of tent-camels and elephants, then the cavalry in the centre of a cloud of dust, and at last, 'rub-a-dub-dub, rub-a-dub-dub,' and the infantry, hot and fagged, and white as bakers, trudge up; then more baggage; then the rear-guard, and three miles of stragglers, and bazaar people.

On the night of 26th April the column crossed the Ganges and entered the province of Rohilkhand. The night and early morning marches continued as the army swept on—the 'Devil's Wind' as the Indians called it—seeking out the mutineers.

Three days later Russell had an accident which was to affect him for the rest of his life. In the early dawn during a halt in the march, he woke up from a quick nap to find:

> All the stallions about us were squeaking and lashing out violently. I ran over to preserve my beast from being eaten alive—but I was sleepy: my leg was stiff from the strain of the day before—and, just as I was getting up to the head of my horse, a powerful Arab, belonging to Stewart, ran back to have a last go in at his enemy, and delivered a murderous fling, from which I could not escape, for my own horse was pressing hard against me. I saw the shoes flash in the moonlight. In an instant I was sent flying along the ground under my horse's belly. One heel had struck me just at the lower part of the stomach, but the steel scabbard of the sword I wore broke the force of the blow there, though the shoe cut out a small piece of skin; the other hoof caught me right in the hollow of the right thigh. Several men ran towards me. Ricketts and Bunny picked me up, and helped me

to one of Tombs' guns, where I managed to hold on by the tumbril seat. I was in great pain, faint, sick, and burning with thirst.

The next day, unable to ride a horse, he was carried in a dooly.

I am to know more of these doolys, it would appear, than I care for. I confess that there is something revolting to my feelings about the mode of progression, though we had our sedan chairs, and were no better than Hindu notables in our day. It is miserable jogging along by the column. Everyone bullies dooly-bearers; therefore, to avoid knocks and whip cuts and bad language, they go off in the open, and expose one to the risk of being cut up by the enemy's cavalry. They were reported to be strong at Shahjahanpur; and it was not pleasant to find myself at dawn this morning out in a wide plain, with only a cloud of dust in the distance to show where our column was marching.

Three days later his leg was much worse.

In great agony last night; up at one this morning and left Shahjahanpur camp at 1 a.m.! bound for Tilhour, twelve miles distant. In much pain all day; a large lump forming in the hollow of the thigh, from near the knee to an inch of the hip. The kick is now really serious. Twenty-five leeches were put on the calf of my leg as soon as we halted. Why on the calf? Bleed, and bear, and ask no questions.

The army was marching all this time through hostile country and there were frequent reports that rebels had been seen. Russell's dooly and those of two other injured officers, were frequently '...the only portions of our force visible for miles. As I have resolved not to be cut up without a fight for it, and giving myself a chance, I had up my syce this morning, and warned him, under terrible pains and penalties, to lead my best horse always close to my litter, ready for mounting, with one revolver loose in the holster.'

The next day, 5th May, the army was on its way to Bareilly where it was rumoured that a large force led by Khan Bahadur Khan, one of the principal rebel leaders, had

The British army on the move. In the foreground is a dooly; Russell was later carried in one after being severely kicked by a horse.

gathered and would fight. Russell was 'tortured by flies, smothered in an atmosphere of dust, prostrated by heat, my sufferings were augmented by loss of blood, by recent leech-bites, and by a fresh blister. Belladonna had lost its influence over the pain in my injured limb.'

At about noon the column halted. There was some firing up ahead and some of the troops were engaged. The heat was fearful and Russell had his dooly taken over to a small *tope* (clump of trees) and set down in the shade. He went to sleep.

I know not what my dreams were, but well I remember the waking. There was a confused clamour of shrieks and shouting in my ear. My dooly was raised from the ground and then let fall violently. I heard my bearers shouting 'Sowar! sowar!' I saw them flying with terror in their faces. All the camp-followers, in wild confusion, were rushing for the road. It was a veritable *stampede* of men and animals. Elephants were trumpeting shrilly as they thundered over the fields, camels slung along at their utmost joggling stride, horse and tats, women, and children, were all pouring in a stream, which converged and tossed in heaps of white as it neared the road—an awful panic! And, heavens above! within a few hundred yards of us, sweeping on like the wind, rushed a great billow of white sowars, their sabres flashing in the sun, the roar of their voices, the thunder of their horse, filling and shaking the air. As they came on, camp-followers fell with cleft skulls and bleeding wounds upon the field; the left wing of the wild cavalry was coming straight for the tope in which we lay. The eye takes in at a glance what tongue cannot tell or hand write in an hour. Here was, it appeared, an inglorious and miserable death swooping down on us in the heart of that yelling crowd. At that instant my faithful syce, with drops of sweat rolling down his black face, ran towards me, dragging my unwilling and plunging horse towards the litter, and shouting to me as if in the greatest affliction. I could scarcely move in the dooly. I don't know how I ever managed to do it, but by the help of poor Ramdeen I got into the saddle. It felt like a plate of red-hot iron; all the flesh of the blistered thigh rolled off in a quid on the flap; the leech-bites burst out afresh; the stirrup-irons seemed like blazing coals; death itself could not be more full of pain. I had nothing on but my shirt. Feet and legs naked—head uncovered—with Ramdeen holding on by one stirrup-leather, whilst, with wild cries, he urged on the horse, and struck him over the flanks with a long strip of thorn—I flew across the plain under that awful sun. I was in a ruck of animals soon, and gave up all chances of life as a troop of sowars dashed in among them. Ramdeen gave a loud

Panoramic sketch of the action at Bareilly that led to the capture of Khan Bahadur Khan, one of the principal rebel leaders in Rohilkhand. Russell nearly lost his life reporting it.

cry, with a look of terror over his shoulder, and leaving the stirrup-leather, disappeared. I followed the direction of his glance, and saw a black-bearded scoundrel, ahead of three sowars, who was coming right at me. I had neither sword nor pistol. Just at that moment, a poor wretch of a camel-driver, leading his beast by the nose-string, rushed right across me, and seeing the sowar so close, darted under his camel's belly. Quick as thought, the sowar reined his horse right round the other side of the camel, and as the man rose, I saw the flash of the tulwar falling on his head like a stroke of lightning. It cleft through both his hands, which he had crossed on his head, and with a feeble gurgle of 'Ram! Ram!' the camel-driver fell close beside me with his skull split to the nose. I felt my time was come. My naked heels could make no impression on the panting horse. I saw, indeed, a cloud of dust and a body of men advancing from the road; but just at that moment a pain so keen shot through my head that my eyes flashed fire. My senses did not leave me; I knew quite well I was cut down, and put my hand up to my head, but there was no blood; for a moment a pleasant dream of home came across me; I thought I was in the hunting-field, that the heart of the pack was all around me; but I could not hold on my horse; my eyes swam, and I remember no more than that I had, as it were, a delicious plunge into a deep cool lake, in which I sank deeper and deeper, till the gurgling waters rushed into my lungs and stifled me.

On recovering my senses I found myself in a dooly by the roadside, but I thought what had passed was a dream. I had been for a long time insensible. I tried to speak, but my mouth was full of blood. Then I was seized with violent spasms in the lungs, from which for more than an hour I coughed up quantities of mucus and blood; my head felt like a ball of molten lead. It is only from others I gathered what happened this day, for my own recollections of the occurrences after the charge of the cavalry are more vague than those of a sick man's night visions. I can remember a long halt in the dooly, amidst an immense multitude of ammunition camels, sick and wounded soldiers, and camp-followers. I remember rows of doolys passing by to the rear, and occasional volleys of musketry, and the firing of field guns close at hand. It appears that I fell from my horse close to the spot where Tombs' guns were unlimbering, and that a soldier who belonged to the ammunition guard, and who was running from the sowars, seeing a body lying in the sun all naked, except a bloody shirt, sent out a dooly when he got to the road for 'a dead officer who had been stript', and I was taken up and carried off to the cover of some trees. Alison and Baird saved themselves also, but they got well away before I could mount. Baird's servant poured some brandy down my throat. After a long interval of pain and half consciousness of life, Simon came to me, chafed my legs and arms, and rubbed my chest. My thirst was insatiable. The heat from twelve o'clock to sunset was tremendous, and this day all over India we lost

literally hundreds of men by sun-stroke. For hours we were halted close behind the 79th and 42nd. At one time I have a dreamy sort of notion that I saw a body of men charge on the latter and the Staff, and a great deal of bayoneting and shooting going on; but I cannot say whether it was real, or if, hearing of the charge of the Gazees that evening, and the descriptions of it given so often whilst I was very weak, I mistake the impressions of one sense for those of another. No surgeon came near me, as well as I recollect, for several hours. The non-attendance of my friends may have tended to save my life. As soon as the flow of blood and mucus from the lungs had somewhat ceased, Simon got me a bottle of *vin ordinaire*, which I drank at a few gulps. My dooly was recovered, and it was lucky I was not in it, for it bore marks of a probing of no friendly character by lance and sword. Tod Brown afterwards told me that some of the sowars came up within a few yards of his guns, and that one fellow was shot when within ten feet of a heavy piece of siege ordnance, which he seemed determined to spike. The Multani horse were wheeled round, and sent out to meet the sowars the moment they were seen to be down on us; but some of them turned, and Tombs, who had come up at a gallop, was obliged to fire into a mass of Multanis and sowars who were all coming pell-mell together upon his guns. This, and the sight of the Carabineers bearing down on them, rapidly sent the sowars flying to the right-about; but the panic produced by their demonstration was very great, and almost as soon as the first was over I believe a second took place.

The sun was going down ere we were moved forward for about half a mile, and there, on a bare sandy plain, was one small tent pitched for Sir Colin, and two or three pall and servants' tents for the officers. I was put into my own pall. Scarcely was I placed in the charpoy ere Sir Colin came in, and, having heard what had happened, congratulated me on the escape from the sun and sowar, and proceeded to give me details of what had occurred. He complained very much of want of information. When he thought he was outside Bareilly he was in reality only outside the ruined cantonments, some miles from the city proper. The enemy were still in the city. They had fallen back, and it was too late to pursue them or to make an attempt to enter the place. The men were quite exhausted. They had suffered fearfully from sun-stroke. Sir Colin described the charge of the Gazees vividly. Just at this moment Walpole came in with a bloody handkerchief round his hand. He had a narrow escape from the Gazees, and was nearly cut to pieces under Sir Colin's eyes. The General sat talking with the Chief for some time; and then Cameron of the 42nd came into my tent to add his narrative of a very narrow shave indeed, for the Gazees dragged him from his horse, his revolver was in the holster, his sword fell out of the scabbard as he was pulled to the ground, and but for the coolness and courage of two or three of his own men he would have been hacked to pieces in a moment. Of the Gazees, but one or two escaped. Languidly and drowsily I listened to all this; all wordly affairs for the time seemed of little consequence to me. I was thinking of home.

The doctors came in at last, Tice and Mackinnon. They saw me—withdrew, consulted in whispers. I can remember so well their figures as they stood at the door of the pall, thrown into dark shade by the blazing bivouac-fires! No tents were pitched; the soldiers lay down in their blankets, or without them, on the sandy plain. The cavalry stretched themselves by their horses, and the artillery lay among their guns. Strong pickets and patrols were posted all round the camp. Ere I went to sleep for the night I was anointed all over back and chest with strong tincture of iodine. I never knew till long afterwards that up to this moment one lung had ceased to act at all, and that a portion of the other was gorged from pulmonary apoplexy, brought on by the sun-stroke or heat; and that in fact my two friends had no expectation of my being alive next morning. Such is my recollection and experience of the Battle of Bareilly.

A lithograph by G.F. Atkinson showing the Horse Artillery in action during the Mutiny.

However, for the British forces the day culminated in the defeat of Khan Bahadur Khan and the occupation of Bareilly.

During the days that followed, although his head became clearer, Russell was still in great pain. He was told by the doctors that:

> Had I not been so weakened by previous bleeding and dosing, the *coup de soleil* would have been fatal to me as it was to many of our poor fellows on the 5th. I am now able to employ amanuensis, but the leg is still very painful, and the swelling is now as hard and as large as an egg; so I shall remember the Rohilkhand campaign for the rest of my life, be it long or short.

His problems seemed intent on multiplying: the following day he found himself in the middle of a sandstorm.

> The day had been, as usual, unbearably hot, but it had been exceedingly sultry. Towards evening the horizon darkened, and a storm, which, for grandeur, fury, and variety of physical phenomena, I never saw surpassed, burst upon our camp. It came on about an hour before sunset, its approach being heralded by strong hot winds, laden with dust, which increased in violence until they became what sailors call half a gale of wind. From the point whence this wind came there was visible, behind and above the clouds of dust, something which looked like a gigantic wall of bright red brick, advancing at a slow and equable pace, and spreading as it approached more widely across the horizon. About it tumbled a confused mass of whirling black clouds, scintillating with incessant lightning, and convulsed by the throes of the thunder which echoed within them.
>
> It was a sight almost appalling—it certainly was all-absorbing—to watch the progress of this awful manifestation. As the wall of sand rose high in the air and came across the track of the setting sun, darkness, as of an eclipse, fell upon the land, though on the opposite side of the horizon there still appeared a sort of pale, sickly twilight through the dust. As the storm approached it seemed as if the earth were beaten by the hoofs of myriads of cavalry. The roar of the wind, the beat of the hail, the rush of the rain, and crashing of the branches of trees, mingled with loud peals of thunder. The lightning flashed out in every variety of form—in narrow streaks, in broad belts of blinding light, in bright blue zigzags, in

balls and bolts of fire, and in snapping jets, which seemed to leap from tree to tree, and to run along the ground amidst the hail.

The storm continued with great ferocity, the hailstones the size of pigeon's eggs, until the arid plain was under two or three inches of water.

As Russell was still prostrated, he employed some of the soldiers to write his letters for him. When he tried to pay one, the soldier refused saying: 'No! Mr Russell, there's not a man in the regiment who was out in the Crimea would take a penny from you, sir. Sure, we ought to do more than that for your honour, for you were the true soldier's friend.' Russell apologises in his diary for quoting this story, but this touching tribute obviously gave him intense pleasure and was especially precious to him because of its source.

In his diary, too, he goes out of his way to pay tribute to the Indian soliders and the many native servants without whom the British army could not have survived in India at the time of the Mutiny. He found it extremely distressing that so many acts of kindness and fidelity were so often repaid with death and torture. Although the rebels had committed acts of barbarous savagery, he goes on to say:

> But were our acts those of civilised Christians, when in this very place we hung a relative of the Nawab of Farrukhabad under circumstances of most disgusting indignity, whilst a chaplain stood by among the spectators? It is actually true that the miserable man entertained one or two officers of a British regiment in his palace the day before his death, and that he believed his statements with respect to his innocence were received; but in a few hours after he had acted as host to a colonel in our army, he was pounced upon by the civil power, and hanged in a way which excited the displeasure of every one who saw it, and particularly of Sir William Peel. All these kinds of vindictive, unchristian, Indian torture, such as sewing Mohammedans in pig-skins, smearing them with pork-fat before execution, and burning their bodies, and forcing Hindus to defile themselves, are disgraceful, and ultimately recoil on ourselves. They are spiritual and mental tortures to which we have no right to resort, and which we dare not perpetrate in the face of Europe.

Russell was a deeply compassionate man and with his impulsive nature he was constantly defending the Indian people against what he saw as the injustices of British rule. Numerous examples of this questioning of British actions appear in his despatches and especially in his private letters to Delane. Although separated by a continent, Editor and correspondent worked together as they had done during the Crimean War. Delane used Russell's letters to good effect, confiding them to those in a position to influence both government and public opinion. But again, it was Russell who required, and possessed, the courage to speak his mind while surrounded by many who strongly disagreed with him, not least the members of the Anglo-Indian press. He was accused of constantly denigrating British rule in India: to which he replied that his criticisms were levelled at 'a base and brutal minority'. In a letter to Delane he begs: 'Could you point out that I never accused the Anglo-Indians of the Company's service, or the old race, of cruelty and roughness? I allude generally to the low, ignorant, and violent newcomers, and non-officials, who come here to make their fortunes.'

Newly arrived army personnel were also guilty of allowing their improved status in India to go to their heads.

> Every man takes ten jumps on the social scale when he comes to India—the private rides a tat; the Sub mounts a buggy; the Captain keeps hunting dogs and a phaeton, and the Colonel: well, he's the Duke of Badminton... As to servants, it's monstrous. I have less than any, but one man in camp, and yet I could parade a lot that could take the shine out of most Chesham Place or country squires' houses.

Above: A group of the 'Heroes of Lucknow'. Thomas Kavanagh is seated in the foreground. *Below:* The army on the march, a lithograph from G.F. Atkinson's *The Campaign in India*.

Loyal Sikhs often joined forces of irregular cavalry, such as these officers of Hodson's Horse.

Russell goes on to lament:

> What I observe with regret is this—that after an Englishmen has been a few years
> in India, unless he is a man of reflection and some education, he forgets altogether
> the principles of his life, the rules of his religion, and the feelings of his civilis-
> ation; he regards rebellion or insurrection not as a political offence but as a
> blasphemy and sacrilege of ineffable magnitude committed against the Deity,
> whom he vicariously (and imperfectly) represents... We are in contact with an
> immensely ancient, obdurate, unyielding civilisation...and we set at once to work
> to improve them, to force them into our clothes, ideas, religion, and boots, and
> then, dissatisfied that they don't at once fit the mould, we call them niggers, deny
> they have souls to be saved, find they have bodies only to be kicked, and at once
> emancipate ourselves in our relations with them from all the teaching of our own
> civilisation.

Replying to a letter from his friend John Sherer, at Cawnpore, he continued his theme:

> I tried to direct public opinion at home, failing any expression of it in India,
> against the Dantons and St Justs who, riding their bloody hobbies, with the war
> cries of 'Sepoy atrocity' and 'white pandies', sought to break through the barriers
> of truth and justice, and were the very Don Quixotes of cruelty, revenge and lust
> of blood. I am open to admit the existence of great and tremendous provocations
> of these evil passions, but I ask what is the use of a superior civilisation, and of
> Christianity itself, if we are to yield to these incitements? You say rightly that the
> manners of the natives are almost as bad as our own, but my John, think of the
> differences of position between the two races.

In his diary Russell gives two examples of the inconsistent behaviour of his countrymen:

> Here is a friend of mine, who has just been winning three steeple-chases, in a
> state of pardonable anger against Government and all mankind, because the
> 'niggers' have just murdered some unfortunate gentlemen who were surveying a
> railway close at hand. If they had been shot in a boundary row, or on a Munster
> jaunting-car, he would think comparatively little of it, however he might grieve
> for their loss. His wrath now is directed against the 'niggers,' and, above all, the
> Government, which has, he declares, encouraged these rebels. 'I would,' he
> exclaims, 'hang every scoundrel within ten miles of the place!' A moment afterwards
> he is eulogizing the syce who had fed his horse. The syce says he has relations
> among the rebels who killed the engineers. Further on I meet a man going out to
> shoot. 'I can't try the best places, about five miles from this, up the Kymore
> Hills,' he says, 'because there are a lot of rascally rebels there,' 'But suppose they
> come down on you?' 'Oh! my fellows' (all natives) 'will keep a sharp look-out,
> and they would all fight for me to the death.' 'Can you trust them, after all that
> has happened?' 'Well: I am going out alone—they carry my guns and everything,
> and I have 500 rupees also, but they won't do me any harm.' 'What is the difference
> between them and sepoys?' 'Well, as to that, you know, they're all niggers alike;
> but I *can* trust my fellows,' etc. etc.

Unusually for an Englishman, Russell once actually asked an Indian what the native
servants thought of their British masters. He replied:

> 'Does the Sahib see those monkeys? They are playing very pleasantly. But the
> Sahib cannot say why they play, nor what they are going to do next. Well, then,
> our poor people look upon you very much as they would on those monkeys, but
> that they know you are very fierce and strong, and would be angry if you were
> laughed at. They are afraid to laugh. But they do regard you as some great

powerful creatures sent to plague them, of whose motives and actions they can comprehend nothing whatever.'

It was not long before Russell's letters, both public and private, began to bear fruit. Delane wrote to him in May:

> The public feeling has righted itself more promptly than was to be expected, and we had before the recess a debate in which the most humane instead of the most blood-thirsty sentiments were uttered. The key to the savage spirit was the 'atrocities,' and these seem to have resolved themselves into simple massacre.

And again in July:

> You will have seen, I hope, how I have backed every one of your suggestions by leading articles. Happily, you have everybody on your side and no enemy, as in the Crimea, to deny or hint denial of every fact. Everybody, too, says, and with perfect truth, that it is you who have first made India known to us, described its aspect and its peculiarities, so that we have before our eyes at last the scene of so many exploits and reverses.

By the end of May, although Lucknow had been retaken, Oudh was still anything but secure and there were frequent clashes with the rebels, who were as elusive as ever. With the rainy season fast approaching, it was clear that another campaign would be required to subjugate the province entirely. Russell, still a very sick man, decided to go to Simla in the Himalayan foothills to convalesce. He would rejoin the army towards the end of October.

On 3rd June, Russell set off for Delhi in a gharry as he was still too ill to ride. He entered Delhi two days later, having passed through countryside devastated by the Mutiny. He found himself in the 'ruined streets of a deserted city, in which every house bore the marks of cannon and musket shot, or the traces of the hand of the spoiler... not a creature was to be seen, except a hungry pariah, or an impudent cow.'

After much searching, he arrived at what he believed to be the house of the British official he was due to stay with. To his embarrassment, he was shown into a room full of strangers in what proved to be the Commissioner of Delhi's dining-room.

> I was fairly installed at table in a few moments. To me the change was as great as it was agreeable. I had not seen the face of an Englishwoman since I left Calcutta. I had lived in camps and in canvas from the time of my arrival at Cawnpore till that moment. I came in dusty—I am afraid, dirty—fagged—a hot, unpleasant-looking stranger. I found myself at once back in civilised life, amid luxuries long unknown, received with a courtesy and frank cordiality which made me feel less like an intruder than an invited and welcome guest. I need say no more.

The same day Russell was taken by the Commissioner to visit the King of Delhi who had been captured by the British after the relief of Delhi.

> The first knowledge the great mass of Englishmen had at home of the King of Delhi was that he was the nominal chief of a revolt which was shaking our Indian empire to its foundations. He was called ungrateful for rising against his bene-factors. He was, no doubt, a weak and cruel old man; but to talk of ingratitude on the part of one who saw that all the dominions of his ancestors had gradually been taken from him, by force or otherwise, till he was left with an empty title, a more empty exchequer, and a palace full of penniless princesses and princes of his own blood, is perfectly preposterous. Was he to be grateful to the Company for the condition in which he found himself?

Russell makes the point that the British could, with perfect justice, execute the king for his apparent backing of the Mutiny and for being an accessory to the murder of British men and women living under his roof. But, until his trial, he was kept a prisoner in his own decaying and deserted palace. Russell goes on to say:

> But, to my mind the position of the King was one of the most intolerable misery long ere the revolt broke out. His palace was in reality a house of bondage; he knew that the few wretched prerogatives which were left to him, as if in mockery of the departed power they represented, would be taken away from his successors; that they would be deprived of even the right to live in their own palace, and would be exiled to some place outside the walls. We denied permission to his royal relatives to enter our service; we condemned them to a degrading existence, in poverty and debt, inside the purlieus of their palace, and then we reproached them with their laziness, meanness, and sensuality. We shut the gates of military preferment upon them—we closed upon them the paths of every pursuit—we took from them every object of honourable ambition—and then our papers and our mess-rooms teemed with invectives against the lazy, slothful, and sensuous princes of his house. Better die a hundred deaths than drag on such a contemptible, degrading existence.

On their arrival at the palace, they found the King:

> In a dingy, dark passage, leading from the open court or terrace in which we stood to a darker room beyond, there sat, crouched on his haunches, a diminutive, attenuated old man, dressed in an ordinary and rather dirty muslin tunic, his small lean feet bare, his head covered by a small thin cambric skull-cup.

They had arrived at a bad moment: 'the ex-King was sick; with bent body he seemed nearly prostrate over a brass basin, into which he was retching violently.' His visitors politely turned their backs and waited until he had finished and then entered. Russell was saddened by what he saw.

Bahadur Shah II, King of Delhi, photographed in 1858 within months of Russell's visit on his way to Simla. The King was tried by the British for his part in the Mutiny and subsequently exiled to Rangoon.

A battery on the Ridge outside Delhi from which the British bombarded
the city during the siege.

That dim-wandering-eyed, dreamy old man, with feeble hanging nether lip and
toothless gums,—was he, indeed, one who had conceived that vast plan of restoring a great empire, who had fomented the most gigantic mutiny in the history
of the world, and who, from the walls of his ancient palace, had hurled defiance
and shot ridicule upon the race that held every throne in India in the hollow of
their palms?

He broke silence. Alas! it was to inform us that he had been very sick, and that
he had retched so violently that he had filled twelve basins. This statement, which
was, it must be admitted, distressingly matter of fact and unromantic, could not, I
think, have been strictly true, and probably was in the matter of numeration
tinctured by the spirit of Oriental exaggeration, aided by the poetic imagination of
His Majesty. He is a poet—rather erotic and warm in his choice of subject and
treatment, but nevertheless, or may be therefore, an esteemed author of no less
than four stout volumes of meritorious verses, and he is not yet satiated with the
muse, for a day or two ago he composed some neat lines on the wall of his prison
by the aid of a burnt stick. Who could look on him without pity? Yes, for one
instant 'pity', till the rush of blood in that pitiless courtyard swept it from the
heart! The passage in which he sat contained nothing that I could see but a
charpoy such as those used by the poorest Indians. The old man cowered on the
floor on his crossed legs, with his back against a mat which was suspended from
doorway to doorway, so as to form a passage about twelve feet wide by twenty-
four in length. Inside the mat we heard whispering, and some curious eyes that
glinted through the mat at the strangers informed us that the King was not quite
alone.

One set of eyes belonged to the King's latest wife, who told the Commissioner:

'Why, the old...fool goes on as if he were a king; he's no king now. I want to go
away from him. He's a troublesome, nasty, cross old fellow, and I'm quite tired of
him.' Bow-strings and sacks! was not this dreadful language? But the ex-Mogul is
a philosopher; he merely asked one of his attendants for a piece of coffee-cake or
chocolate, put a small piece in his mouth, mumbled it, smiled, and pointing with

his thumbs over his shoulder in the direction from which the shrill and angry accents of queenly wrath were coming, said, with all the shrug and *bonhomie* of a withered little French marquis of the old school '*Mon Dieu!*—I mean, Allah! listen to her!' And so we left him alone in his misery. He numbers upwards of eighty-two years; but they are said to be only of lunar months, and that his real age is seventy-eight. It is needless to say that he will never, if sent, reach Caffraria alive.

While in Delhi, Russell visited the Ridge from which the British had for months besieged the mutineers in the city before they retook it at the end of September of the previous year.

It was with no ordinary emotions I visited the remains of our trenches, and looked out over the decaying parapets upon the city and its great circling sweep of wall, and bastion, and battery; for I saw it was the pride, self-reliance, and greatness of a conquering race alone, which had enabled a handful of men to sustain and successfully conduct the most hopeless military enterprise that was ever undertaken. But at the same time I felt that had we been demi-gods we must have failed, if the enemy, to whom we were opposed, had possessed the ordinary intelligence and military skill of any European soldiery. At every step the audacity of the siege, the grandness of courage, the desperation of our position, grew upon me.

He just had time to visit the Jumma Masjid before continuing on his way to Simla. 'It is one of the grandest temples ever raised by man. There is a chaste richness, an elegance of proportion, and grandeur of design in all its parts, which are in painful contrast to the *mesquin* and paltry architecture of our Christian churches.'

On 14th June Russell arrived in Simla where he was to spend the next four months. For a long time he was too crippled to go about at all and was further incapacitated by a general malaise peculiar to Simla. He passed his days sitting on the verandah of his

The hill station of Simla where Russell convalesced from his leg injury. British officers and their families retreated there in the dry season to escape the fearful heat of the plains.

bungalow, looking out on the Himalayas and receiving a stream of visitors. He also collected quite a menagerie which included two hill bears, a mynah bird and a monkey. He seemed to take more pleasure in the daily antics of his pets than in the frivolous social life of the town: 'Here we have ball after ball, each followed by a little backbiting; the great event of the day being the promenade.'

He was shocked by the boisterous and undisciplined behaviour of some of the young officers who were in Simla either on leave or to convalesce.

I think that every Englishman in India ought to look upon himself as a sort of unrecognised, unpaid servant of the State, on whose conduct and demeanour towards the natives may depend some of the political *prestige* of our rule in the whole Empire. He is bound to keep the peace, to obey the law, to maintain order and good government. In the hill stations he certainly does not exhibit any strong inclination to adopt this view of his position.

Having spent September on a shooting expedition with friends, he had recovered sufficiently to return to the plains and rejoin Sir Colin Campbell (now Lord Clyde) for the renewed campaign in Oudh. When he reached Ambala he received an invitation to visit the Rajah of Puttiala, which he accepted with alacrity. Russell and the Deputy Commissioner, Mr Melville, set off on the eighteen-mile journey to Puttiala and, nearing their destination, they saw a dust-cloud approaching.

Mr Melville said, 'There is the Rajah! He has come a long way out to meet us.' I knew enough of Oriental etiquette to be aware, that the distance to which the potentate moves from his seat or his palace to meet the stranger-visitor, was the exact measure of the honour and respect which he intended to exhibit to him; and it never occurred to me but that the advance of the Rajah, who was more than a mile from the gates of his capital, was meant for Mr Melville, the deputy commissioner.

Looking along the road to our front, I could make out a pleasant sheen of arms under a tope of trees; a certain play of bright colours, and a tossing of banners, and faint shadowings of elephants, as if Turner had been at work on a late canvas in some giant effort at 'The March of an Eastern King'. By degrees these forms became plainer. The bright colours were resolved into turbans, shawls, scarfs, and robes, whose wearers were mounted on richly-caparisoned horses; the banners were great streamers of gold-encrusted satin, rising above a turmoiling crowd, which was marshalling itself into order as we came up; and the elephantine outline hardened into huge, substantial monsters, covered with silver howdahs, and dressed in the most brilliant crimson velvet, and in cloths of many hues, richly adorned with lace. The howdah of one was empty, that of the other was occupied by a large, fair, fat man of some thirty-five years of age, who flashed like a prism in the sun as he advanced to meet us.

It rapidly became apparent that Russell and Mr Melville were expected to mount the elephant with the empty howdah.

The ladder to the howdah was short, the elephant was high, the sun was hot, and as I toiled up—may I confess the fact that—I wished the Rajah had not been kind enough to receive me, and that I was clambering up to get a drink of fresh water instead of a glimpse of the elevated countenance which was awaiting me at the other side? When I had, with much labour, gained the howdah height, closely followed by Mr Melville, a new trouble awaited me. The mahout of the Rajah had brought up his elephant alongside ours, and I was requested to step across to the Rajah's howdah and take the place of honour on his right-hand side, on his own royal pachyderm. In vain I solicited Mr Melville by words and by looks: 'Pray don't ask me; do you go.' 'No; the Rajah requests you will, and as this visit

The Maharajah of Puttiala with Ministers and Suite—not the Maharajah
who fêted Russell, but his successor who played host to the Prince of
Wales on his tour of India in 1875.

is from you, there is no option but to obey. Will you be good enough to step
across?'

Across what?—a chasm of uncertain and varying breadth, full fifteen feet deep!
There is no beast so mobile as an elephant. Flies vex him, mahouts persecute him;
(*e pur si muove*)—he is never at rest. There sat his Highness the Rajah, and here
stood his lowness the correspondent, *claudo pede*, afraid, by reason of his lameness, to make a leap; and the bulging sides of the two elephants kept their howdahs
as far apart as the main-chains of two line-of-battle ships would separate their
hammock-nettings. I could not make an explanatory speech to the Rajah, who sat
smiling with extended hand, the finger tips some good six feet away; and thus I
stood, supremely foolish, and very uncertain what to do, till a sudden lurch, a *vis
a tergo*, a desperate resolution, all combined, and with a desperate ponderous
flop, full thirteen stone and ten pounds (it was in the time of Plancus, and after
much exudation of ichor in the hills), I dropped on the Rajah's feet, and took my
seat at his side. Dear good man! Kings have long and unfeeling arms; but I presume their toes are as sensitive as those of most mortal men. The Rajah of Puttiala
never winced, and yet I am nearly certain I alighted, or preponderated, upon his
feet, and I am perfectly certain his feet were quite naked, with the exception of
some rings of precious metal set round his Highness's most-favoured pedal digits.
I sat at his right-hand side. The elephant of Mr Melville was on his Highness's left
hand; and, as Mr Melville was my interpreter, the intercourse between the Rajah
and myself was rather embarrassed and difficult.

'The Rajah says he is very glad to see you.' (In reality he said, 'Would your
kindness cause it to be conveyed to the great lord that my eyes are brighter for
beholding him, and that his servant's health has been considerably improved since
he had the pleasure of seeing him safe in Puttiala.')

The Taj Mahal, visited by Russell on his way back from Simla to rejoin
Sir Colin Campbell at Allahabad.

'Pray tell the Rajah I am very much obliged to him.' (Translated by the deputy
commissioner into fine Court Hindoostanee)...

By some ingenious usage of the Court tongue it was intimated to the Rajah that
if we had a wish on earth it was to see him enter Puttiala; but he would not deign
to yield till he had made particular inquiries as to the general health of the Queen
of England, of myself, of my relations and friends, and acquired some geographi-
cal notes as to my route, the length of time I had been in India, and such matters
of etiquette.

Finally, to Russell's intense relief, the procession turned towards the Rajah's palace.
He described the magnificent scene around him.

There were men with wands of silver, and batons of silver-gilt, with banners and
silver spears, with gold sticks in waiting, with musical instruments of silver in the
shape of serpents, with kettledrums and trumpets of the same previous metal,
with swords and lances flashing in the sun. There were men dressed in harlequin
suits of red and yellow, with masks and vizards, with skins of bears and wild
beasts, who danced and leaped to the sound of the wild music of the band, like
the mummers and mystery-men of our old plays. There were grey-bearded, black-
bearded, white-bearded, stern, long-nosed grave Sikh chiefs on fine horses,
dressed in the noble and rich simplicity of forms and colours which seem to be a
heritage of their race. There were braceleted, ear-ringed, necklaced courtiers on
prancing chargers; there were wild, fierce-looking sowars on lean, restive, fiery
horses; there were quaint fantassins with matchlock, musket, tulwar, and bow;
and in our front there was a section of some eighteen or twenty camels, capar-
isoned in the Rajah's colours of red and white, with zomboruks, or swivel guns,
mounted on their backs, and an artilleryman or two to each. As we moved the
trumpets fanfared, the drums rattled, the morrice-dancers leaped and tumbled,
the horses neighed, and just in front of the elephants, the men with gold and

silver badges and sticks, and the heralds with blazons, in loud voices shouted out the names and honours and titles of the Rajah in chorus, and invoked blessings on him whom the king delighted to honour.

To Russell's further consternation he observed that he was to be the object of a six-gun salute.

I felt supremely ridiculous, and had I been possessed of the use of both my legs I should probably have thought of leaping down off the elephant and running away. I had no official or unofficial position which could justify me in receiving such marks of honour, and the commissioner steadfastly repudiated them; and there was I, helpless, on the back of the Rajah's elephant.

At the Durbar itself Russell was astonished at the splendour of the Court. He was presented with tray upon tray of priceless jewels and asked to select one. Still labouring under the conviction that his position was a false one, he carefully took the plainest he could find. The final temptation was the hardest to refuse—a snow-white Arab horse —but refuse it he did. In spite of pressing invitations to remain at Puttiala for several days, they managed to extricate themselves without offending their host and set off for Ambala.

As Russell points out in his diary, the Rajah had been a good friend to the British during the Mutiny. He had raised and equipped a large force, in addition to his own army, which he had placed at the government's disposal; he had supplied money and transport and, together with the neighbouring chiefs, had kept open the vital lines of communication between the Punjab and Delhi. There had, it was true, been rumours that the Rajah had been in touch with the King of Delhi. Russell exclaims indignantly:

And who are we that we should claim the allegiance of the hearts of all the Indian princes? What rule is there in the world which can challenge the affections of the whole mass of its subjects? Can England believe that her reign needs no stronger support than willing fidelity in the breasts of a large mass of the Irish Roman Catholics? Could the early Georges have ventured to rely on the devotion of the English Tories? Does Napoleon the Third live in the love of the Faubourg St. Germain?—No. There is not a European State which is not vexed more or less by the political disaffection of some section or other of its subjects. How, then, can we expect such an abnormal government as that of Great Britain in Hindostan, where our governors are, indeed, alien in blood, religion, and language, to command the absolute love of all classes of natives? Or what right have we to demand anything beyond actual service and co-operation in time of need on the part of our tributaries and allies? We must be content with such aid as we get, provided it be effectual.

Russell continued his journey by gharry, pausing briefly at Agra where he was overwhelmed by the beauty of the Taj Mahal:

The moon had just risen on the right, and I was about sinking back in my gharry, having ordered the driver to proceed to the Artillery Quarters, when suddenly my eye rested on a dome of dazzling whiteness—so white, so clear, so sharp, that, for the instant, one might be pardoned for fancying that the crest of an Alp had thrust itself through the baked crust of this arid India. Four glittering pinnacles shooting up beside it, completed the notion of the rounded summit of Mont Blanc flanked by its own aiguilles. The whole vision disappeared in a moment, as the vehicle whisked round the corner, but I knew that I had seen that Pearl of architecture, the wonder of the world—The Taj of Agra.

Russell reached Allahabad at the end of October where he found Lord Clyde and many of his friends, some of whom had sweated out the hot weather in the plains. The main army was preparing to cross the mile-wide Ganges by a bridge of boats in readiness for the opening of the Oudh campaign.

On 1st November, from a specially erected platform near the fort, Lord Canning read the Queen's Proclamation, announcing the transference of the government of India from the East India Company to the Crown and the British Parliament, and pardoning those rebel chiefs not responsible for the murder of Europeans.

That night Russell crossed the Ganges with Lord Clyde, who informed him that none of the chiefs would be attacked until it was certain that they had received copies of the Proclamation:

> …and this, indeed, seems to be but just and reasonable, because it would, first, certainly be hypocritical and absurd on our part to pretend to offer these chiefs terms, on condition that they surrender, and then to destroy their forts and kill themselves and followers ere they could become acquainted with the alternative offered to them by submission.

With the army now assembled, the campaign commenced. Russell gives a colourful description in his diary of the column on the move:

> November 8th.—It is a wonderful sight to see an Indian army on the march as it approaches its camping ground. The square head of the column seems enveloped by the myriads of animals and men, and up-towering elephants and camels, made taller than nature by heaps of tents and baggage and furniture piled upon their backs. The elephants are provident enough to look for the sugar-cane as they march along the roadside, and generally each of these quadrupeds marches laden with a large mass of cut cane, in addition to the chairs and tables and mountains of canvas piled upon its back.
>
> The mass, dense and small in the distance, grows larger and looser all over the wide plain, as it approaches, till it seems to fill the space from horizon to horizon —to cover the fields and permeate the forests with a shifting mass of life. Through all this the column of troops bores steadily onwards till the first battalion or squadron halts.

The army, with Sir Colin Campbell at its head, crossing the Ganges into Oudh on 1st November 1858.

Then a more detailed description:

Here is one's life at present:—First bugle at 5.15 a.m.: strike tents, a cup of tea before starting, a grouping, stumbling ride out through tent-pegs, camp-followers *regardant*, camels *couchant*, elephants *passant*, and horses *rampant*, to the road; very cold, and chill ere the sun rises; then jog, jog, at the rate of two miles an hour or so, with a halt of a few minutes every hour, to allow the baggage and the rear-guard to close up; artfully riding from one flank to another as the breeze, or rather current of air, drives the smothering clouds of dust across the line of march, in order to evade the nuisance as much as possible.

At last about two o'clock p.m. the welcome sight of the assistant quartermaster-general riding over the plain in front, and directing the movements of his flagmen, who mark out the lines of the camp, announces that we are at our resting-place; but it is long ere the camels stalk in upon us, and cone after cone of canvas offers brief shelter to the Rechabite. Each man is choked with dust, and fagged by heat and slow riding. The water-skin of the bheesty gives a refreshing shower-bath; but it is nearly four o'clock ere the tent is all in order, for the furniture drops in slowly and fitfully, as the coolies behave on the road. Then darkness closes in, and if with an effort, of the violence of which in my own case I can speak conscientiously, one has sat down to write, the slow beat of the camp gong soon announces that the dinner hour—about 6.30 p.m.—is near at hand. The meal lasts nearly an hour, and there are few who can resist the temptation of the charpoy on returning to their tents from dinner, about 8.30 or 9 o'clock p.m. How our servants exist I cannot ascertain by any reference to my own experiences. No English servant could—or, if he could, he certainly would not—exhibit the patience and powers of endurance of these bearers, syces, and grass-cutters. My syce follows me all day, for six or seven hours, at a jog-trot, not a sign of fatigue on his dusty face, or a drop of perspiration on his dark skin. He is heavily weighted, too, for he carries a horse-cloth, a telescope, a bag of gram (part for himself and part for his horse), and odds and ends useful on a march. When we halt he is at hand to hold the horse. At the end of the march there is no rest for him; he grooms the horse with assiduity, hand-rubs him, washes out his nostrils and ears and hoofs, waters him,

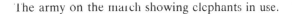

The army on the march showing elephants in use.

soaks his grain, and feeds him; then he has to clean saddlery, and bits, and spurs; finally, at some obscure hour of night, he manages to cook a cake or two of wheat-flour, to get a drink of water, to smoke his hubble-bubble, and then, after a fantasia or so on the tom-tom, aided by a snuffling solo through the nose in honour of some unknown beauty, wraps himself up, head and all, in his calico robe, and sleeps, *sub Jove frigido*, till the first bugle rouses him out to feed and prepare his horse for the march. If any true Briton maintains that beef and beer are essential to develop a man in stature, or strength, or 'lasting,' let him look at our camp-servants and own his error. The grass-cutter has an equally hard existence; the kelassies, or tent-pitchers, keep pace with the camels, and your bheesty is ready with his mussuck the moment you ride into camp. And here at this moment is my bearer, with a clean snow-white turban and robe, sliding into my tent to tell me dinner is ready, to wait on me till I go to sleep, and to wake me betimes in the morning. And so farewell for to-day.

The Oudh campaign was nothing if not frustrating. There were frequent alarms and skirmishes, accompanied by conflicting reports as to the intentions of the rebel chiefs. Russell suspected that the spies employed by the British forces were 'impartial in their services to both sides'. Rebel strongholds which appeared ready to put up a fight were discovered to have been evacuated during the night, the mutineers having slipped through the net, taking with them their guns, treasure, women and belongings. The forts were often surrounded by dense, prickly jungle which further aided their escape.

At this time their principal quarry was the rebel chief Bene Madho, who led them a weary dance. One moment he appeared ready to parley and the next he had slipped quietly away to reappear some miles distant. After a bad night sleeping on a nettle 'of the most stinging and relentless character', Russell sums up the following day's tasks:

> ...site of new cantonments to be decided on; Rae Bareilly to be examined; Bene Madho to be discovered. We have 'certain' intelligence that he is at all points of the compass at exactly the same hour of the same day, and we have not thirty-one columns to spare to verify these reports.

This cat and mouse game continued throughout November and into December, the prey neatly eluding them time and again. Russell was saddened by the terrible damage done by the camp followers of the army, although Lord Clyde and his officers never ceased their efforts to prevent it from happening:

> Those insatiable 'looters'—men, women, and children, all are at it; a field is gobbled, crunched, and sucked up in ten minutes... Why, the race is suckled on loot, fed on theft, swaddled in plunder, and weaned on robbery... But I do not suppose for a moment they are worse than other camp-followers...in other parts of the world. Whatever the soldier may be, the creatures who follow are kites and vultures, actually and metaphorically.

By the middle of December they were in sight of the 'Snowy Range', the foothills of the Himalayas, with the Terai, a belt of forest and jungle, separating them. It was now known that the Nana Sahib, Britain's most hated enemy in India, was somewhere in this wilderness.

The army celebrated Christmas Day with a day of rest. The Commander-in-Chief and his guests, who included Russell, sat down to a magnificent meal, magically produced miles from civilisation, after six weeks on the move.

> Here we have barons of beef, great turkeys, which, in Irish phrase, are 'big enough to draw a gig'; mutton of grass-fed sheep, game, fish without the flavour of tin and rosin, truffled fowl, rissoles, and all the various triumphs of the French *cuisine*, spread on snowy white table-cloths in well-lighted tents, served by

Life in camp was made extremely comfortable by a host of indefatigable
native servants.

numerous hands. Here, too, were beakers of pale ale from distant Trent or
Glasgow, Dublin or London porter, Champagne, Moselle, sherry, curious old
port (rather bothered by travelling twenty miles a day on the backs of camels),
plum-puddings, mince-pies, and other luxuries not often found in camps. The
artillery sang their Christmas carols; the Rifle band played its best, and there was
rejoicing in the wide expanse of tents till ten o'clock came, and then the voices
gradually died away, and lights went out by degrees till midnight came, and
Christmas Day had passed in India.

By the end of December it seemed that Lord Clyde had the Nana, now joined by Bene
Madho, within his grasp. In spite of a daring night attack, the rebels slipped through his
fingers once again and into Nepalese territory. Lord Clyde's work in Oudh was now
completed and, leaving sufficient forces to keep the Nana out of India, he returned to
Lucknow. Russell made his way back to Calcutta where he stayed with Sir James
Outram until he could secure a passage home. He wrote some reflective letters to
Delane:

January 20th, 1859. I believe that some great effort must be made to check the
aggressive and antipathetic treatment of the natives. I believe that India is the
talisman now by which England is the greatest Power in the world, and that by its
loss we lose the magic and *prestige* of the name which now holds the world in awe.
I believe that we never can preserve India by brute force alone except at a cost
which will swallow up all the wealth of the Home country, and that we can only
hold it by brute force unless we make some changes in our system of government.
I am told that our policy is changed. I hear that the Queen has proclaimed the
rights of native States, and seeks no increment of territory, and yet at this very

moment the conversation of every Indian officer at the Mess table, or wherever the affairs of India may be discussed, clearly reveals the conviction that sooner or later we must absorb every State between Ceylon and Peshawur.

And again in February:

Our rule is now more secure in India than it has ever been before, and nothing but extreme oppression and injustice, and the misery and wretchedness and despair which may arise from these, can produce another rising; but, at the same time, there are more doubts as to our intentions, more suspicions of our motives, greater jealousy of our race, than there ever was before; and these feelings are mixed up with the animosities of a defeated nationality, such as it is, and with resentment against those who in their indiscriminate zeal and desire of vengeance punished the innocent with the guilty.

The final paragraph in his diary gives Russell's recipe for peace in India:

Let us be just, and fear not—popularize our rule—reform our laws—adapt our saddle to the back which bears it. Let us govern India by superior intelligence, honesty, virtue, morality, not by the mere force of heavier metal—proselytize by the force of example—keep our promises loyally in the spirit, nor seek by the exercise of Asiatic subtlety to reach the profundity of Asiatic fraud. Otherwise, the statesman was never born who can render India either safe or profitable; and our arms will be paralysed in the money-market, for the cost of keeping that glorious Empire will be far greater than the profit we derive from its possession; and such a result, in these days, is considered quite sufficient ground for the relinquishment of the greatest heritage that the devotion, courage, and energy of her sons ever bequeathed to a nation.

The History of The Times sums up Russell's contribution to the Mutiny thus:

The settlement of the Indian troubles without recourse to reprisals, which would rankle for ever, was a high Imperial purpose and one which Russell and *The Times* served with eminent success. The interior of India might have held the secret of many harsh tyrannies if Russell had not exposed, and thereby prevented, the deeds of subordinate officials whose acts (in Russell's published words) 'resemble the manifestations of vindictiveness and fright rather than those of justice and punishment.' By giving the names of such officials to the world, *The Times* used its power to refound the Indian Empire upon a new and humaner basis.

Calcutta Harbour from which Russell embarked for England in March 1859 with part of his Simla menagerie, including a bear cub.

The American Civil War

The interest of Russell's stay in America at the beginning of the Civil War lies less in his battle reporting, which had played such a major part in his work in the Crimea and India, than in the personal and evocative accounts he gave of a nation becoming increasingly divided against itself.

Before going to America, Russell admits, he was 'almost entirely ignorant of the nature of the crisis and of the issues at stake' but, once there, he explored both the country and its people with a fresh and, as usual, remarkably objective eye.

He was not alone in his ignorance of American affairs in the mid-nineteenth century. Leslie Stephen wrote that in 1865: 'The name of America called up to the ordinary English mind nothing but a vague cluster of associations, compounded of Mrs Trollope, *Martin Chuzzlewit*, and *Uncle Tom's Cabin*. There was a vague understanding that some of the Southern states wanted to break away from the Union and run their affairs in their own way; it was also thought that the right of the Southern states to own slaves was not one of the fundamental issues. In reality, the slavery question had become the central issue in American politics by the 1850s. The phenomenal success of Harriet Beecher Stowe's *Uncle Tom's Cabin* had accelerated an awareness of the slavery problem in Britain; by the end of 1852, the year of its publication, a million copies had been sold in this country alone, and, in Winston Churchill's words, it 'rolled round the world in every language and was read with passion and emotion in every country. It was the herald of the storm'.

Generally, British sympathies tended towards the South. The upper classes saw the Southern gentleman as a latter-day cavalier and therefore felt an affinity with him and his way of life; the North was rude and crude, dominated by commercialism, and 'trade' —always a term of abuse when employed by the Victorian gentry. Russell himself refers to New York as having 'all the air of a nouveau-riche'. The second factor was an economic one: the South was the sole supplier of the cotton that was so vital to a large section of British industry.

In November 1860 Abraham Lincoln, a little-known provincial lawyer, was elected President. As far as the American people were concerned, his election finally brought the slavery question to a head; but this was not appreciated in Europe at that time. Lincoln was morally opposed to slavery but the institution was legal in the South, and his respect for the law and his wish for a united country prevented him from forcing abolition on the Southern states. Had *The Times* and its readership realised that the North was also fighting for emancipation of the slaves, they would undoubtedly have supported it. Instead, it was understood that the South was prepared to fight for states' rights and the North for the preservation of the Union. This belief was further reinforced by Lincoln's inaugural address in March 1861 when he declared: 'I have no purpose, directly or indirectly, to interfere with the institution of slavery in the states where it exists. I believe I have no lawful right to do so, and I have no inclination to do so.'

Meanwhile, the Union had begun to disintegrate around him. A month after his election South Carolina had seceded from the Union because it feared for its right to independence. It was quickly followed by Mississippi, Florida, Alabama, Georgia, Louisiana and Texas and, in February 1861, the seven secessionist states proclaimed the existence of a new nation, the Confederate States of America. Jefferson Davis was elected as its President and authorised to raise an army of 100,000 men. He was to remain President of the Confederacy until its surrender, and was throughout a champion of states' rights and a firm believer that slavery should be extended into the Western territories of America.

Abraham Lincoln photographed by Matthew Brady in February 1860,
nine months before he was elected President of the United States.

A month after these momentous events, Russell set sail for America as Special Correspondent for *The Times*.

I had no theories to uphold, no prejudices to subserve, no interests to advance, no instructions to fulfil; I was a free agent, bound to communicate to the powerful organ of public opinion I represented, my own daily impressions of the men, scenes, and actions around me, without fear, favour, or affection of or for anything but that which seemed to me to be the truth.

Although Russell was impartial at this stage, the management and Editor of *The Times* certainly were not. They were all, and for varying reasons, pro-Southern in their sympathies—a fact which was to complicate Russell's life in America considerably. Even on the ship bound for New York, Russell's fellow passengers soon made him aware of the enormous divergence of feeling in that troubled continent. He observed that North and South 'sat apart, ate apart, talked apart—two distinct nations, with intense antipathies on the part of the South which was active and aggressive in all its demonstrations'.

On his arrival in New York, Russell found himself in a coach 'rattling over a most abominable pavement, plunging into mudholes, squashing through snow-heaps in ill-lighted, narrow streets of low, mean-looking wooden houses, of which an unusual proportion appeared to be lager-beer salons, whiskey shops, oyster-houses, and billiard and smoking establishments'. He found that all the talk was of the two forts situated in the South but still in Federal hands: Fort Pickens and Fort Sumter. Both were rapidly running out of supplies and the South had declared its intention of preventing any attempt to resupply the two garrisons. The situation must come to a head very soon.

Russell was 'astonished to find little sympathy and no respect for the newly installed government. They were regarded as obscure and undistinguished men'. The journals continued to refer to Lincoln 'in the most contemptuous manner, and to designate him as the great "Rail-Splitter" '. In a letter to Delane, Russell notes that 'New York would do anything rather than fight—her delight is to eat her bread and honey and count her dollars in peace'. He found himself 'plunged into a chaos of opinions' and

The New York waterfront, about 1870.

William Russell photographed in Washington, D.C. in 1861.

went on: 'As far as I can make out, there is no one with any faith in anything stronger than the march of events. Every man is an atom in a gale.'

After a brief stay in New York, Russell travelled by train to Washington.

...The passengers were crowded as close as they could pack, and as there was an immense iron stove in the centre of the car, the heat and stuffiness became most trying, although I had been undergoing the ordeal of the stove-heated New York houses for nearly a week. Once a minute, at least, the door at either end of the carriage was opened, and then closed with a sharp crashing noise, that jarred the nerves, and effectually prevented sleep...

Unfortunately a party of prize-fighters had mind to make themselves comfortable, and the result was anything but conducive to sleep. They had plenty of whiskey, and were full of song and fight, nor was it possible to escape their urgent solicitations 'to take a drink,' by feigning the soundest sleep. One of these, a big man, with a broken nose, a mellow eye, and a very large display of rings, jewels, chains and pins, was in very high spirits, and informed us he was 'Going to Washington to get a foreign mission from Bill Seward. He wouldn't take Paris, as he didn't care much about French or Frenchmen; but he'd just like to show John Bull how to do it; or he'd take Japan if they were very pressing... Any attempts to persuade them to retire to rest made by the conductors were treated with thesovereign contempt, but at last whiskey asserted its supremacy, and having established the point that they 'would not sleep unless they — pleased,' they slept and snored.

At 6.00 a.m., we were roused up by the arrival of the train at Washington, having crossed great rivers and traversed cities without knowing it during the night. I looked out and saw a vast mass of white marble towering above us on the left, stretching out in colonnaded porticoes, and long flanks of windowed masonry, and surmounted by an unfinished cupola, from which scaffold and cranes raised their black arms. This was the Capitol.

Arriving in Washington on 26th March, Russell stayed in the

...great pile of Willards Hotel, now occupied by applicants for office in the new government, and by the members of the newly-assembled Congress. It is a quadrangular mass of rooms, six stories high, and some hundred yards square; and it probably contains at this moment more scheming, plotting, planning heads than any building of the same size ever held in the world... Crowds of long-limbed, nervous, eager-looking men, in loose black garments, undulating shirt collars, vast conceptions in hatting and booting, angular with documents and pregnant with demand, throng every avenue.

Russell goes on to describe the immense dining-room of the hotel:

At present not less than twenty-five hundred people dine in the public room every day. On the kitchen floor there is a vast apartment, a hall without carpets or any furniture but plain chairs and tables, which are ranged in close rows, at which flocks of people are feeding, or discoursing, or from which they are flying away. The servants never cease shoving the chairs to and fro with a harsh screeching noise over the floor, so that one can scarce hear his neighbour speak. If he did, he would probably hear, as I did, at this very hotel, a man order breakfast, 'Black tea and toast, scrambled eggs, fresh spring shad, wild pigeon, pigs' feet, two robins on toast, oysters,' and a quantity of breads and cakes of various denominations. The tumult, the miscellaneous nature of the company—my friends the prize-fighters are already in possession of the doorway—the heated, muggy rooms, not to speak of the great abominableness of the passages and halls, despite a most liberal provision of spittoons, conduce to render these institutions by no means agreeable to a European.

Russell found that his arrival in America had been keenly awaited 'as the most famous newspaper correspondent the world has ever seen'. He was described in a New York newspaper as follows:

He had short iron locks parted down the middle, a greyish moustache and a strong tendency to double chin, a very broad and very full but not lofty forehead: eyes of a clear, keen blue, sharply observant in their expression, rather prominently set and indicating abundant language... You must imagine this portly and pleasant-looking gentleman, dressed in the extreme elaboration of Piccadilly full evening dress, his massive throat encased in the neatest and most dazzling of snowy ties; his broad chest making an immense display of fine linen; his waistcoat a miracle of embroidered silk, dark in color save where illuminated by flowers or traversed by his heavy watch-chain—another thinner chain running round his neck, meandering over his cambric frills and terminating in a pair of eyeglasses which he is very fond of fiddling with while speaking. As a speaker he is rather nervous and hesitating... He is given to humming and hawing before the commencement of each sentence...but in the *matter* of his speech we have seldom heard any orator more lucid, compact and self-balanced than Mr. Russell.

The respect commanded by Russell and *The Times* was such that he was invited everywhere and met everyone of any consequence. Within days of arriving in Washington, he was introduced to Mr Seward who, as Secretary of State, was second only to the President in importance and was to have a great influence on affairs during the next four years:

Mr Seward is a slight, middle-sized man, of feeble build, with the stoop contracted from sedentary habits and application to the desk, and has a peculiar attitude when seated, which immediately attracts attention. A well-formed and large head is placed on a long slender neck, and projects over the chest in an argumentative kind of way, as if the keen eyes were seeking for an adversary; the mouth is remarkably flexible, large but well-formed, the nose prominent and aquiline, the eyes secret, but penetrating, and lively with humour of some kind twinkling about them; the brow bold a broad, but not remarkably elevated; the white hair silvery and fine.

Seward expressed a 'supreme contempt for those who thought there was anything serious in secession. "Why," said he, "I myself, my brothers, and sisters, have been all secessionists—we seceded from home when we were young, but we all went back to it sooner or later. These States will all come back in the same way." ' Russell was treated with great courtesy by Seward, who saw to it that he was kept up to date with events the whole time he was in America—although Russell's Bull Run despatch was later to make relations rather strained. It was Seward who arranged for Russell to meet Abraham Lincoln very soon after his arrival in the capital, and Russell's description of this extraordinary man is both revealing and perceptive. He was taken by Seward to the still unfinished White House and into a 'handsome, spacious room, richly and rather gorgeously furnished'.

Soon afterward there entered, with a shambling, loose, irregular, almost unsteady gait, a tall, lank, lean man, considerably over six feet in height, with stooping shoulders, long pendulous arms, terminating in hands of extraordinary dimensions, which, however, were far exceeded in proportion by his feet. He was dressed in an ill-fitting, wrinkled suit of black, which put one in mind of an undertaker's uniform at a funeral; round his neck a rope of black silk was knotted in a large bulb, with flying ends projecting beyond the collar of his coat; his turned-down shirt-collar disclosed a sinewy muscular yellow neck, and above that, nestling in a great black mass of hair, bristling and compact like a riff of mourning pins, rose the strange quaint face and head, covered with its thatch of wild republican hair, of President Lincoln. The impression produced by the size of his extremities, and by his flapping and wide projecting ears, may be removed by the appearance of kindliness, sagacity, and the awkward bon-hommie of his face; the mouth is absolutely prodigious; the lips, straggling and extending almost from one line of black beard to the other, are only kept in order by two deep furrows from the nostril to the chin; the nose itself—a prominent organ—stands out from the face with an inquiring, anxious air, as though it were sniffing for some good thing in the wind; the eyes dark, full, and deeply set, are penetrating, but full of an expression which almost amounts to tenderness; and above them projects the shaggy brow, running into the small hard frontal space, the development of which can scarcely be estimated accurately, owing to the irregular flocks of thick hair carelessly brushed across it. One would say that, although the mouth was made to enjoy a joke, it could also utter the severest sentence which the head could dictate, but that Mr Lincoln would be ever more willing to temper justice with mercy, and to enjoy what he considers the amenities of life, than to take a harsh view of men's nature and of the world, and to estimate things in an ascetic or puritan spirit. A person who met Mr Lincoln in the street would not take him to be what —according to the usages of European society—is called a 'gentleman'; and, indeed, since I came to the United States, I have heard more disparaging allusions made by Americans to him on that account than I could have expected among simple republicans, where all should be equals; but at the same time, it would not be possible for the most indifferent observer to pass him in the street without notice...

Mr Seward then took me by the hand and said—Mr President, allow me to present to you Mr Russell of the London *Times'*. On which Mr Lincoln put out his hand in a very friendly manner, and said 'Mr Russell, I am very glad to make your acquaintance, and to see you in this country. The London *Times* is one of the greatest powers in the world—in fact, I don't know anything which has much more power—except perhaps the Mississippi. I am glad to know you as its minister.' Conversation ensued for some minutes, which the President enlivened by two or three peculiar little sallies, and I left agreeably impressed with his shrewdness, humour, and natural sagacity.

Some days later Russell was again asked to the White House, this time to dine and to be introduced to many of the most influential men in the Federal government. He also met Mrs Lincoln whom he described as follows:

She is of middle age and height, of a plumpness degenerating to the *embonpoint* natural to her years; her features are plain, her nose and mouth of an ordinary type, and her manners and appearance homely, stiffened, however, by the consciousness that her position requires her to be something more than plain Mrs Lincoln, the wife of the Illinois lawyer...

In the conversation which occurred before dinner, I was amused to observe the manner in which Mr Lincoln used the anecdotes for which he is famous. Where men bred in courts, accustomed to the world, or versed in diplomacy, would use some subterfuge, or would make a polite speech, or give a shrug of the shoulders as the means of getting out of an embarrassing position, Mr Lincoln raises a laugh by some bold west-country anecdote, and moves off in the cloud of merriment produced by his joke.

Russell had arrived in America at a strange point in its history. After Lincoln's inauguration there was a period of suspense—somewhat similar to the mood in Great Britain after Munich in 1938. Neither the President nor his government were highly regarded. Many government officials were Southerners and were busy packing their bags and heading for home. Russell's view that 'the South will never go back to the Union' was made clear in his first despatch sent at the end of March. On 1st April he wrote:

From all I have seen and heard my belief is that the Southern States have gone from the Union, if not for ever, at least for such time as will secure for their government an absolute independence till it be terminated by war, or, if their opponents be right, by the certain processes of internal decay arising from inherent vices in their system, faulty organisation, and want of population, vigour and wealth.

He was to hold this view for as long as he remained in America, and his writings are full of reasons for supporting it. For instance, when he met the three Southern commissioners sent by President Davis to talk with the Federal government, he commented that they 'have the idea they are ministers of a foreign power treating with Yankeedom, and their indignation is moved by the refusal of Government to negotiate with them'.

Undoubtedly, the Southerners considered themselves a superior race and were confident that, should it come to a fight, they had the better soldiers and finer officers. Russell's own description of the appearance of the Southerners when he first encountered them justifies the impression he already had that America was made up of two separate nations: 'The people, I observe, are of a new and marked type, very tall, loosely yet powerfully made, with dark complexions, strongly-marked features, prominent noses, large angular mouths in square jaws, deep-seated bright eyes, low, narrow foreheads —and are all of them much given to ruminate tobacco.'

After a month in the North, Russell began to feel that he must go South 'and see with my own eyes how affairs stand there, before the two sections come to open rupture'. Just as he was leaving Washington he heard that the government had restated its intention of resupplying Fort Sumter, in spite of the Confederate threat. By the time he had reached Norfolk, Virginia, the South had replied to Lincoln's declaration by opening fire on the fort on 12th April and forcing it to surrender. When he saw the electrifying effect this had on the South, Russell wrote: 'Now I confess I could not share in the excitement at all. The act seemed to me the prelude to certain war.' From now on, the issues at stake had become clear, and public opinion, both in the North and in the

The 1st Michigan Regiment on parade on the Campus Martius, Detroit. It was one of the regiments of 3-month volunteers that were to fight in the First Battle of Bull Run.

The Confederate flag flying over Fort Sumter after the rebels captured it in April 1861.

South, had crystallised. There was no going back now and Russell noted that: 'All was noise, dust and patriotism.'

On 15th April, Lincoln published a proclamation calling for 75,000 volunteers. Over the next three months four more Southern states seceded: Virginia, Arkansas, North Carolina and Tennessee. West Virginia remained loyal to the Union and, most important, so did Kentucky. Lincoln was reported to have said 'I should like to have God on my side, but I must have Kentucky'.

A letter to Russell from Bancroft Davis, the New York correspondent of *The Times*, gives a very clear account of the feeling engendered in the North by the surrender of Fort Sumter:

> You have missed the most extraordinary demonstration in history—the rising of the Northern people *en masse* for their institutions. Fifty thousand men are enlisted in the city of New York alone, and ready to go as soon as they can be supplied with arms and equipments. Broadway is a cloud of stars and stripes. Business is abandoned and every man is a soldier. The same spirit prevails throughout the interior. The indifference, the Southern preference, the indecision which prevailed when you were here are vanished. The attack on Sumter and the call of the President swept them away in a single night, and now no man dare avow himself a traitor.

To balance this Russell wrote in his diary:

> The utter contempt and loathing for the venerated Stars and Stripes, the abhorrence of the very words United States, the intense hatred of the Yankees on the part of these people, cannot be conceived by anyone who has not seen them. I am more satisfied than ever that the Union can never be restored as it was.

Russell continued his journey south and, having crossed the flat, marshy land around Charleston, saw the new Stars and Bars flag of the Confederacy flying above Fort Sumter, smoke still rising, as if symbolically, from one corner. He was introduced to General Beauregard who was in command of the assault and found him 'a small, compact man, about 36 years of age, with a quick and intelligent eye and action, and a good deal of the Frenchman in his manner and look'. After some conversation, the General told Russell:

> You shall go everywhere and see everything. We rely on your discretion and knowledge of what is fair in dealing with what you see'... I answered the General, that he might rely on my making no improper use of what I saw in this country, but... 'Unless you tell me to the contrary, I shall write an account of all I see to the other side of the water, and if, when it comes back, there are things you would rather not have known, you must not blame me.' He smiled and said, 'I dare say we'll have great changes by that time.'

Russell related an incident at this point which brought home to him with considerable force the realities of slavery: 'About 8.30 p.m. a deep bell began to toll. "What is that?" "It's for all the coloured people to clear out of the street, and go home. The guards will arrest any who are found out without passes in half an hour".'

When the Civil War began, more than one-third of the population was made up of black slaves. A strong male slave could cost up to $2,000 and therefore represented a substantial investment. Southerners were proud of their 'peculiar institution', as they called it, and would defend it thus:

> We are an agricultural people, pursuing our own system, and working out our own destiny, breeding up women and men with some other purpose than to make them vulgar, fanatical, cheating Yankees... We have gentlemen and gentlewomen in your sense of it. We have a system which enables us to reap the fruits of the earth by a race which we save from barbarism in restoring them to their real place

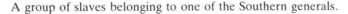

A group of slaves belonging to one of the Southern generals.

in the world as labourers, whilst we are enabled to cultivate the arts, the graces, and accomplishments of life, to develop science, to apply ourselves to the duties of government, and to understand the affairs of the country.

Russell was baffled by their conviction that they had right on their side: 'Assaulted by reason, by logic, argument, philanthropy, progress, directed against this peculiar institution, the Southerner at last is driven to a fanaticism—a sacred faith which is above all reason or logical attack in the propriety, righteousness and divinity of slavery.'

As a readily available representative of Britain, Russell was always being questioned about the British view of the conflict. In the South, a great affection was professed for the 'old country' and it was assumed that Britain would come down on the side of the South, if not for emotional reasons, then for economic ones: 'They presume that the British crown rests on a cotton bale, as the Lord Chancellor sits on a pack of wool.' The North, in its turn, assumed that a country such as Britain, which had already fought against slavery, would support them in their hour of need.

Curious to see what was inside the now famous Fort Sumter, Russell set off from Charleston with some companions in a rowing boat. One of its occupants

...was dressed in the blue frock coat of a civilian, round which he had tied a red silk sash—his waistbelt supported a straight sword, something like those worn with Court dress. His muscular neck was surrounded with a loosely-fastened silk handkerchief; and wild masses of black hair, tinged with grey, fell from under a civilian's hat over his collar; his unstrapped trousers were gathered up high on his legs, displaying ample boots, garnished with formidable brass spurs. But his face was not one to be forgotten—a straight, broad brow, from which the hair rose up like the vegetation on a riverbank, beetling black eyebrows—a mouth coarse and grim, yet full of power, a square jaw—a thick argumentative nose—a new growth of scrubby beard and moustache—these were relieved by eyes of wonderful depth and light, such as I never saw before but in the head of a wild beast. If you look some day when the sun is not too bright into the eye of the Bengal tiger, in the Regent's Park, as the keeper is coming round, you will form some notion of the expression I mean. It was flashing, fierce, yet calm—with a well of fire burning behind and spouting through it, an eye pitiless in anger, which now and then sought to conceal its expression beneath half-closed lids, and then burst out with an angry glare, as if disdaining concealment.

This was none other than Louis T. Wigfall, Colonel (then of his own creation) in the Confederate Army, and Senator from Texas in the United States—a good type of the men whom the institutions of the country produce or throw off—a remarkable man, noted for his ready, natural eloquence; his exceeding ability as a quick, bitter debater; the acerbity of his taunts; and his readiness for personal encounter...

The other day, when the fire against Sumter was at its height, and the fort, in flames, was reduced almost to silence, a small boat put off from the shore, and steered through the shot and the splashing waters right for the walls. It bore the Colonel and a Negro oarsman. Holding up a white handkerchief on the end of his sword, Wigfall landed on the quay, clambered through an embrasure, and presented himself before the astonished Federals with a proposal to surrender, quite unauthorised, and 'on his own hook,' which led to the final capitulation of Major Anderson.

I am sorry to say, our distinguished friend had just been paying his respect *sans bornes* to Bacchus or Bourbon, for he was decidedly unsteady in his gait and thick in speech; but his head was quite clear, and he was determined I should know all about his exploit.

He...I forgot to say that he has the name, particularly in the North, of having killed more than half a dozen men in duels—(I had an escape of being another)—conducted me through the casemates with uneven steps, stopping at every traverse to expatiate on some phase of his personal experiences, with his sword dangling between his legs, and spurs involved in rubbish and soldiers' blankets.

After this exciting encounter, Russell proceeded with his journey to the new capital of the Confederate states at Montgomery. Arriving, he found himself in a hotel which, by his standards, was even worse than Willards in Washington:

Three gentlemen and myself were crammed into a filthy room which already contained two strangers, and as there were only three beds in the apartment it was apparent that we were intended to 'double up considerably'; but after strenuous efforts, a little bribery and cajoling, we succeeded in procuring mattresses to put on the floor, which was regarded by our neighbours as proof of miserable aristocratic fastidiousness. Had it not been for the flies, the fleas would have been intolerable, but one nuisance neutralised the other. Then, as to food—nothing could be had in the hotel—but one of the waiters led us to a restaurant, where we selected from a choice bill of fare, which contained, I think, as many odd dishes as ever I saw, some unknown fishes, oyster-plants, 'possums, raccoons, frogs, and other delicacies, and eschewing toads and the like, really made a good meal off dirty plates on a vile tablecloth, our appetites being sharpened by the best of condiments.

While in Montgomery, Russell was 'much affected' by a slave auction:

The auctioneer, who was an ill-favoured, dissipated-looking rascal, had his 'article' beside him on, not in, a deal packing-case, a stout young negro, badly dressed and ill-shod, who stood with all his goods fastened in a small bundle in his hand, looking out at the small and listless gathering of men, who, whistling and chewing, had moved out from the shady side of the street as they saw the man put up. The chattel character of slavery in the States renders it most repulsive...

A man in a cart, some volunteers in coarse uniforms, a few Irish labourers in a long van, and four or five men in the usual black coat, satin waistcoat and black hat, constituted the audience, whom the auctioneer addressed volubly: 'A prime field hand! Just look at him—good-natured, well-tempered; no marks, nary signs of bad about him! En-i-ne hunthered—only nine-hun-ther-ed and fifty dol'rs for 'em! Why, it's quite rad-aklous! Nine hundred and fifty dol'rs! I can't raly—That's good. Thank you, sir. Twenty-five bid—nine-hun-therd and seventy-five dol'rs for this most useful hand.' The price rose to one thousand dollars, at which the useful hand was knocked down to one of the black hats near me. The auctioneer and the negro and his buyer all walked off together to settle the transaction, and the crowd moved away.

'That nigger went cheap,' said one of them to a companion, as he walked towards the shade. 'Yes, sirr! Niggers is cheap now—that's a fact.' I must admit that I felt myself indulging in a sort of reflection whether it would not be nice to own a man as absolutely as one might possess a horse, to hold him subject to my will and pleasure as if he were a brute beast without the power of kicking or biting—to make him work for me—to hold his fate in my hands; but the thought was for a moment. It was followed by disgust.

He was also introduced to President Davis who

...did not impress me as favourably as I had expected, though he is certainly a very different looking man from Mr Lincoln...wonderful to relate, he does not chew, and is neat and clean-looking, with hair trimmed and boots brushed. The expression of his face is anxious, he has a very haggard, care-worn, and pain-

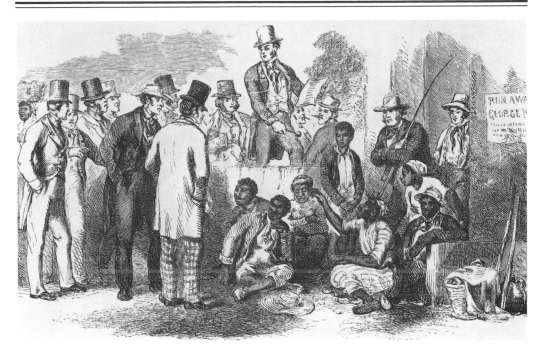

A Southern slave auction similar to one seen by Russell.

drawn look, though no trace of anything but the utmost confidence and greatest decision could be detected in his conversation.

On 9th May Russell left Montgomery and travelled by steamer down the Alabama river to Mobile. During the trip he had the leisure to observe the negro crew,

> ...male and female, acting as stewards and stewardesses, at their morning meal, which they took with much good spirits and decorum. They were nicely dressed —clean and neat. I was forced to admit to myself that their Ashantee grandsires and grandmothers, or their Kroo and Dahomey progenitors were certainly less comfortable and well clad, and that these slaves had other social advantages.

Several of the male slaves were responsible for keeping the steamer's boilers supplied with wood and had to work ceaselessly to do so. Watching the slaves dancing in the evening, Russell was constantly assured by the Irish captain: 'Yes, sir, they're the happiest people on the face of the airth!' Russell drily adds: 'When "wooding" and firing up they don't seem to be in the possession of the same exquisite felicity.'

Mobile, situated on the western shore of Mobile Bay which opens out into the Gulf of Mexico, seems to have found more favour with Russell than many of the other American cities he had visited; he particularly enjoyed the 'great oyster saloons'.

The US navy had blockaded the mouth of the bay, but two forts, Morgan and Gaines, once in Federal hands, had now been taken over by the Confederacy. Russell was able to visit them and make a tour of inspection. However, his real aim was to gain access to two more forts further east along the coast of the gulf. One of these, Fort MacRae, was in Confederate hands and the other, Fort Pickens, was still controlled by the North. He arranged to hire a small schooner and with some friends set off down the coast towards the forts. They were soon apprehended by one of the US naval ships and taken to meet the commander of the blockading squadron, Captain Adams. Russell's conversation with Adams reveals an example of the way in which families were broken up by the war. Adams, though born in the North 'married a lady of Louisiana, where he resided

A Confederate camp at Warrington Navy Yard, Pensacola, Florida in 1861, at a stage when the soldiers had no formal uniform.

on his plantation till his ship was commissioned. He was absent on foreign service when the feud first began, and received orders at sea...to repair direct to blockade Pensacola. He has just heard that one of his sons is enlisted in the Confederate Army, and that two others have joined the forces in Virginia; and as he said sadly, "God knows, when I open my broadside, but that I may be killing my own children." ' But that was not all. One of the Mobile gentlemen [with Russell] brought Adams a letter from his daughter, 'in which she informs him that she has been elected *vivandière* to a New Orleans regiment, with which she intends to push on to Washington, and get a lock of old Abe Lincoln's hair; and the letter concluded with the charitable wish that her father might starve to death if he persisted in his wicked blockade.'

Russell was given permission to visit the Confederate Fort MacRae where he met General Bragg, a soldier who had distinguished himself in the Mexican War of 1845. The General's views on the war were quite clear: 'The North was bent on subjugating the South, and as long as he had a drop of blood in his body, he would resist such an infamous attempt.' After being shown round all the defences, Russell concluded that the Southern newspapers had 'lied consumedly', which was nothing unusual. Bragg was reported to have 30,000 to 50,000 men at his command, whereas in reality he had barely 10,000 and only enough ammunition for one day's normal firing.

Russell returned to his hired schooner and, deciding to leave his fellow passengers behind as they would assuredly not be allowed into Fort Pickens, ordered the young captain to make for the Federal stronghold. Having achieved his aim and seen round the fort, Russell returned in the schooner to Mobile but set off again almost immediately for New Orleans, where he found:

> ...the streets are badly paved, as those of most American cities, if not all that I have ever been in, but in other respects they are more worthy of a great city than are those of New York. There is an air thoroughly French about the people—

cafés, restaurants, billiard rooms abound, with oyster and lager-beer saloons interspersed. The shops are all *magazins;* the people in the streets are speaking French, particularly the Negroes, who are going out shopping with their masters and mistresses, exceedingly well dressed, noisy and not unhappy-looking.

The newspapers were full of the news that Virginia had been invaded by Federal troops and the town of Alexandria seized. 'It is impossible to describe the excitement and rage of the people,' Russell reported. The Federal troops were considered no more than a band of 'thieves, robbers and assassins', and they had come to 'violate the territory of a sovereign state'.

It was at this time that the Confederacy decided to move its capital from Montgomery to Richmond, thus making the capitals of both North and South no more than 100 miles apart. Russell prophesied in his diary that 'the selection must cause a collision between the two armies in front of the rival capitals'.

After ten days in New Orleans, Russell once more took to the water, this time up the mighty Mississippi river. On his way to Montgomery he had visited several plantations but he now broke his journey to see another, which he described in his diary:

We entered, by a wicket gate, a square enclosure, lined with negro huts, built of wood... The ground round the huts was covered with litter and dust, heaps of old shoes, fragments of clothing and feathers, amidst which pigs and poultry were recreating. Curs of low degree scampered in and out of the shade, or around two huge dogs, *chiens de garde*, which are let loose at night to guard the precincts; belly deep, in a pool of stagnant water, thirty or forty mules were swinking in the sun and enjoying their day of rest.

The huts of the negroes engaged in the house are separated from those of the slaves devoted to field labour out of doors by a wooden paling. I looked into several of the houses, but somehow or other felt a repugnance, I dare say unjustifiable, to examine the penetralia, although invited—indeed, urged, to do so by

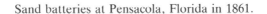

Sand batteries at Pensacola, Florida in 1861.

1st Virginia Regiment, photographed early in 1861.

the Governor. It was not that I expected to come upon anything dreadful, but I could not divest myself of some regard for the feelings of the poor creatures, slaves though they were, who stood by, shy, curtseying, and silent, as I broke in upon their family circle, felt their beds, and turned over their clothing. What right had I to do so?

General view of the Port of New Orleans, showing the great accumulation
of cotton caused by the blockade of the Southern ports by the Union
navy. This photograph was probably taken later in the war.

Swarms of flies, tin cooking utensils attracting them by remnants of molasses,
crockery, broken and old, on the dressers, more or less old clothes on the wall,
these varied over and over again, were found in all the huts; not a sign of
ornament or decoration was visible; not the most tawdry print, image of Virgin or
Saviour; not a prayerbook or printed volume. The slaves are not encouraged, or
indeed permitted to read, and some communities of slave-owners punish heavily
those attempting to instruct them.

All the slaves seemed respectful to their master; dressed in their best, they
curtseyed, and came up to shake hands with him and with me. Among them were
some very old men and women, the canker-worms of the estate, who were dozing
away into eternity, mindful only of hominy, and pig, and molasses...

It struck me more and more, however, as I examined the expression of the
faces of the slaves, that deep dejection is the prevailing, if not universal, characteristic of the race. Here there were abundant evidences that they were well
treated; they had good clothing of its kind, food, and a master who wittingly
could do them no injustice, as he is, I am sure, incapable of it. Still, they all
looked sad, and even the old woman who boasted that she had held her old owner
in her arms when he was an infant, did not smile cheerfully, as the nurse at home
would have done, at the sight of her ancient charge...

Early the next morning, Russell rode out over the fields with the owner,

...through fields crisp with dew. In a few minutes our horses were traversing
narrow alleys between the tall fields of maize, which rose far above our heads...
through vast fields, hedgeless, wall-less, and unfenced... In the midst of this
expanse white dots were visible...the gangs of hands at work.

He saw their breakfast waiting in a cart and pronounced it 'ample, and... wholesome;
such as any labouring man would be well content with'. He also noticed that their
clothing:

...seemed heavy for the climate; their shoes, ponderous and ill-made, had worn away the feet of their thick stockings, which hung in fringes over the upper leathers. Coarse straw hats and bright cotton handkerchiefs protected their heads from the sun. The silence which I have already alluded to, prevailed among these gangs also—not a sound could be heard but the blows of the hoe on the heavy clods. In the rear of each gang stood a black overseer, with a heavy-thonged whip over his shoulder...

When the frost comes, the cane is rendered worthless—one touch destroys the sugar. But if frost is the enemy of the white planter, the sun is scarcely the friend of the black man. The sun condemns him to slavery, because it is the heat which is the barrier to the white man's labour. The Governor told me that, in August, when the crops are close, thick set, and high, and the vertical sun beats down on the labourers, nothing but a black skin and head covered with wool can enable a man to walk out in the open and live.

In the planter's house the assembled company dined:

Here was old France again. One might imagine a lord of the seventeenth century in his hall, but for the black faces of the servitors and the strange dishes of tropical origin. There was the old French abundance, the numerous dishes and efflorescence of napkins, and the long-necked bottles of Bordeaux, with a steady current of pleasant small talk.

Russell draws an interesting parallel between the children of slaves and those of a similar age in the mining and manufacturing districts of England, where they would already be working long hours in dreadful conditions. The negro children, on the other hand, were not expected to work, although they were kept in what Russell calls 'a kind of forcing-house', where they were quite simply being fattened up into strong and healthy workers. The 'kindly' overseer who showed Russell round spoke of his charges with satisfaction. To him it was the most natural thing in the world, but Russell observes:

Now, in this one quarter there were no less than 80 children...No education—no God—their whole life—food and play, to strengthen their muscles and fit them for the work of a slave...

I declare that to me the more orderly, methodical, and perfect the arrangements for economising slave labour—regulating slaves—are, the more hateful and odious does slavery become. I would much rather be the animated human chattel of a Turk, Egyptian, Spaniard, or French creole, than the labouring beast of a Yankee or of a New England capitalist.

He found some relief from his distress by ridiculing the diverse ways in which the Southerners justified their belief in slavery:

The Negro skull won't hold as many ounces of shot as the white man's. Potent proof that the white man has a right to sell and to own the creature! He is plantigrade, and curved as to the tibia! Cogent demonstration that he was made expressly to work for the arch-footed, straight-tibiaed Caucasian. He has a *rete mucosum* and a coloured pigment! Surely he cannot have a soul of the same colour as that of an Italian or a Spaniard, far less of a flaxen-haired Saxon! See these peculiarities in the frontal sinus—in siniciput or occiput! Can you doubt that the being with a head of that shape was made only to till, hoe, and dig for another race? Besides, the Bible says that he is a son of Ham, and prophecy must be carried out in the rice-swamps, sugar-canes, and maize-fields of the Southern Confederation. It is flat blasphemy to set yourself against it. Our Saviour sanctions slavery because he does not say a word against it, and it is very likely that St Paul was a slave-owner. Had cotton and sugar been known, the apostle might

Slaves working in the fields.

have been a planter! Furthermore, the Negro is civilised by being away from Africa and set to work, instead of idling in native inutility. What hope is there of Christianising the African races, except by the agency of the apostles from New Orleans, Mobile, or Charleston, who sing the sweet songs of Zion with such vehemence, and clamour so fervently for baptism in the waters of the 'Jawdam'?

Meanwhile, both North and South seemed to be running into financial problems; the Southern newspapers were clamouring for an immediate attack on Washington and the North was demanding the same for Richmond; both sides kept repositioning their troops and, most significantly, a large mass of Confederate soldiers had been assembled at Manassas Junction on the railway, some 30 miles south of Washington.

Still using the Mississippi steamers as his mode of travel, Russell reached the town of Jackson. He wrote hilariously about some of the conversations he had with those he encountered. The Governor of Mississippi, for one, 'evinced that wonderful confidence in his own people which, whether it arises from ignorance of the power of the North, or a conviction of greater resources, is to me so remarkable':

'Well, sir,' said he, dropping a portentous plug of tobacco just outside the spittoon, with the air of a man who wished to show he could have hit the centre if he liked, 'England is no doubt a great country, and has got fleets and the like of that, and may have a good deal to do in Eu-rope; but the sovereign State of Mississippi can do a great deal better without England than England can do without her.'

Later, with tongue well in cheek, Russell recounted how a companionable chat taught him 'many valuable facts':

I was warned, for example, against the impolicy of trusting to small-bored pistols or to pocket six-shooters in case of a close fight, because suppose you hit your man mortally he may still run in upon you and rip you up with a bowie knife before he falls dead; whereas if you drive a good heavy bullet into him, or make a hole in him with a 'Derringer' ball, he gets faintish and drops at once... [and] if a gentleman with whom you are engaged in altercation moves his hand towards his breeches pocket, or behind his back, you must smash him or shoot him at once, for he is either going to draw his six-shooter, to pull out a bowie knife, or to shoot you through the lining of his pocket. The latter practice is considered rather ungentlemanly, but it has been somewhat more honoured lately in the observance than in the breach.

On one occasion Russell fell in with a General Gideon J. Pillow who conducted him round his fort on the Mississippi:

The General ordered some practice to be made with round shot down the river. An old forty-two pound carronade was loaded with some difficulty, and pointed at a tree about seventeen hundred yards—which I was told, however, was not less than twenty-five hundred yards—distant. The General and his staff took their posts on the parapet to the leeward, and I ventured to say, 'I think, General, the smoke will prevent your seeing the shot.' To which the General replied, 'No, sir,' in a tone which indicated, 'I beg you to understand I have been wounded in Mexico, and know all about this kind of thing.' 'Fire,' the string was pulled, and out of the touch-hole popped a piece of metal with a little chirrup. 'Darn these friction tubes! I prefer the linstock and match,' quoth one of the staff, *sotto voce*, 'but General Pillow will have us use friction tubes made at Memphis, that aren't worth a cuss.' Tube No. 2, however, did explode, but where the ball went no one could say, as the smoke drifted right into our eyes.

The General then moved to the other side of the gun, which was fired a third time, the shot falling short in good line, but without any ricochet. Gun No. 3 was next fired. Off went the ball down the river, but off went the gun, too, and with a frantic leap it jumped, carriage and all, clear off the platform. Nor was it at all wonderful, for the poor old-fashioned chamber carronade had been loaded with a charge and a solid shot heavy enough to make it burst with indignation. Most of us felt relieved when the firing was over, and, for my own part, I would much rather have been close to the target than to the battery.

On 18th June, Russell was forced to make the decision to return immediately to Washington as the US navy had succeeded in closing the Southern ports, thus preventing his despatches from reaching England. He therefore left the river and boarded a train from Memphis to Cairo; the town was a Unionist camp and full to bursting for the quaint reason that: 'These camps are such novelties in the country, and there is such romance in the mere fact of a man living in a tent, that people come far and wide to see their friends under such extraordinary circumstances.'

By this time Russell had been in the South for two months, and an entry in his diary on 20th June is perhaps a fair summing up of his abhorrence of slavery: 'Slavery is a curse, with its time of accomplishment not quite at hand—it is a cancer, the ravages of which are covered by fair outward show, and by the apparent health of the sufferer.'

On 23rd June he wrote: 'The latest information which I received today is of a nature to hasten my departure for Washington—it can no longer be doubted that a battle between the two armies assembled in the neighbourhood of the capital is imminent. At four o'clock in the evening I started by train on the famous Central Illinois line from Cairo to Chicago.' On his arrival in Chicago he found his mail and a variety of criticisms of him in the New York newspapers.

When I left England the prevalent opinion, as far as I could judge, was, that a family quarrel, in which the South was in the wrong, had taken place, and that it would be better to stand by and let the Government put forth its strength to chastise rebellious children. But now we see the house is divided against itself, and that the family are determined to set up two separate establishments. These remarks occur to me with the more force because I see the New York papers are attacking me because I described a calm in a sea which was afterwards agitated by a storm. 'What a false witness is this.' they cry, 'See how angry and how vexed is our Bermoothes, and yet the fellow says it was quite placid.'

I have already seen so many statements respecting my sayings, my doings, and my opinions, in the American papers, that I have resolved to follow a general rule, with few exceptions indeed, which prescribes as the best course to pursue, not so much an indifference to these remarks as a fixed purpose to abstain from the hopeless task of correcting them.

Russell was continually shocked by the lies told by the press of both North and South: 'The Southerners are told there is a reign of terror in New York—that the 7th New York Regiment has been captured by the Baltimore people—that Abe Lincoln is always drunk—that General Lee has seized Arlington Heights, and is bombarding Washington. The New York people are regaled with similar stories from the South.'

The Union general, Irvin McDowell, once said to Russell: 'I have made arrangements for the correspondents to take the field...and I have suggested to them that they should wear a white uniform to indicate the purity of their character.'

Sadly, the bulk of the American press did not live up to this pious hope and its coverage of the war was a catalogue of lies, distortions and propaganda. It was the first war in which the telegraph was widely used, and news coverage was not only more immediate but also more extensive than ever before. But this marvel of modern science was not matched by the skill of its users, many of whom had little or no previous journalistic experience, were grossly underpaid and, in most cases, under 30 years old. The majority did not last more than a year. They were employed by demanding and often unscrupulous editors who wanted news at any price. Wilbur F. Storey of the *Chicago Times* sent the following order to one of his correspondents: 'Telegraph fully all news you can get and when there is no news send rumours.' When they were not tailoring facts to keep up morale, they were not above telling the army generals what to do. Russell says: 'I could not help observing the arrogant tone with which writers of stupendous ignorance on military matters write of the operations which they think the Generals should undertake.'

After three days, Russell continued with his journey and reached New York on 2nd July. A spectacular change had taken place since he was last there in April.

Instead of peaceful citizens, men in military uniforms thronged the pathways, and such multitudes of United States' flags floated from the windows and roofs of the houses as to convey the impression that it was a great holiday festival. The appearance of New York when I first saw it was very different... Now, fully a third of the people carried arms, and were dressed in some kind of martial garb.

The walls are covered with placards from military companies offering inducements to recruits. An outburst of military tailors has taken place in the streets; shops are devoted to militia equipments; rifles, pistols, swords, plumes, long boots, saddle, bridle, camp beds, canteens, tents, knapsacks, have usurped the place of the ordinary articles of traffic. Pictures and engravings—bad, and very bad—of the 'battles' of Big Bethel and Vienna, full of furious charges, smoke and dismembered bodies, have driven the French prints out of the windows. Innumerable General Scotts glower at you from every turn, making the General look wiser than he or any man ever was...

Wall Street and Pine Street are bent on battle. And so this day, hot from the South and impressed with the firm resolve of the people, and finding that the North has been lashing itself into fury, I sit down and write to England, on my return from the city. 'At present dismiss entirely the idea, no matter how it may originate, that there will be, or can be peace, compromise, union, or secession, till war has determined the issue.'

The change in manner, in tone, in argument, is most remarkable. I met men to-day who last March argued coolly and philosophically about the right of Secession. They are now furious at the idea of such wickedness—furious with England, because she does not deny their own famous doctrine of the sacred right of insur-rection. 'We must maintain our glorious Union, sir.' 'We must have a country.' 'We cannot allow two nations to grow up on this Continent, sir.' 'We must possess the entire control of the Mississippi.' These 'musts,' 'can'ts', and 'won'ts', are the angry utterances of a spirited people who have had their will so long that they at last believe it is omnipotent. Assuredly, they will not have it over the South without a tremendous and long-sustained contest, in which they must put forth every exertion, and use all the resources and superior means they so abundantly possess.

The clergy are active on both sides; and their flocks approve of their holy violence. One journal tells with much gusto of a blasphemous chaplain, a remarkably good rifle shot, who went into one of the skirmishes lately, and killed a number of rebels—the joke being in the fact, that each time he fired and brought down his man, he exclaimed, piously, 'May Heaven have mercy on your soul!' One Father Mooney, who performed the novel act for a clergymen of 'christening' a big gun at Washington the other day, wound up the speech he made on the occasion, by declaring 'the echo of its voice would be *sweet music*, inviting the children of Columbia to share the comforts of his father's home.' Can impiety and folly, and bad taste, go further?

Russell hastened to the capital by train, passing through countryside now dotted with the tents of army camps. He wrote in his diary on 3rd July:

The fields around Washington resounded with the words of command and tramp of men, and flashed with wheeling arms. Parks of artillery studded the waste ground, and long trains of white-covered wagons filled up the open spaces in the suburbs of Washington.

To me all this was a wonderful sight. As I drove up Pennsylvania Avenue I could scarce credit that busy thoroughfare—all red, white, and blue with flags, filled with dust from galloping chargers and commissariat carts; the sidewalks thronged with people, of whom a large proportion carried sword or bayonet; shops full of life and activity—was the same as that through which I had driven the first morning of my arrival. Washington now, indeed, is the capital of the United States; but it is no longer the scene of beneficent legislation and of peaceful government. It is the representative of armed force engaged in war—menaced whilst in the very act of raising its army by the enemy it seeks to strike.

With his usual energy, Russell made a tour of the army camps on either side of the Potomac river and estimated that the American press had exaggerated the number of soldiers by at least 45,000. He found them ill-equipped, poorly officered, dirty to excess and, worst of all, with miserably deficient artillery. Most of the soldiers had volun-teered for three months only and were rejoicing in the fact that their time was nearly up. This was to have considerable significance later. Russell's final opinion was: 'And it is with this rabblement that the North propose not only to subdue the South but according to some of their papers, to humiliate Great Britain, and conquer Canada afterwards.'

He followed this visit with another to Fort Monroe near Baltimore and seems to have been rather more favourably impressed. He gave an amusing account of his return journey to Washington by steamer down the Chesapeake river:

July 15th. I need not speak much of the events of last night, which were not unimportant, perhaps, to some of the insects which played a leading part in them ...Need I repeat the horrors of this day? Stewed, boiled, baked and grilled

Left: Wide variation in uniform between two commanders of Union cavalry regiments at the First Battle of Bull Run. *Right:* Studio photograph of Private Francis E. Brownell of the 11th New York Fire Zouaves. He was to fight in the First Battle of Bull Run.

on board this miserable *Elizabeth*... The captain was a shy, silent man, much given to short naps in my temporary berth, and the mate was so wild, he might have swam off with perfect propriety to the woods on either side of us, and taken to a tree as an aborigine or chimpanzee. Two men of most retiring habits, the Negro, a black boy, and a very fat Negress who officiated as cook filled up the 'balance' of the crew.

I could not write, for the vibration of the deck of the little craft gave a St Vitus' dance to pen and pencil; reading was out of the question from the heat and flies; and below stairs the fat cook banished repose by vapours from her dreadful cauldrons, where, Medea-like, she was boiling some death broth. Our breakfast was of the simplest and—may I add?—the least enticing; and if the dinner could have been worse it was so; though it was rendered attractive by hunger, and by the kindness of the sailors who shared it with me. The old pilot had the most wholesome hatred of the Britishers, and not having the least idea till late in the day that I belonged to the old country, favoured me with some very remarkable views respecting their general mischievousness and inutility. As soon as he found out my secret he became more reserved, and explained to me that he had some reason for not liking us, because all he had in the world, as pretty a schooner as ever floated and a fine cargo, had been taken and burnt by the English when they sailed up the Potomac to Washington. He served against us at Bladensburg. I did not ask him how fast he ran; but he had a good rejoinder ready if I had done so, inasmuch as he was up West under Commodore Perry on the lakes when we suffered our most serious reverses. Six knots an hour! Hour after hour! And nothing to do but listen to the pilot.

Russell had already had a short interview with Mr Seward and had found him 'more worn and haggard' than when he had seen him three months previously. He had also met General McDowell who was in command of the army of the Potomac under the overall command of General Winfield Scott. Russell said of McDowell: 'His manner is frank, simple, and agreeable, and he did not hesitate to speak with great openness of the difficulties he had to contend with, and the imperfection of all the arrangements of the Army.' The General had made clear his willingness to allow Russell to accompany the army which was at that moment poised ready for the march to the town of Centreville 'directly in front of which, at a place called Manassas, stands the army of the Southern enemy.'

Rumours were already rampant among the population of Washington, fuelled by accounts in the newspapers:

Along Pennsylvania Avenue, along the various shops, hotels, and drinking bars, groups of people were collected, listening to the most exaggerated accounts of desperate fighting and of the utter demoralisation of the rebels. I was rather amused by hearing the florid accounts which were given in the hall of Willard's by various inebriated officers, who were drawing upon their imagination for their facts, knowing, as I did, that the entrenchments at Fairfax had been abandoned without a shot on the advance of the Federal troops. The New York papers came in with glowing descriptions of the magnificent march of the Grand Army of the Potomac, which was stated to consist of upwards of seventy thousand men; whereas I knew not half that number were actually on the field.

Russell also gave an endearing glimpse in his diary of Lincoln hurrying to the White House, '...striding like a crane in a bullrush swamp among the great blocks of marble, dressed in an oddly cut suit of grey, with a felt hat on the back of his head, wiping his face with a red pocket handkerchief.'

All this time Russell had been making energetic efforts to procure a horse so that he would be mobile when the army moved. He found that 'every carriage, gig, wagon, and

The 7th New York Regiment assembled on the Bowery below Cooper
Union on the day of their departure for Bull Run in July 1861.

hack had been engaged by people going out to see the fight.' In their number were
members of Congress and the Cabinet, senators with their ladies, picnic hampers and
other comforts, intent on witnessing a splendid Federal victory.

Russell's original plan had been to set off for Centreville on the night of 20th July, in
order to be well up with the army should battle commence. However, when he applied
for the necessary pass at General Scott's headquarters, he was told that he could have

one only if it was signed by the General himself who, regrettably, was asleep. Russell suspected that difficulty was being put in his way to discourage him from seeing the battle. It had not gone unnoticed by the authorities that the newspaper he represented was clearly in sympathy with the rebels, although it was equally clear to those who knew him or had read his despatches carefully, that Russell by that stage was convinced of the justness of the Union cause.

As 21st July dawned, Russell finally set off in a gig with a spare horse and a Mr Warre, who had delayed their departure by two hours—a fact which Russell was to regret bitterly.

General Beauregard, on orders from the South's Commander-in-Chief, General Robert E. Lee, had positioned his main army of 20,000 men across the principal highway from Washington to Richmond, based at the Manassas Railway Junction. In the centre of the position was a small tributary of the Potomac river called Bull's Run. A second and smaller Confederate army under General Joseph E. Johnston was drawn up at Harper's Ferry on Beauregard's left.

On the Union side, General McDowell's main army was drawn up to face the Confederates and consisted of 30,000 men, most of whom were 'three months' volunteers. A second force of some 15,000, under the command of the aged General Patterson, was to carry out a flanking movement on McDowell's right intended to pin down General Johnston and prevent him from joining forces with Beauregard. However, by the night of the 20th, Johnston had already managed to elude Patterson and the two Confederate armies had combined. Beauregard had also ordered up General Jackson's Virginia Brigade, consisting of 2,600 men, who had made the journey from Winchester partly on foot and partly by train. This was the first time that the railway had ever been used for strategic transportation in war. In fact, the railways were to play a vital role in the American Civil War, to the distinct advantage of the Federal army, as two-thirds of the railway tracks were in the North.

The First Battle of Bull Run, 21st July 1861, showing the Confederates defending their position on Henry House Hill. One of the mounted figures on the hill is probably General Thomas J. Jackson.

General Thomas J. Jackson, Commander of the First Brigade in the Confederate Army of the Shenandoah. It was during his stand on Henry House Hill at the Battle of Bull Run that he was nicknamed Stonewall Jackson.

The Federal General, William Sherman, called McDowell's plan of attack 'the best planned and worst fought battle of the war'. McDowell had ordered a wide turning movement to take place at dawn on the 21st. This was intended to envelop the enemy's left and rear, but the inexperienced troops took too long to execute it and the element of surprise was all but lost. Nonetheless, with the added advantage of superior artillery, the Federals had succeeded in pushing the rebel line back until it was forced to retreat up Henry House Hill. Had McDowell immediately pursued the retreating Confederates, the outcome of the battle might have been very different, but he was hampered by the loss of many of his experienced officers. The Confederates were given valuable time in which to re-form a strong right flank, based on the brigade of General Jackson.

General Beauregard had had outflanking plans of his own—against the Federal left—but by midday he was forced to the conclusion that he was in the wrong place, and that the main battle was now being fought on the Henry House Hill plateau.

When McDowell was ready to re-attack he found himself up against the 'stonewall' defence of General Jackson. It was this magnificent stand which earned the General his nickname. He was eventually reinforced by Beauregard who had now rallied all his troops into the main Confederate line. For the next three hours both sides fought hard; the advantage passing from one side to the other (one battery of guns changed hands three times during the afternoon). But the Union troops, after a night of marching and a day of fierce fighting under a roasting sun, began to falter. They had had enough. Some began, quite simply, to go home. The weakened Federal lines started to cave in and the trickle became a flood. Then panic ensued.

It was into this panic-stricken retreat that Russell rode in his gig, although he did not fully realise what was happening at the time. He had already encountered a great many soldiers on their way back from the front and on questioning them had been told: 'We are going home because, as you see, the men's time's up, sir. We have had three months of this sort of work, and that's quite enough of it.' Russell had hurried on, frantic to get to the front, and had eventually reached Centreville at about noon. Driving up to the highest point near the town, he found himself looking down on a densely wooded country which spread ahead of him for five or six miles. In the middle distance he could see what proved to be Manassas junction.

> The intervening space was not a dead level; undulating lines of forest marked the course of the streams which intersected it, and gave, by their variety of colour and shading, an additional charm to the landscape which, enclosed in a framework of blue and purple hills, softened into violet in the extreme distance, presented one of the most agreeable displays of simple pastoral woodland scenery that could be conceived.
>
> But the sounds which came upon the breeze, and the sights which met our eyes, were in terrible variance with the tranquil character of the landscape. The woods far and near echoed to the roar of cannon, and thin frayed lines of blue smoke marked the spots whence came the muttering sound of rolling musketry; the white puffs of smoke burst high above the tree-tops, and the gunners' rings from shell and howitzer marked the fire of the artillery.
>
> Clouds of dust shifted and moved through the forest; and through the wavering mists of light blue smoke, and the thicker masses which rose commingling from the feet of men and the mouths of cannon, I could see the gleam of arms and the twinkling of bayonets. On the hill beside me there was a crowd of civilians on horseback, and in all sorts of vehicles, with a few of the fairer, if not gentler sex.

A Union officer galloped up declaring: 'We've whipped them on all points', to the complete satisfaction of the Congress men and their ladies. Russell was determined to get nearer the action; mounting the spare horse, which he had prudently insisted on hiring, he set off on a four-mile ride across country until he was forced back on to a road by a wide stream. As he was threading his way towards a bridge his attention was attracted by loud shouts. Ahead of him he saw:

> ...several wagons coming from the direction of the battlefield, the drivers of which were endeavouring to force their horses past the ammunition carts going in the contrary direction near the bridge; a thick cloud of dust rose behind them, and running by the side of the wagons were a number of men in uniform... My first impression was that the wagons were returning for fresh supplies of ammunition. But every moment the crowd increased; drivers and men cried out with the most vehement gestures, 'Turn back! turn back! we are whipped.' They seized the heads of the horses and swore at the opposing drivers. Emerging from the crowd a breathless man in the uniform of an officer with an empty scabbard dangling by his side was cut off by getting between my horse and a cart for a moment. 'What is the matter, sir? What is all this about?' 'Why, it means we are pretty badly

The Federal army retreating in disorder to the town of Centreville, Maryland; the Reserve Division covering the retreat and attempting to repel the Confederate cavalry.

whipped, that's the truth,' he gasped, and continued. By this time the confusion had been communicating itself through the line of wagons towards the rear, and the drivers endeavoured to turn round their vehicles in the narrow road, which caused the usual amount of imprecations from the men, and plunging and kicking from the horses...

Again I asked an officer, who was on foot with his sword under his arm, 'What is all this for?' 'We are whipped, sir. We are all in retreat. You are all to go back.' 'Can you tell me where I can find General McDowell?' 'No, nor can anyone else.'

A few shells could be heard bursting not very far off but there was nothing to account for such an extraordinary scene. A third officer, however, confirmed the report that the whole army was in retreat, and that the Federals were beaten on all points, but there was nothing in this disorder to indicate a general rout.

All these things took place in a few seconds. I got up out of the road into a corn-field, through which men were hastily walking or running, their faces streaming with perspiration, and generally without arms, and worked my way for about half a mile or so, as well as I could judge, against an increasing stream of fugitives, the ground being strewed with coats, blankets, fire-locks, cooking tins, caps, belts, bayonets—asking in vain where General McDowell was.

Again I was compelled by the condition of the fields to come into the road; and having passed a piece of wood and a regiment which seemed to be moving back in column of march in tolerably good order, I turned once more into an opening close to a white house, not far from the lane, beyond which there was a belt of forest. Two field-pieces unlimbered near the house, with panting horses in the rear, were pointed towards the front, and along the road beside them there swept a tolerably steady column of men mingled with field ambulances and light baggage carts, back to Centreville. I had just stretched out my hand to get a cigarlight from a German gunner, when the dropping shots which had been sounding through the woods in front of us, suddenly swelled into an animated fire. In a few seconds a crowd of men rushed out of the wood down towards the guns, and the artillerymen near me seized the trail of a piece, and were wheeling it round to fire, when an officer or sergeant called out, 'Stop! stop! They are our own men'; and in two or three minutes the whole battalion came sweeping past the guns at the double, and in the utmost disorder. Some of the artillerymen dragged the horses out of the tumbrils; and for a moment the confusion was so great I could not understand what had taken place; but a soldier whom I stopped, said, 'We are pursued by their cavalry; they have cut us all to pieces.'

The scene on the road had now assumed an aspect which has not a parallel in any description I have ever read. Infantry soldiers on mules and draught horses, with the harness clinging to their heels, as much frightened as their riders; negro servants on their masters' chargers; ambulances crowded with unwounded soldiers; wagons swarming with men who threw out the contents in the road to make room, grinding through a shouting, screaming mass of men on foot, who were literally yelling with rage at every halt, and shrieking out, 'Here are the cavalry! Will you get on?' This portion of the force was evidently in discord.

There was nothing left for it but to go with the current one could not stem. I turned round my horse from the deserted guns, and endeavoured to find out what had occurred as I rode quietly back on the skirts of the crowd. I talked with those on all sides of me. Some uttered prodigious nonsense, describing batteries tier over tier, and ambuscades, and blood running knee deep. Others described how their boys had carried whole lines of entrenchments, but were beaten back for want of reinforcements. The names of many regiments were mentioned as being utterly destroyed. Cavalry and bayonet charges and masked batteries played prominent parts in all the narrations. Some of the officers seemed to feel the disgrace of defeat; but the strangest thing was the general indifference with which the event seemed to be regarded by those who collected their senses as soon as they got out of fire, and who said they were just going as far as Centreville, and would have a big fight to-morrow.

By this time I was unwillingly approaching Centreville in the midst of heat, dust, confusions, imprecations inconceivable. On arriving at the place where a small rivulet crossed the road, the throng increased still more... The runaways ran alongside the wagons, striving to force themselves in among the occupants, who resisted tooth and nail. The drivers spurred, and whipped, and urged the horses to the utmost of their bent. I felt an inclination to laugh, which was overcome by disgust, and by that vague sense of something extraordinary taking place which is experienced when a man sees a number of people acting as if driven by some unknown terror...

For my own part, I wanted to get out of the ruck as fast as I could, for the heat and dust were very distressing, particularly to a half-starved man. Many of the fugitives were in the last stages of exhaustion, and some actually sank down by the fences, at the risk of being trampled to death. Above the roar of the flight, which was like the rush of a great river, the guns burst forth from time to time.

The road at last became somewhat clearer; for I had got ahead of some of the ammunition train and waggons, and the others were dashing up the hill towards Centreville...

It never occurred to me that this was a grand débâcle. All along I believed the mass of the army was not broken, and that all I saw around was the result of confusion created in a crude organisation by a forced retreat.

Arriving at Centreville, Russell searched high and low for Mr Warre and the gig but was told that they had left for Washington some time ago.

Nothing was left for it but to brace up the girths for a ride to the Capitol, for which, hungry and fagged as I was, I felt very little inclination. I was trotting quietly down the hill road beyond Centreville, when suddenly the guns on the other side, or from a battery very near, opened fire, and a fresh outburst of artillery sounded through the woods. In an instant the mass of vehicles and retreating soldiers, teamsters, and civilians, as if agonised by an electric shock, quivered throughout the tortuous line. With dreadful shouts and cursings, the drivers lashed their maddened horses, and leaping from the carts, left them to their fate, and ran on foot. Artillery-men and foot soldiers, and negroes mounted on gun horses, with the chain traces and loose trappings trailing in the dust, spurred and flogged their steeds down the road or by the side paths. The firing continued and seemed to approach the hill, and at every report the agitated body of horsemen and wagons was seized, as it were, with a fresh convulsion.

Once more the dreaded cry, 'The cavalry! cavalry are coming!' rang through the crowd, and looking back to Centreville I perceived coming down the hill-between me and the sky, a number of mounted men, who might at a hasty glance be taken for horsemen in the act of sabreing the fugitives. In reality they were soldiers and civilians, with, I regret to say, some officers among them, who were whipping and striking their horses with sticks or whatever else they could lay hands on. I called out to the men who were frantic with terror beside me, 'They are not cavalry at all; they're your own men'—but they did not heed me. A fellow who was shouting out, 'Run! run!' as loud as he could beside me, seemed to take delight in creating alarm; and as he was perfectly collected as far as I could judge, I said, 'What on earth are you running for? What are you afraid of?' He was in the roadside below me, and at once turning on me, and exclaiming, 'I'm not afraid of you,' presented his piece and pulled the trigger so instantaneously, that had it gone off I could not have swerved from the ball. As the scoundrel deliberately drew up to examine the nipple, I judged it best not to give him another chance, and spurred on through the crowd, where any man could have shot as many as he pleased without interruption. The only conclusion I came to was, that he was mad or drunken. When I was passing by the line of the bivouacs a battalion of men came tumbling down the bank from the field into the road, with fixed bayonets, and as some fell in the road and others tumbled on top of them, there must have been a few ingloriously wounded.

After surviving many other small incidents on the way, Russell and his stalwart horse reached Washington. At the time, he was quite certain that he would be riding out again in a day or two to see McDowell's army attack the Confederates afresh. In the edited version of his diaries, he wrote:

Little did I conceive the greatness of the defeat, the magnitude of the disasters which it had entailed upon the United States or the interval that would elapse before another army set out from the banks of the Potomac onward to Richmond. Had I sat down that night to write my letter, quite ignorant at the time of the great calamity which had befallen his army, in all probability I would have stated that McDowell had received a severe repulse, and had fallen back upon Centreville, that a disgraceful panic and confusion had attended the retreat of a portion of his army, but that the appearance of the reserves would probably prevent the enemy taking any advantage of the disorder; and as I would have merely been able to describe such incidents as fell under my own observation, and would have left the American journals to narrate the actual details, and the despatches of the American Generals the strategical events of the day, I should have led the world at home to believe, as, in fact, I believed myself, that McDowell's retrograde movement would be arrested at some point between Centreville and Fairfax Court House.

He made a valiant attempt to write his despatch when he returned, but fatigue overtook him and he fell asleep with his head on the blotter. When he awoke next morning it was to see, to his intense surprise,

> ...a steady stream of men covered with mud, soaked through with rain, who were pouring irregularly, without any semblance of order, up Pennsylvania Avenue towards the Capitol. A dense stream of vapour rose from the multitude; but looking closely at the men, I perceived they belonged to different regiments... mingled pellmell together. Many of them were without knapsacks, crossbelts, and firelocks. Some had neither greatcoats nor shoes, others were covered with blankets.

The talk in the streets was all of disorder; there was general agreement that the army was hopelessly disorganised and Russell commented that 'many think the contest is now over; but the gentlemen of Washington have Southern sympathies, and I, on the contrary, am persuaded this prick in the great Northern balloon will let out a quantity of poisonous gas, and rouse the people to a sense of the nature of the conflict on which they have entered.' These words were to prove prophetic.

All next day, 23rd July, the defeated army continued to tramp into the city. 'Today the aspect of Washington is more unseemly and disgraceful, if that were possible, than yesterday afternoon... The grand army of the Potomac is in the streets of Washington, instead of being on its way to Richmond.'

General McDowell had paid immediately and highly for the failure of the North in its first battle. Russell met and talked to him and was very impressed by his 'calm self-

One of the army camps near Washington, D.C., probably photographed shortly after the First Battle of Bull Run when the North had begun to reorganise its army.

possession and perfect amiability which could only proceed from a philosophic temperament and a consciousness that he would outlive the calumnies of his country-men.' General McClellan was appointed in his place.

On 27th July, Russell contracted some sort of fever and a doctor prescribed powders to be taken in mint juleps. 'Now mint juleps are made of whiskey, sugar, ice, very little water, and sprigs of fresh mint...—"A powder every two hours, with a mint julep. Why, that's six a day, Doctor, Won't that be—eh?—won't that be rather intoxicating?" '

Days passed in a haze of mint juleps, but he recovered and on going out on to the streets again, found that Washington was a changed city—no more 'drunken rabble-ment' but patrols and guards and general order prevailed. Thousands of men were pouring in from all parts of the Union in response to the vote of Congress to raise 500,000 long-term volunteers.

As Russell had foreseen, the disaster of Bull Run was of more benefit to the North in the long run than it was to the South. The Union was shaken sharply out of its complacency and set to with a national will to win the war. The South did the reverse: it sat back and congratulated itself and, in doing so, allowed the North to overtake it.

For a month after the battle, Russell retained his position as the respected correspondent of *The Times*. As soon as his version of events in *The Times* reached America the storm broke over his head with astonishing violence. The day after the battle the American press reports had been largely accurate: they had admitted to 'the repulse, the losses, the disastrous retreat, the loss of guns, in strange contrast to their prophecies and wondrous hyperboles about the hyperbolic grand army. Now they set themselves to stem the current they have made.' By 20th August they had stemmed the current so completely that Russell's version of events seemed to have come as a complete shock.

From Russell's diary:

> August 21st—The echoes of Bull Run are coming back with a vengeance. This day month the miserable fragments of a beaten, washed out, demoralised army, were flooding in disorder and dismay the streets of the capital from which they had issued forth to repel the tide of invasion. This day month and all the editors and journalists in the States, weeping, wailing, and gnashing their teeth, infused extra gall into their ink, and poured out invective, abuse, and obloquy on their defeated general and their broken hosts. The President and his ministers, stunned by the tremendous calamity, sat listening in fear and trembling for the sound of the enemy's cannon. The veteran soldier, on whom the boasted hopes of the nation rested, heart-sick and beaten down, had neither counsel to give nor action to offer. At any moment the Confederate columns might be expected in Pennsylvania Avenue to receive the welcome of their friends and the submission of their helpless and disheartened enemies.
>
> All this is forgotten—and much more, which need not now be repeated. Saved from a great peril, even the bitterness of death, they forget the danger that has passed, deny that they uttered cries of distress and appeals for help, and swagger in all the insolence of recovered strength. Not only that, but they turn and rend those whose writing has been dug up after 30 days and comes back as a rebuke to their pride.

The 'rending' came from every quarter: he received assassination threats; libellous articles and even poems appeared in every newspaper; he was nicknamed 'Bull Run' Russell and one man even asserted that he had met up with Russell on that fateful day and could emphatically deny everything that he had written. Russell, indeed, remem-bered the man and had even felt obliged to take pity on him as he was obviously badly frightened by events and extremely unsafe on his horse.

Russell's supporters were few but they did exist. The *New York Times* was almost alone among the Press in praising him:

The terrible epistle has been read with quite as much avidity as an average President's message. We scarcely exaggerate the fact when we say the first and foremost thought in the minds of a very large portion of our people after the repulse of Bull Run was, What will Russell say?...

He does not, for he cannot, in the least exaggerate its horrible disorder or the disgraceful behaviour of the incompetent officers, by whom it was aided instead of being checked. He saw nothing whatever of the fighting, and therefore says nothing whatever of its quality. He gives a clear, fair, and perfectly just and accurate, as it is spirited and graphic, account of the extraordinary scenes which passed under his observation. Discreditable as those scenes were to our Army, we have nothing in connection with them whereof to accuse the reporter. He has done justice alike to himself, his subject, and the country.

General McDowell was another supporter. When he met Russell he said:

I must confess, I am much rejoiced to find you are as much abused as I have been. I hope you mind it as little as I did. Bull's Run was an unfortunate affair for both of us, for had I won it, you would have had to describe the pursuit of a flying enemy, and then you would have been the most popular writer in America, and I would have been lauded as the greatest of generals. See what measure has been meted to us now. I'm accused of drunkness and gambling, and you Mr Russell —well!—I really do hope you are not so black as you are painted.

General Sherman was of the same opinion:

Mr Russell, I can endorse every word that you wrote; your statements about the battle, which you say you did not witness, are equally correct. All the stories about charging batteries and attacks with bayonets are simply falsehoods, so far as my command is concerned, though some of the troops did fight well.

Russell found universal dislike and distrust for the American Press among the military. The photographer, Matthew Brady, was also able to verify every word of Russell's description. He, his photographic van and apparatus had become inextricably caught up in the retreat and he had seen it all at first hand.

During August Russell received his first two letters from Delane since his arrival in America. Delane had lost an eye and writing had obviously become a burden to him. He praised Russell for his letters which 'are as fresh and crisp as if you were nearer twenty than forty. I don't believe you ever wrote better; the interest has been through-out maintained, and the skill with which you managed your Southern raid has delighted everybody here.' Of the Bull Run despatch he said: 'I can't describe to you the delight with which I, and I believe everybody else, read your vivid account of the repulse at Bull Run and the terrible débâcle which ensued. My fear is only that U.S. will not be able to bear the truth so plainly told.'

However, the policy of *The Times* was still clearly pro-Southern and Russell wrote to Delane in September of the 'incessant attacks' being made on him by the newspapers and that the 'only thing that makes me stick out here is the determination not to show a white feather for these fellows'. He goes on:

Davis writes from New York that it is the bitter leaders in *The Times* that do the harm and excite the people, and that I shall be made the scapegoat of people's sins at home. It is quite obvious, I think, that the North will succeed in reducing the South. There is an iron will in McClellan, and he will not move till he is able to do so with an enormous force, well drilled and secure against defeat as far as man can give guarantees...The situation in which I am placed, at a moment, too, when I am as weak as a cat from Potomac fever, is anything but agreeable, and I look out for articles in *The Times* very much as a wounded man looks out for a marauder with a knife in his hand on the battlefield. I don't want to ask you to

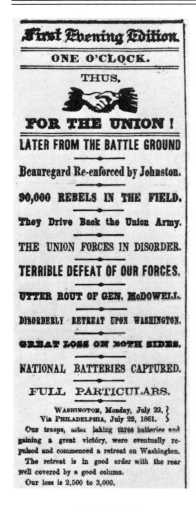

Left: Northern newspaper report of the First Battle of Bull Run, unreservedly admitting the 'terrible defeat of our forces'—a piece of honest reporting that was later refuted. *Right:* The photographer Matthew Brady, who, like Russell, became involved in the retreat from Bull Run.

sacrifice the policy of *The Times* to me, but I would like you, if possible, not to sacrifice me (and no end of children and a wife) to the leaders in *The Times*.

The History of The Times points out that Russell's letters 'showed a remarkable political acumen' and goes on to say: 'His judgements, had Delane and Morris taken heed of them, might have saved the paper from serious errors, but both were blinded by an understandable though none the less regrettable prejudice.'

As the difficulties of his situation multiplied, Russell was obviously in two minds about staying on in America. However, both Morris and Delane urged him strongly to do so. Although he made a short trip around some of the Western states, he had to resign himself to his somewhat tiresome and still much abused existence in Washington.

Towards the end of November, an incident occurred which very nearly precipitated war between America and Great Britain. The Confederate government proposed to send two diplomatic envoys, James Mason and John Slidell, to Europe to plead the South's case. Having successfully run the blockade, Mason and Slidell transferred to a British ship, H.M.S. *Trent.* A Federal ship intercepted her in the Bahama Channel and arrested the two envoys. Uproar ensued. The affair was declared 'an outrage upon the British flag', among other things, and Lord Palmerston (then Prime Minister of Great Britain) drafted a note to the Federal government which, if it had been sent, could only have led to war. However, the Prince Consort, only weeks before his death, counselled moderation. The final note gave the US government an escape clause if it declared that the action of the Federal ship was unauthorised. Lincoln, who was reported as saying: 'One war at a time', gave orders for Mason and Slidell to be released. Both nations breathed a sigh of relief.

On 19th November Russell had written: 'I rarely sat down to write under a sense of greater responsibility, for it is just possible my letter may contain the first account of the seizure of the Southern Commissioners which will reach England.' He was quite aware of the gravity of the situation and felt sure that the Union would not climb down over the affair. Public opinion was at fever pitch and Russell was once more a handy scapegoat for the country's rage against all things British. Happily, his political antennae were for once at fault.

When the dust had settled, Russell left for New York where he became ill with typhoid fever. Matters went from bad to worse. He was accused by the *New York Herald*, his most implacable enemy among the American Press, of financial speculation during the *Trent* affair. Russell felt that his integrity had been brought into question and he was profoundly upset by the incident. He was also finding it extremely difficult to obtain the necessary pass to accompany General McClellan and the Union army when it made its next move. As if all this was not enough, he found that he was just as unpopular in New York as he had been in the capital. He expressed his general mood in a letter to Delane on 27th January:

If I am ever in another Bull's Run you may depend on it I will never get out of it alive... It is a dead load round a man's neck to be feeling always that he is disliked and is liable to insult and outrage. I'm the only English thing they can vent their anger on, and *The Times* is regarded as so dead against the North that everyone connected with it in the North is exposed to popular anger whilst I am especially obnoxious to it as I am supposed to be the cause of all the ill will of the paper to the Federal government. It's hard work playing a neutral game unless you're on neutral ground I can tell you.

He was confident that McClellan would not move until the weather had improved and so took the opportunity of making a trip to Canada for a month. This prompted a rebuke from J.C. MacDonald, Manager of *The Times*: 'Delane doesn't like letters from Canada when he wants them from the Potomac. And Morris is tremendously riled with you for writing long grumbles ending in nothing specific.' Russell had, indeed, written Morris a long letter in February, bemoaning his circumstances and had received a rather sharp one in reply saying: 'You must either go to the front or come home.... Up to the beginning of this year you did well; but since then you seem to have lost heart and to have thrown us overboard.'

On his return to Washington on 1st March, Russell found little had changed. His application for a pass to no less than five generals had not borne fruit. He had even written to the President who was unable to help. McClellan had actually given him a pass on his return, but it was subsequently withdrawn by Stanton, the Secretary of War. It was rumoured that there was considerable animosity between the two men and Russell was perhaps being used as a weapon by Stanton against the General.

Towards the end of March, Russell wrote in his diary:

It was plain I had now but one course left. My mission in the United States was to describe military events and operations, or, in defect of them, to deal with such subjects as might be interesting to people at home... When to the press and populace of the United States, the President and the Government of Washington added their power, resistance would be unwise and impracticable. In no camp could I have been received—in no place useful. I went to America to witness and describe the operations of the great army before Washington in the field, and when I was forbidden by the proper authorities to do so, my mission terminated at once.

The American historian, J.F. Rhodes, once described Russell as 'this intelligent and fair-minded man who sympathized with the North because he hated slavery...it was not Delane who called this sound and able writer home. We drove him away'.

Delane was not well pleased when Russell returned home: 'I wish I could think you had done right in coming home so precipitately in the very crisis of the war. It is lamentable that at such a time we should be practically unrepresented.' However, although Russell wrote no more for the paper on American affairs, he was awarded a generous pension. He continued to voice his own opinions about the war in the *Army and Navy Gazette*, of which he was by then Editor, and which he subsequently bought.

Army wagons in the shadow of the Capitol, Washington. The dome of the huge building is clearly still under construction.

The Franco–Prussian War

In March 1863, although still editing the *Army and Navy Gazette*, Russell received a letter from Delane which was to add a new dimension to his life. Delane had been offered a place at the forthcoming marriage of the Prince of Wales to Princess Alexandra: 'But, you who wrote the Coronation of Moscow as never man wrote—don't you feel it a duty to describe the marriage of the Prince of Wales? I am sure you do, and that you will not let a work so peculiarly your own fall to any other scholar of the school that you have founded.' Russell, of course, agreed. His splendid description of the wedding was later expanded into a handsome book which became the official account of the event. This first contact with the royal couple was to lead to a life-long friendship.

In 1865 he was the only correspondent on board the Great Eastern steamship during the laying of the Transatlantic Cable. He obviously felt that his account had lacked lustre in some way, as an apology to Delane prompted the following praise: 'Everybody I have met is delighted with it and considers it a miracle of lucidity, which on such a subject was not easy. Anything like garnish would have been altogether out of place.' Russell continued to undertake special assignments for Delane from time to time.

A year later the Austro-Prussian War broke out and Russell reported it for *The Times* from the Austrian side. The Battle of Sadowa saw the decisive defeat of the Austrians by Prussia. Russell viewed the whole affair from a 'lofty tower'.

> Nothing but a delicate and yet bold panorama on a gigantic scale could convey any idea of such a scene, filled with half a million of men, moving over its surface like the waves of the sea or as a vast driving cloud in a gale, a scene in which every village was vomiting forth fire and smoke, every knoll the scene of murderous conflict, every valley the indiscriminate grave of thousands of men, every cornfield covered with the full harvest of death, and trodden under foot by furious legions before the day was done, while the church spire, rising aloft from its blood-stained base and the flames of the little hamlet, seemed to bear witness to Heaven against the wickedness of man.

Russell was distinctly impressed by the Prussian needle-gun and did his utmost to convince the British Government of its desirability. He wrote to Delane:

> Let there be no mistake about it. The needle-gun has pricked the Austrian Army to the heart. If we do not *at once* arm our troops with a breach-loader with fixed ammunition (no d----d humbug about 'capping') we are howling idiots, and deserve to be smashed in our first fight... *Do press this on the authorities if they have the smallest doubt about it.*

Due to a breakdown in the health of *The Times's* permanent correspondent in Vienna, Russell stood in for him for a short time. It was this experience which made him aware of the inevitability of a struggle between the German States and France. 'The non-Prussian German States would rather a thousand times be swallowed up by the great northern monarchy [Prussia] than see an inch of German soil handed over to France.'

In January 1867 Russell's wife died after years of illness. He buried himself in the country to write a novel and to try to forget—the attempt was not a success. He then stood for Parliament as a Conservative, but this also ended in failure. The year 1870 saw the beginning of the Franco-Prussian War and Russell's fiftieth birthday. It was a period in his life which was to test him in many ways.

Officer's wives of the *Garde du corps* during the Austro-Prussian War of 1866 scraping linen for the wounded in the Officer's Mess.

The conflict began in February of that year when Spain offered her vacant throne to Prince Leopold of Hohenzollern-Sigmaringen, a distant relation of King William I of Prussia. Leopold accepted. The French were deeply disturbed at the prospect of a German monarch on the throne of Spain and felt that the balance of European power would be seriously threatened. France protested to William (as head of the house of Hohenzollern) in the strongest terms, asking him to persuade Leopold to withdraw his candidature. William, who had disliked the scheme from the first, readily complied. Within 48 hours Leopold had withdrawn his acceptance. The French, however, now demanded guarantees that the offer would never be renewed and sent their ambassador to see the King who was taking the waters at Bad Ems. Having already obtained Prince Leopold's renunciation, William saw no point in taking the matter further and politely but firmly declined to give the French Ambassador an interview. He sent a telegram to his Chancellor, Count Otto von Bismarck, bringing him up to date with events. Bismarck was aghast. This development did not advance his plans in any way. For years his driving ambition had been the unification of the German states and, with it, their supremacy in Europe. He now felt that the King's easy compliance with France's peremptory demands was a humiliation, and that the German people would see it as such. If it came to a war, he was confident that a united Germany could win. So, seizing the opportunity with which fate had presented him, he skilfully altered the King's telegram so that the French Ambassador appeared to have been soundly snubbed by William, and released it to the world press. The result was instantaneous. The French government and people erupted with anger and indignation. France declared war on Prussia within the week.

France's fatal mistake was in her underestimation of the Prussian army and her unrealistic assessment of her own. General von Moltke was an organising genius and had modernised not only the army, but also the railway system to transport it. Within

Above: The French Cabinet which declared war against Prussia on 2nd January 1870. Emperor Napoleon III is easily recognisable by his splendid waxed moustache. *Left:* King William I, who took nominal command of the Prussian armies during the war. *Right:* Crown Prince Frederick, commander of the Prussian Third Army, described by Russell as 'looking a soldier every inch of all his great height.'

eighteen days, Prussia was able to mobilise an army of 1,183,000 men, led by a 72-year-old king who was the first professional soldier to rule Prussia since Frederick the Great, and who was aided by a superb general staff.

Napoleon III had also put in motion the reform of the French army, but in 1870 it was still woefully unprepared for what was to come. Once mobilisation began, the army soon degenerated into chaos. Soldiers were wandering about all over the country looking for their units, the railway system clogged up completely and there seemed to be a shortage of everything.

As to armaments, the French had their 'secret weapon' the *mitrailleuse*: this consisted of 25 revolving barrels which, when the handle was turned, could fire all at once or in rapid succession. But the Prussian guns fired further, faster and with more accuracy. Russell himself was to comment in his diary in October of that year: 'The superiority of the Prussian breech-loaders over the French muzzle-loaders is terribly manifest in every action.'

Napoleon set up his headquarters at the town of Metz in Lorraine, dominated by its great, but as yet unfinished, fortress. The French plan was to invade Prussia across its border with Lorraine, but, by the beginning of August, with the army still scattered behind him, Napoleon had made no move.

Meanwhile, *The Times* was doing some mobilising of its own. Correspondents were despatched to various strategic points. Delane had originally planned that Russell would join the French imperial staff, but Napoleon, with a lamentable lack of foresight, refused to have any foreign correspondents with his army. Writing in his expanded diary of 1874, Russell felt that:

> ...[had] special correspondents been admitted to the French armies, the system of deception and falsehood which paralysed the energies of the nation would have failed at the outset, and Frenchmen would have known the truth which they never knew until it was too late. The War Minister who informed France that the Army was ready for war to the very last button of the soldier's gaiter, and who allowed the armies of France to enter upon a campaign without tents, medicines, transports, supplies, shoes, or maps, was perhaps aware that the keen eyes of neutral observers might perceive the deficiencies which correspondents of the French Press either could not detect or were afraid to indicate.

Although Russell felt that the French might make some early gains, he was in no doubt that the allied German armies would be the final victors. He had not forgotten Sadowa. Delane, however, did not share this view, as a letter to Russell demonstrates: 'Nothing shall ever persuade me—except the event—that the Prussians will withstand the French, and I would lay my last shilling upon Casquette against Pumpernickel.' Delane was soon to alter his opinion and *The Times* gained credit for correctly predicting success for the Germans.

Having failed to get Russell accepted by the French, application was now made to the Prussian army. He was immediately given permission to join the staff of Crown Prince Frederick. July 20th found him rattling through Belgium in a train on his way to Berlin, surrounded by the fever and bustle of war. The excitement was heightened by the fact that the Queen of Prussia, Queen Augusta, was on the same train. When it stopped at Potsdam, the private station for the royal palace, Russell wrote:

> A carriage with well-appointed postillions and out-riders and handsome horses was waiting—a tall old man in military uniform, with a star on his breast, heavy grey moustache, bold front, and fixed and hautain eye stood in the doorway of the station, and received her tenderly. It was the King.

Russell was accompanied at this stage by Lord Ronald Gower and by Lieutenant Colonel Pemberton, who had canvassed long and hard to be attached to *The Times*. Gower was to act as Russell's 'jackal'. On their arrival in Berlin their paramount objective was to get their 'Legitimation' to join the Crown Prince's army. Although they were constantly assured that it was coming, it was not until 29th July that it actually materialised. Russell, however, was enjoying himself hugely, as a letter to his daughter shows:

> Nothing could exceed the reception I have had here. I have been presented to the King; the Queen talked with me for an hour, and I dined with them and all the bigwigs at the Palace at Potsdam on Sunday when the Princess was christened —the Crown Prince, the Princess Royal, etc. Everyone is ready to give me every facility to be killed, and I am to accompany either the King or the Crown Prince on the field... It will be an awful conflict. The Palace is in tears—Queen and Princesses. But all full of hope in the confidence that God blesses their cause. The French think the same... The christening was a gloomily splendid affair—the poor little baby protested against the sermon with all her lungs. The great Bismarck gave me a full hour's talk, and has very much interested himself about me.

As Russell's relationship with Bismarck was to prove a difficult one, it is interesting to read his first impressions of this great man:

> He rose, and advanced to meet me with outstretched hand and a most charming frankness of manner... The face is one that can never be mistaken. The coarsest caricatures are like, just as the finest photographs or most delicate engravings fail to convey an idea of the infinite subtlety of expression, the play of the mouth, and—need it be said—the varying expression of the eye. First, business. He said, 'You shall go. I have no power to give you an order; that is the War Minister's business. We put up a general defence against newspaper corespondents going with our army. But you shall be an exception, and in a short time you will receive your *Legitimation.*' Then, for more than an hour Count Bismarck found time to expound the situation, to give his views of France, Frenchmen, French statesmen and the Emperor; to retrace the story of French interference in German politics, and his own policy in his interviews with the Emperor, speaking of matters of the highest importance with a frankness and unreserve characteristic of the man, but embarrassing to one in my position. His English is excellent.

News was coming in that Napoleon III was close to the frontier near Saarbrücken but apparently not yet advancing beyond it.

> Every hour gained for the Germans is an immense advantage. All the plans for concentration are so exceedingly fine that a rough intrusion may shatter the scheme altogether. So the great anxiety is to know if the French are moving; and when hour after hour comes with its telegrams reporting 'nothing doing along the front', or insignificant appearances of patrols, men rub their hands and look cheerful. An irruption of 30,000 or 40,000 men, upon say, Treves, a few days ago, would have marred Von Moltke's plans. The German hosts are getting stronger every hour. The streams have gathered towards the border, and have now formed a sea of bayonets; fast augmenting trains roll ceaselessly on, setting from north and east and south towards the narrow frontier between Strasbourg and Luxembourg.

After scouring Berlin for some means of transport, Russell and Pemberton managed to buy horses and two wagons. Russell had his family crest, a gigantic goat, painted on the side of his wagon, which was to give rise to much amusement and conjecture during the coming weeks.

On 31st July the King left Berlin for the frontier to take nominal command of his armies in the field. Bismarck went with him.

The next day Russell and his five horses, five men and two wagons also left by train, to creep slowly south west through Prussia to Cologne on the river Rhine. It then

Excited crowds cheering King William as he leaves Berlin for the front on 31st July 1870. According to Russell, the departure was rendered all the more impressive by a terrific thunderstorm which crashed overhead as the Royal carriages moved off.

followed the river south to Bingen and then on to Mayence. Here it was decided that Pemberton would join the staff of Prince Frederick Charles—presuming that he could find him.

While they had been on the train, the French had won what proved to be their one and only victory—at Saarbrücken. But it was enough for the Parisians who went mad with delight.

Frantic to catch up with the elusive Crown Prince, Russell and Gower set off in a hired carriage by road (all the trains being full), leaving the rest of his lumbering entourage to follow as best it could. Arriving in Worms and finding no news of his quarry, Russell, who was feeling far from well, despaired of ever catching up with him. 'It is plain that we are "out of the hunt". A great army, headed by a great prince, is somewhere about; but we cannot find it. It is evident that it is not on German soil as yet that the contest is to be worked out.

He set off again for Neustadt and, on entering the town, heard that French prisoners and wounded Germans were coming in by train and that there was fighting around the town of Wissembourg. The Crown Prince was thought to be at Landau, but how to get there? The railway lines were all blocked; '...the Mayence man positively refused to stir another step—Not if the Crown Prince himself asked him. His horses could not do it.'

Eventually, they managed to hire another carriage 'at some fabulous rate', and were soon entering Landau. 'Here we were in the full tide of war. The streets, the market-place thronged with soldiers; guards at every gate; troops encamped—though that is not the proper word, for the Germans carry no tents—bivouacked along the ramparts and in the fields between the moats.' But still no Crown Prince. Russell was in a quandary. He dared not go on without his wagons and horses, which were still toiling along behind him; to be separated from his transport and baggage in the middle of a campaign he knew could be fatal. There was still no room on the trains and no place to stay in

Landau. Throwing caution to the winds, Russell made a dash for it and just managed to slip out of the town before the gates were closed for the night. They plunged on towards Wissembourg through the most terrific thunderstorm, along roads which were choked by the tramping columns of the German army:

> It really was an awful night. The pine-groves which lined the road were crowded with soldiers taking shelter, who were revealed by the lightning, standing around the fires, which were every moment extinguished, only to be lighted again and fed with pine cones till they blazed fiercely up and again expired. Scarcely a sound was heard amidst these enormous masses of men, only the roar of watercourses and falling rain, and rolling of thunder and the echoes thereof. Great bodies of cavalry dismounted and stood by their horses.

Their troubles did not end at Wissembourg. There was no shelter of any kind and they were forced to sleep in one of the wagons. During the night they were virtually arrested as spies, but luckily the officious Bavarian who suspected them disappeared during the night. They set off again next morning, heading westwards. Russell was now becoming exhausted by the long journey, lack of sleep and the uncertainty of his position. His leg, badly injured in India,

> ...[had] become swollen from the hip, and was racked with shooting pains. I wished with all my heart that I had never set out to join a belligerent army. The weakness caused by continued indisposition, the want of rest, and of proper food, had produced in me a strange mental condition—lethargy—intense despondency. My mind was filled with most melancholy forebodings. I was a very croaky Cassandra indeed—a prophet of all evil. We should never see the Crown Prince—never come up to him. We should never see our horses again, nor our grooms, nor our van. My companion, to whom this scene was new, took it all in for gospel. After some faint attempts to rouse me to take a more hopeful view of circumstances, he became tinged with a soft melancholy himself. Had he been despondent and croaky, I was just in such a mood as would have induced me to resist obstinately any suggestions of a depressing nature upon his part; but as he sank down, I was determined to go lower, and so, from the loss of horses and carriages and Crown Prince, I proceeded to absolute loss of life; we should certainly be cut up; I should be hanged as the correspondent of the hated *Times,* and as a spy; and he, as an English lord, provided with German military papers, would be treated as a contraband of war, laden with chains and sent off to the galleys for life.

At last, Russell heard positive news of the Crown Prince's whereabouts. He was at Soultz-sous-Forêts, a short distance ahead. As they straggled into the town, the first person they saw was an old friend of Russell's, Count Seckendorff, who greeted him warmly saying: 'Welcome! welcome! we have been expecting you. You are to breakfast with the Crown Prince at 12 o'clock.'

But this was not to be: there were sounds of a heavy cannonade somewhere ahead and rumours of a battle in progress. The Crown Prince and all his staff clattered out of town in the direction of the firing. Russell was mad with frustration. His horses were still far behind, the Mayence man was no longer open to persuasion, financial or otherwise, and there was not a fresh mount to be had anywhere. Russell's lameness made it impossible for him to walk to the battle, a good ten miles away.

Thus Russell—the only newspaper correspondent within miles—missed the Battle of Wörth, and all for want of a horse. He spent the day

> ...in a horrible trance, a waking sleep, which left me conscious of what was passing, and yet deprived me of power of movement. At 4 o'clock the sounds of firing had died away. I awoke and went out. Crowds of soldiers in the street. They reported that their comrades had gained another great victory, that the French were in full

retreat, that the French army of Alsace under the command of Marshal MacMahon was utterly routed with great loss.

In fact, the German Third Army had also been severely mauled by the contest, with 10,500 dead and wounded. Russell spent a dreadful night in quarters which were appropriated for wounded soldiers:

> The wounded men in the room below died almost as fast as they were carried in. Their bodies were taken out from the bloody straw, only to be succeeded by those of men scarcely living. The sounds came up through the thin floor. Then, in the middle of the night, there came great convoys, and the tramp of troops over the stony street. Sleep was difficult under such circumstances, hardened as I am; and my couch was curved, so that whether I lay in it or on it, I was obliged to look at my feet high in air above my head, my body being bent as if I were a fish tied up head and tail to accommodate the pot in which it was to be boiled. Then, to console myself, I thought of what the wounded must suffer. But who can hold a fire in his hand by thinking of the frosty Caucasus?

However, the next day saw him breakfasting at the Crown Prince's table, where he was 'much struck by the number of young, intelligent, active-looking fellows on the staff... The prince smoked a pipe with a porcelain bowl, on which were the Royal arms of Prussia, painted, it was said, by the fair hand of the Crown Princess.'

Having at last gained the protection of the Crown Prince's headquarters' staff, Russell was absorbed into it and given his place in the column. Each carriage had its own number and when the order was given to move, it merely fell into place in numerical order. About a mile out of Soultz Russell described the following:

> In a large field were assembled some eight or ten acres (I cannot use any other phrase) of French prisoners, guarded by a double line of sentries, without covering or equipage of any kind. They were grouped together according to the various

A remarkable photograph showing a vast camp of French prisoners. Conditions here were much better than those at the camp described by Russell after the Battle of Wörth.

regiments or arms of the service. A young cavalry officer in charge of the mounted men on the road courteously gave orders for us to be permitted to ride into the field to have a closer view of the prisoners. I confess I did so with reluctance. One feels a sort of shame at staring, out of mere curiosity, at brave men whom fortune has placed in such a sorry plight... It was a very curious sight, and one I never thought I should have seen. At a distance, the variety of uniforms gave it the appearance of a bed of flowers.

They passed through the battlefield of Wörth. 'What a rout it must have been! It would seem as if the regiments must have been completely annihilated, as for upwards of two miles signs of utter ruin met the eye on both sides of the road in the fields.' Hanging over this scene was the foul, sour smell of decay.

A life of perpetual movement gave a special significance to Russell's nightly billets, which were assigned to him by the Intendant of the Crown Prince's staff. He was near the bottom of the list and some of his quarters reflected his lowly status. He described one in particular:

After hard knocking at the gate...the door was opened by a gnarled, withered, and excessively foul old man...who did not appear to have washed his hands or face, or to have allowed any cleaning process on his person or in his house...He led us into a dirty courtyard, and showed a loathesome stable to put up the horses, but it was almost better than our bedroom... It was a chamber of horrors. The air seemed to be thick with an invisible preparation of rancid cheese, through which myriads of flies whizzed and buzzed, rising in swarms at the smallest movement, and settling down in masses on the rafters, ceiling, and walls.

The meal prepared for him was worse:

...An awful soup thick with Michael's cheese, served up in a tin dish and the beef from which it was made, an enormous cucumber, a bottle of a terrible preparation, which, he said, 'he had made from his own grapes,' and a pet cheese, which was instantly ordered into the outer darkness.

Yet, on another occasion he found himself ascending 'an imposing staircase to charming rooms, handsomely furnished', where he was installed in great luxury. 'Such are the chances of war! Sèvres vases, pictures, ormulu [sic] clocks, damasked furniture, buhl cabinets, rich carpets, and couches one day; the next a cabin and straw.'

The Third Army was now marching through Lorraine, where the Prussians were neither liked nor welcomed by the local population, who were distinctly French. Their attitude to the invaders was not improved by the swingeing requisitions made by the army. There seemed to be little enough of everything as it was, but when the army moved on, it left famine in its wake. Russell commented on this: 'The Prussians must be cock-sure of victory or they would never lay up stores of enmity in case of defeat.'

The First and Second German armies had surrounded the fortress town of Metz and Marshal Bazaine and his forces were bottled up inside. But the French had not fallen back on the town without a terrific struggle. The Battle of Gravelotte on 17th August had inflicted severe losses on the Prussians—the highest of the war—and their generals had made some appalling mistakes. MacMahon was said to be falling back on Châlons.

Russell appears to have been a welcome guest at the Crown Prince's table. This enabled him to keep in touch with the mood at headquarters and catch up on the latest news.

The Crown Prince told us of great fights before Metz. He seemed much affected by the loss. 'Where is this all to end? It is quite frightful.' He told us of regiments that had lost 20 and 30 officers and many hundreds of men. 'My father,' he said, 'felt it very deeply; it made him quite unwell.'

Arriving at Ligny on 23rd August, Russell learned that MacMahon had now abandoned Châlons and was thought to be on his way to Paris. Four days later, after much confusion and speculation, it was discovered to everyone's utter amazement that he was not en route to Paris at all, but making for Metz, in the opposite direction, in a desperate and futile attempt to relieve it.

The Prussian Third Army of 150,000 men, which had originally been marching due west, now executed a right-angled turn, covered 50 miles in a forced march north, and caught up with MacMahon, all in the space of three days—an astonishing feat.

There was an air of expectancy at the Crown Prince's headquarters. A major, and possibly decisive, battle was felt to be imminent. But there was still a good deal of ground to cover and the night of 29th August found Russell at Ste Menehould. He describes the scene that night:

> A last look before I turned in…revealed a beautiful sight: all the stars of heaven seemed to have settled on the face of the earth, and, far as the eye could sweep, the watch-fires burned on hill-side, valley, and rolling plain—near at hand, lighting up the figures of the soldiers in their bivouacs and justifying Rembrandt at every flash, and far away gathering closely into asteroids and nebulous clouds which closed in the horizon. Some 80,000 men are resting all around us on their arms, and yet no sound is heard except the neigh of a horse now and then, or the voice of a sentry challenging.

Russell's letter to *The Times* that night had this expectant sentence: 'Before dawn the Crown Prince may have to prepare for the battle for which Paris is dying and France quivering with excitement.'

The next day the German and French armies collided at Beaumont, fifteen miles south east of the frontier fortress town of Sedan, the birthplace of the great French general, Turenne. MacMahon now realised that the relief of Metz had become a pipe-dream. Retreating into Sedan, he turned to face the enemy which surrounded him on three sides, with the Belgian frontier at his back barely seven miles to the north. The desperately ill French Emperor was with him, now almost crippled by the pain of a stone as 'big as a pigeon's egg' which was lodged in his bladder. In the pungent words of General Ducrot, a veteran of the Crimea: '*Nous sommes dans un pot de chambre et nous y serons emmerdés!*'

With two days still to go before the battle, Russell had been observing the members of the Crown Prince's staff as tension mounted:

> There is a good deal said of men being 'cool under fire'. One has seen men very cool under it, but I have never met with one yet who is not a little excited *before* he goes into action. It may be pleasurably so. Still there is a glisten in the eye, and a heightened colour in the cheek, and a *timbre* in the voice, not derived from internal coolness. Our staff is tremendously civil. We go about exchanging lights and even cigars; men look into their holsters and see what there is to support life upon, and happy is he who has a nice sausage-end and a hunk of bread and some hard-boiled eggs.

That night the Crown Prince's staff came to rest in a small village called Oches. Russell found himself spending it in

> …a sort of wigwam inhabited by two witches, a cave of Endor, with a smell which no spirit would face. The difficulty is to find any time to write. I have plenty of notes, but there is scarcely a minute to transcribe them. Human nature will assert its rights; and after 14 hours in the saddle or else in the open without much food, sleep is with most natures an imperative necessity, from which I, at any rate, am not exempt. As I tried to write, the pen slipped out of my hand, and I had just waking sense enough to throw myself in the corner of the room on the bed… I

King William with his Chief of Staff, Field Marshall von Moltke, the man largely responsible for the superb reorganisation of the Prussian army.

wish I could have explained to the fleas that I was not a German. They burned with the fire of insatiable patriotism, and, between the snores of the tired warriors in the straw, and the keening of the old hags by the fire-side, and insect activity, I had but a sorry night when I most needed rest.

He was not alone in his misery. The rest of the staff, most of whom boasted royal blood, had endured a night of equal horror and Russell claimed that the small Prince of Weimar 'seemed to have aged ten years from the sufferings of the night'.

August 31st saw more jockeying for position, the Prussian cavalry harrying the French at every opportunity. The Crown Prince decided to carry out an inspection of his men which gave an added boost to morale, already high after the victory at Beaumont the day before. Russell went off with a companion on a little sortie of his own, which included watching an artillery bombardment of the town of Bazeilles, to the east of Sedan. They returned to a few hasty hours of sleep.

He was awoken by loud knocking and a voice calling out: 'The Crown Prince has sent to tell you to come to the battle.' It was still pitch dark. By the time he had collected himself, his groom and his horse, the village was already deserted and they rode out alone, heading north for the river Meuse and Sedan beyond it. At one point they fell in with a marching column: 'The men had laid out in the fields; their uniforms were soiled; their boots muddy; their faces unwashed; there was profound silence in the ranks; and, as they marched along, the jingling of their equipments, cooking-vessels, and canteens, was the only sound which arose above the tramp of their feet.'

The early morning mist began to clear and they had a beautiful ride through the dewy countryside. All was silent except for the occasional growl of distant artillery. Cresting a ridge, Russell found himself looking across the valley of the Meuse towards Sedan which seemed to him 'to be placed in a lake, its ancient bastions and battlements, spires and steeples, reflected in the placid waters'. The artillery bombardment had increased. Russell, spellbound on his hilltop, 'could almost look into Sedan. I could see the soldiers on the ramparts, citizens in the streets'. The struggle for Bazeilles was still raging and, watching it, Russell admitted:

It is not a pleasant thing to be a mere spectator of such scenes. There is something cold-blooded in standing with a glass to your eye, seeing men blown to pieces, or dragging their shattered bodies to places of safety, or writhing on the ground too far for help, even if you could render it.

Turning westwards, he rode through a wood 'fragrant with pine cones, and so dense that it almost shut out the signs of the contest outside, you could hear the rustling of the leaves as game bounded across the rides'. Coming out of the trees he saw a group of officers, dismounted, looking through their glasses.

I thought it was the Crown Prince's escort, and exclaiming, 'Here they are!' I was galloping joyously towards the group, when an officer rushed at me angrily, and exlaimed,—'Dismount, Sir! Don't you see who it is? It is the King!' And, just at that moment, a shot or shell from Sedan whistled through the air and plunged into the bank close to the spot where the King himself, Moltke, Bismarck, and three or four of his staff, were standing. This caused an immediate commotion. Whether I was the unlucky cause of the notice taken of us by the French or not I cannot say, but certainly the looks of several of the *entourage* seemed to imply that I was a criminal of no ordinary magnitude. The escort was directed to retire still further to the rear. The officers close to the King were ordered also to disseminate themselves, and the group drew back a little from the spur of the ridge. The King was dressed in his ordinary uniform, tightly buttoned and strapped; Bismarck, in his white cuirassier flat cap with the yellow band, and uniform. The King spoke but little, pulled his moustache frequently, and now and then addressed a word to Von Moltke, Von Roon, or Podbielski, the chief of his staff. A large telescope was mounted on a tripod, through which Generals Moltke and Roon peered eagerly from time to time towards the east, but I don't think they could very well see the position of the Crown Prince of Saxony, owing to the nature of the ground. What took place to their right, however, was very plain

A rare action photograph showing Prussian infantry during the Battle of Sedan on 1st and 2nd September 1870. The French lost 20,000 soldiers, with 80,000 taken prisoner. This disastrous defeat precipitated the fall of the French Second Empire.

indeed. The position between Donchery and Sedan was laid out for them as if they were looking at a diorama in a peep-show...

How I was pestered for a look through my glass and a peep at my map as I sat down a little apart from the great personages, and tried to make out what it was all about! A glance to the left showed me that the Crown Prince had commenced his tremendous attack upon the French positions to the north and west of Sedan. In the plains below us, in a bend of the Meuse, were drawn up, in most beautiful order, great blocks of cavalry. On the hills above marched the long dark masses of Prussian infantry, their positions indicated by the play of their bayonets and the sun reflected from their helmet spikes. In front of them, from every knoll, and from the edges of detached clumps of trees, spurted continual jets of smoke from literally dozens of batteries, which seemed to have worked round for a part of a semi-circle towards the north, directing a concentrated fire upon the French, who, we could see, were suffering horribly on the position over the village of Floing... The sun was exceeding powerful; the day had become so clear, that through a good glass, the movements of individual men were plainly discernible.

As yet it was evident that the whole force of the French resistance was directed against the Crown Prince of Saxony. It had, in fact, become an attack upon him. The motion of the columns was all in his direction. But, if the French General could have stood beside the Prussian King, he would have already felt the day was desperate; for how could the position of Floing, and the heights around Sedan upon the west and north-west, be defended with one corps against the prodigious force which was encompassing them round about, whose bayonets glittered for miles, and whose columns darkened the ground, advancing, as sure as fate itself, in one great cloud of war against an almost helpless enemy?

Bazeilles was still the centre of fierce fighting and 'vast clouds of black smoke rising above the trees marked the work of destruction going on in that ill-fated town'.

As he was unable to find the Crown Prince and his staff, Russell remained with the King's entourage, observing everything and writing furiously. He was fascinated by the King, Bismarck and Moltke—'the three terrible "Fates" before whose eyes the power of imperial France was being broken to atoms.'

At about 11 o'clock he caught sight of Seckendorff who greeted him with: 'Where on earth have you been? We all thought you were lost.'

As we rode together he told me all he had seen, and I acquainted him with my own proceedings. 'These devils of French are fighting very hard, but we have got them fast and sure; still they are causing us heavy loss. The Emperor is in there. All we are afraid of is that they may break through and escape to Belgium before the two Armies can shake hands round them.'

Rejoining the Crown Prince, whose view of the battle was even clearer than that of the King's, Russell continued to take notes every five minutes. 'As fast as a sheet was filled, I cut it off with a knife and put it into an envelope in my sabertache.' (Unhappily, his exhaustive account of that momentous day was intercepted by the French a never reached its destination.)

In spite of the devastation caused by the German guns and the increasing chaos within Sedan itself, the French cavalry in particular made some magnificent attacks on the encroaching Prussian infantry. Russell watched in admiration as:

...a splendid-looking body of Cuirassiers, shook themselves up, and, sitting low, charged out of the recess in which they were concealed, and swooped upon the Prussians. Those who were aware of the coming wrath turned and fled. Others went on placidly, advancing and firing almost till the wave was upon them. In another minute the great current, steed and man, had swept over the plateau, trampling or sabring the luckless skirmishers, and in a thick cloud of dust, crashed

Left: Napoleon III's letter of capitulation to King William, 2nd September 1870. It reads: 'Since I could not die in the midst of my troops, I can only put my sword in Your Majesty's hands. I am Your Majesty's good brother. Napoleon.' *Right:* An exhausted Emperor, as Russell probably saw him on the day of his surrender to the Prussians. Napoleon was also in great pain from a stone the size 'of a pigeon's egg' in his bladder.

over the hedge into the village of Floing. In an instant they were gone clean out of sight... Down there a terrible tragedy must have been enacted. The Cuirassiers went pell-mell down the descent—so steep that I saw several next day—horses and men—with broken necks.

Again and again the French charged, but Sedan was doomed.

The toils were closing around the prey. Indeed, it occurred to me over and over again that I was looking at some of those spectacles familiar to Indian sportsmen, where a circle of beaters closes gradually in on a wild beast marked in his lair. The angry despairing rushes of the French here and there—the convulsive struggles at one point—the hasty and tumultuous flight from others—gave one an idea of the supreme efforts of some wounded tiger.

By early afternoon the armies of the Prince of Saxony and the Crown Prince had shaken hands. Soon after, the watchers on the ridge saw the white flag of surrender. France had suffered a terrible defeat, with the loss of 17,000 killed and wounded, and 104,000 taken prisoner. The stricken town of Sedan was to see history repeat itself in 1940.

Russell hastened back to his quarters to finish and send off his despatch. 'Ere I lost sight of Sedan, a vast pillar of smoke shot up into the sky, which spread out until it assumed the form of a gigantic tree, overshadowing the whole town. In a few miles we were in solitude. The agony of France was hidden by the ridges of the Meuse.'

That night he dined at the Crown Prince's table and learned of the capture of Napoleon and the terms of surrender. He was struck by the grave and modest demeanour of those present, and although they drank a toast to the King, there were no overt expressions of triumph.

Two days later he visited the battlefield and was shaken by what he saw.

With many years' experience of the work of war, I had never seen the like before—never beheld death in such horrible shapes—because the dead had on

Bismarck and Napoleon meet at the weaver's cottage at Donchery to discuss the French capitulation.

their faces the expression of terror—mental and bodily agony such as I never should have thought it possible for mortal clay to retain after the spirit had fled through the hideous portals fashioned by the iron hand of artillery. There were human hands detached from the arms and hanging up in the trees; feet and legs lying far apart from the bodies to which they belonged.

Russell spent a bad night wandering about Donchery in the drenching rain looking for his van and billet. When he eventually found both, he and his two companions (Mr Skinner of the *Daily News* and Mr Landells, artist for *The Illustrated London News*) settled down for the night. But they were suddenly aroused by Mr Landells who cried: 'Here comes the Emperor.' They rushed out into the street.

The soldiers had turned out of the houses and flocked to the windows as a troop of the Black Hussars came along at a trot, preceding the *cortège*. There was a vision of fourgons crowded with lackeys and officers in French uniforms—of piqueurs, Imperial cockades, and servants' hats covered with oilskin, from which the rain streamed; but I saw only the one *coupé*, in which sat the 'Man of Destiny', and, seeing, scarce believed. And yet there he was, who last I had seen, as it seemed, but a few weeks before, when his glittering squadrons were displayed at Longchamps for the Prince and Princess of Wales as they were returning from the journey in the East, on which I had accompanied them—the most dreaded, and esteemed the most powerful, Sovereign in the world! With one hand he twisted the end of his waxed moustache; the other was placed on his hip, rather back, as if to ease off the jolting of the carriage over the rough stones. An officer—I think Achille Murat—was by his side. The Emperor scanned the crowd at each side wistfully. As he passed, I took off my cap, and he at once returned the salutation, as I thought with an expression of inquiry in his face. But my servant, quite overcome, was on his knees; and certainly a flash of recognition came upon the Emperor's countenance as he caught sight of the man; for, strange caprice! the house in which Louis Napoleon first lodged when he came to London belonged to the man who there, with clasped hands, in the streets of Donchery, was praying Heaven to bless the Captive of Sedan. It was all over in a moment.

Hot on the heels of this moving encounter Russell received news that his friend Colonel Pemberton had been killed at Sedan. During that night he made the sudden decision to leave immediately for London and deliver his account of recent events to *The Times* himself. He could then rendezvous with the Crown Prince on the road to Paris.

The next morning he set off in the company—much to their joint surprise—of Mr Skinner. They had both been pretending to each other that they were sending their despatch via the German Field Post in the normal way. They now laughingly admitted their deception and set off for the Belgian frontier together. On their way they visited the now famous weaver's cottage at Donchery, where Bismarck met with Napoleon after the capitulation. The Emperor was now en route to exile in Germany and thence to Chislehust in Kent, where he was to remain until his death in 1873. Their road lay through miles of still unburied French dead. Russell wrote in his diary: 'I do not remember ever having a ride through more horrible sights, or ever experiencing such loathing and disgust. The smells were vile. It was a true vulture land.'

After catching a train to Brussels, they continued to Ostend and were in London on 5th September. Russell dictated his despatch well into the night and had the satisfaction of seeing it in *The Times* the following morning. Although Russell's was the only complete account of the battle and of the great events succeeding it, the newspapers had already carried news of the action two days previously. This was a clear demonstration of how the style of news reporting was changing, very much to Russell's disadvantage.

He left London the same evening and was in Libremont the next. Hearing that the Crown Prince was already at Rheims, he hurried on. He was forced to spend a night in Sedan which was in turmoil. Riddled with typhus, cholera and smallpox, it reeked of pestilence and decay. The towns and villages were filled with French prisoners. Everywhere were herds of horses, many of them wounded; the Germans were shooting them at the rate of 400 a day and throwing their carcases into the Meuse where they floated slowly downstream, 'forming great parti-coloured islands'.

He reached Rheims on 11th September to find that he had caught up with the King's headquarters. One of the first people he saw was Bismarck 'cleaving his way through the crowd, with his head erect, puffing his cigar. "Why," he said, "we thought you were lost or killed! No one knew what had become of you. For several days there was great anxiety on your account." He then invited Russell to come and talk over matters with him. Bismarck proceeded to give him a detailed account of his interview with Napoleon at Donchery when the Emperor had capitulated with 104,000 troops:

'I was fast asleep in bed, and very much tired after the day, when an aide-de-camp woke me up to say that the Emperor was coming into Donchery to see me. When I heard he was coming I was astonished. I thought, under all the circumstances, I should have been the last man in the world that he would have cared to see. I had sat up till half-past 1 o'clock the night before, and it was just 5 when I was awakened by the news. I pulled on my coat, called for my horse, and was off immediately to meet him...

'I received him with the same respect that I would have shown to my own King. He alighted, and I proposed we should walk into a little cottage close at hand. But the house was a weaver's, and not clean, and so chairs were brought outside, and we sat together talking. Then the Count told the story about the Emperor's anxiety to see the King. I told him it could not be done till the terms of the capitulation had been signed. He urged it again and again, and I always gave him the same reply. Then I pointed out that it was no use for him to affect to treat with the King after his declaration that he had no power whatever, and that all the authority over the army and the country rested with the Regent and with the Government. As the conversation became unpleasant, at last I proposed we should talk on a different subject. Finally, you know what occurred.'

As he still had to catch up with the Crown Prince, Russell set off in a hired cabriolet, his own horse being quite unfit to go any further until it had rested. This conveyance also foundered and he was offered a lift by a passing cart driven by a 'beetle-browed, bull-necked, flat-faced fellow, with a cringing smile and a horrible eye, who was seated with a companion scarcely less objectionable.' This proved to be a near fatal mistake as the two men had planned to rob him. Luckily he was warned that he was in bad company and so was on his guard. When the attack came, Russell acted with speed and coolness and managed to elude his assailants and reached the next village intact.

This incident highlights the difficulties and occasional dangers that beset the life of a foreign correspondent accompanying an invading army. When actually part of the Crown Prince's column, Russell could claim some measure of protection, but the moment he strayed from it, he was responsible for his own safety. The uncertainty of his situation must have been a perpetual strain.

Russell reached Montmirail on 12th September and was given a 'most gracious reception' by the Crown Prince. Apparently, there had been mounting concern at headquarters as to his whereabouts, the more so when it was heard that a *Times* correspondent (Pemberton) had been killed. The Crown Prince then referred to the inaccurate newspaper reports that followed of the meeting between the King and Napoleon after the latter's interview with Bismarck at Donchery. He then went on to say: 'I will tell you exactly what occurred, as it was repeated to me by the King immediately afterwards. You know I was outside the room which His Majesty my father and the Emperor entered to speak together. I closed the door, and remained outside like a sentry on duty till the interview was over.' When the Crown Prince had finished his account, Russell thanked him and said: 'I am glad, sir, to know the exact facts on such authority.' The British Military Attaché was standing by during this discourse and remarked to Russell: 'There now, you have the full story in detail and

A Prussian ammunition dump outside the vast citadel of Sedan after its capitulation on 2nd September.

During the siege, cattle and sheep were driven into the Bois de Boulogne,
which became the larder of Paris.

from the fountainhead.' Russell included a detailed summary of his conversation in his
next letter to *The Times*. It was this version of events which Bismarck later refuted.

The army continued on its way to Paris, passing through country which Russell
described as 'a sylvan landscape of great beauty', punctuated by charming villages. The
landscape was not improved by the looting of enormous quantities of wine by the
German armies. According to General Sheridan (the American Civil War general),
they left 'two almost continuous lines of broken bottles along the roadside all the way
down from Sedan'.

Russell was perplexed by the German assumption that Paris would yield without a
fight. His companions assured him that the French were—'too much cowed. They are a
frivolous set, and when they see us on the ridges they will soon come to terms'.
However they were not too frivolous to precipitate a stiff action over Châtillon, one of
the most important redoubts overlooking Paris. But this, their first major action since
Sedan, also ended in defeat.

By 19th September the Prussians had completely surrounded Paris. Inside the city
great changes had already taken place. On 4th September Empress Eugénie had fled
from the Tuileries and was now in London. The following day the Third Republic was
proclaimed and General Louis Trochu became President of the new government. Jules
Favre, its Foreign Minister, had an interview with Bismarck to discuss the terms of
peace. These proved to be extremely tough and when Favre returned to Paris and
published the terms, public opinion in both Paris and abroad hardened in favour of the
French. A siege of Paris now seemed inevitable.

The city itself was not totally undefended. In those days it was surrounded by a wall
80 feet high with a moat ten feet wide, and beyond the moat, at distances of one to
three miles, was a chain of sixteen powerful forts. Inside the walls were now assembled
over half a million soldiers, made up of the Paris National Guard, those who had escaped from Sedan, and others. There were also about 3,000 cannon. Many of the
principal buildings had been taken over for war-like purposes: the half-finished Opera
House was a military depot, and theatres and the various palaces had become hospitals.

The besieged city contained well over 2 million people who needed to be fed. Some provision had been made for this too: in the Bois de Boulogne there were said to be 250,000 sheep and 40,000 oxen, but no cows for milking. The wisdom of rationing does not seem to have occurred to anyone. However, no-one at that stage could have fore-seen a siege which was to last well over four months.

Russell, though, with his usual perception, wrote to *The Times* on 22nd September:

> The Prussians are not in Paris yet; and although there does not appear to be any fair reason to doubt they can reduce Paris at last by close investment, and that the other towns must fall as soon as the siege trains come up, it must be admitted that the mere investment of Paris will not lead to a surrender for weeks to come if the city be supplied as it is said to be; and, with winter imminent, a tedious operation of that kind ought to be avoided if possible. As to bombardment, even if practicable at present, I doubt if many Prussians would not shrink from such a measure. I am sure their leaders would. If the necessities of war-making are tremendous, would a bombardment, however ensure a surrender? A partial and feeble bombardment only exasperates, and at last almost creates contemptuous indifference amongst determined men.

He was also aware that a 'really vigorous' sortie by the French could break through the German ring around Paris, which was attenuated and weak in places.

The Crown Prince was to establish his headquarters at Versailles, and Russell, although troubled by memories of the town as he had known it in happier days, found himself in comfortable quarters for the first time for many weeks. Everyone began to settle in, or as he expressed it: 'The process of Germanising Versailles is going on with marvellous rapidity.' The huge Château had become a hospital and Russell visited it soon after his arrival. 'It was very hot, the sun was blazing, the windows were all open, and the juxtaposition of the wounded men as they lay in their little iron beds beneath the pictures was very strange.'

The Hall of Mirrors, Versailles, converted into a German hospital.

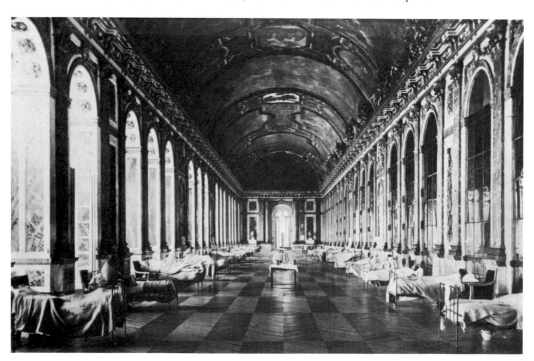

One of the only ways of escaping the siege of Paris: Léon Gambetta leaving for Tours in a Nadar balloon to raise a provincial French army with the aim of breaking the siege from the outside.

He notes in his diary at this time that it was frustrating to be within twelve hours travel of London and yet be five days off by post. This estimate was to prove wishful thinking on his part: a letter from Mowbray Morris on 23rd September informed Russell that his despatches were taking seven to ten days to reach the paper and that this would not do. The *Daily News*, in particular (with the intrepid Archibald Forbes as its chief reporter), was outstripping *The Times* with every story. Morris followed this relatively mild protest with another, more urgent, five days later:

> On your part, I beg you to use the telegraph *freely*. After any important event, go yourself with all speed to the nearest telegraph station that has communication with London, and send by the wires not a scrap of a few lines but a whole letter. This is what the correspondents of the *Daily News* have been doing frequently.

But it was easier said than done for a man like Russell. His whole reputation had been built on the power of his descriptive writing and the attention to detail of his eye-witness accounts. 'I am one of those who cannot describe what I do not see.' He never learnt to use the telegraph with the same fluency as his pen. But he was acutely aware of the great changes in his profession and made every effort to co-operate with *The Times* in finding ways of getting the news back to London more quickly. He even entrusted one despatch to a Mlle Penay who was arrested as a spy at Dieppe. She subsequently spent five weeks in jail as a direct result of the despatch being found on her person.

An intriguing aspect of the siege of Paris was the French use of hot-air balloons. Russell mentions in his diary that,

Count Otto von Bismarck, the Prussian Chancellor.

...much excitement was caused at the outposts by the appearance of the great Captive Balloon, which rose above Paris laden with officers, who could be seen, I am told, reconnoitring the Prussian lines. What a use of the aerial machine in which so many of us mounted during the Jubilee of all Nations at the Paris Exposition!

This was, in all probability, the first attempt the Parisians made to break the blockade in this novel way. It was so successful—although highly dangerous—that a 'Balloon Post' was established forthwith. One of the most important loads the balloons were to carry was a man called Léon Gambetta. Early in November he sailed out of Paris, landed near Tours, and began to raise a new provincial French army with the aim of breaking the siege from the outside.

At the beginning of October, Russell was bemoaning the boredom of life at Versailles—one day followed another with very little to report. However, his life of *ennui* was rudely interrupted on 10th October, when a friend showed him a paragraph which had appeared in the *Standard*, 'which fairly took my breath away'.

It had not appeared in the *Times*; but there it was, plain enough, under the head of 'Latest News,' with the name of Bismarck attached to it—a distinct, unmistakable affirmation that the account of the interview between the Emperor and the King after the battle of Sedan given in the *Times* by its correspondent was quite destitute of any foundation. I saw at once the difficulty of the situation. The quarter from which I had received the statement, which I had written down almost on the spot, was of the very highest; but it was perfectly obvious that I could not drag into controversy with Count Bismarck the name of the exalted person [the Crown Prince] from whom I had derived my information.

Realising that his professional reputation was in some danger, Russell rushed off to Bismarck's quarters intending to confront the Chancellor and demand an explanation. Bismarck was out and Russell was faced with the prospect of several agonising hours of suspense until he returned. To pass the time, Russell went for a ride in the park, and by chance saw the Count striding up the steps of the Château of Versailles. Although it was obvious by his behaviour that Bismarck was trying to avoid a meeting, Russell pursued him relentlessly and caught up with him in time to say:

'Count Bismarck I desire very much to have a few moments' conversation with you.' He seemed a little surprised at first. I had not seen him, except once at the Hôtel des Réservoirs, since our interview at Rheims, when he had been particularly gracious and friendly; but although he held out his hand, there was an evident reserve in his manner. 'Certainly,' he said; 'what is it?' 'I have to ask you about a telegram which I have just seen by accident, and to which your Excellency's name is appended, wherein it is stated that my account of the interview between the King and the Emperor of the French, after the battle of Sedan, has no foundation in truth.' 'I never put my name to a telegram to a newspaper in my life.' I said, 'Here it is, Count,' handing him at the same time the little piece cut out of the *Standard*. He looked at it attentively, and said: 'I never authorised this message to be sent. I never should have dreamed of applying such terms to a statement you made, or certainly I should have let you know first. But, in fact, the use of my name to this statement is quite unauthorised. Leave me the paper; I will inquire into it.' 'Then,' pursued I, 'I have your Excellency's authority for stating that this telegram, which appears to have been furnished to Reuter's Agency by someone, is quite without your sanction or knowledge?' The Count was walking all the time at a slackened pace, and we had gained the courtyard, where, as he said, he was proceeding when I overtook him, 'to refresh his memory of the old days of Louis the Great,' when he observed with some appearance of humour in his tone: 'It is sometimes inconvenient that these statements should be made, and reserve is necessary.' 'But,' retorted I, 'this statement rested upon the very best foundation, and was made, as I understand, to rectify erroneous reports of the same matters which previously appeared. My reputation is very dear to me; in fact, it is of vital importance that this telegram should be contradicted, and I assume, from what you have said, that I can do so in your name, and upon your authority?' This the Count did not reply to, and I again renewed my demand. He was standing by the statue of Condé at the time, and, as if to change the subject, exclaimed, 'What a position that is! What an attitude! Does he not look like a pirate on the stage?' or words to that effect. But still I hammered away about my telegram, when, turning to me with some irritation, he said: 'My attention was called to that report of yours, or rather to the translation of it in a German newspaper, by the King, who declared it to be untrue, and desired it to be set right, and I gave general instructions that a communication should be made, in which your name was not to be mentioned, and certainly not sanctioning the use of my name in any way to the effect that it was not authentic.' Here I was placed in a difficult position, and I had no alternative but to say: 'I received, as I have assured you, the whole of that information from the very best authority, short of that of the Emperor or the King. I was not present on the occasion, nor was your Excellency, but I heard from the lips of one to whom, as I understood, the whole of what passed had been repeated the instant the interview was over, every word of that which is set down. You know, sir, that I cannot call that exalted personage into the controversy; and that, after what you have mentioned to me, I am only anxious to be able to affirm that you gave no authority whatever for the special contradiction, in such terms, applied to myself and my communication, as was attributed to you, or that any authority was given by you for your name to be put to it.' The Count said: 'I will make inquiry into all the circumstances.' 'But you have already told me that the telegram was sent without your authority, and I shall ask you to let me send, as it is of the utmost importance to contradict the statement immediately, a telegram to the *Times*, through the Foreign Office Bureau.' The Count nodded, and said: 'I am in a hurry now, but call upon me to-morrow at the Chancellerie. I will then know how this telegram came to be printed,

The Crown Prince Frederick and his staff outside their Headquarters at Les Ombrages, a house near Versailles belonging to the widow of a wealthy banker. Russell was a frequent visitor there.

and will see what is best to be done.' And so, without offering his hand at first, until he saw that mine was stretched out as in expectation of the honour, the great Chancellor turned and walked off toward the Prefecture.

Russell called the next morning. Bismarck had told Russell that he would discuss the situation with the King to try and establish what, if anything, had been inaccurate in Russell's report—but this he had not done. Russell went on to request that he should be allowed to send a telegram to the newspapers pointing out that the original telegram had not been authorised by Bismarck. The Chancellor was now becoming impatient,

> ...and began to speak in general terms of the necessity of discretion on the part of those who were placed near the persons of the great in courts and camps, reminding me that he had procured leave for me to join the Army, as my reputation, as he was good enough to say, was so high that I might be trusted not to divulge military or political secrets, but that I had not taken due heed of what I had written. I remarked that the matters to which he seemed to refer were well known—that reports of the interview had appeared in other papers coming from the same sources, and that what I wrote had been repeated before others,mentioning one name in particular. At that name the Count appeared to be *en tout humeur*. He struck the table with his hand, and exclaimed, 'I will have such an *auditorium* removed.' I reminded him that on the several occasions on which he had spoken to me of the very highest topics, and with the utmost apparent freedom, I had not made capital by reporting what he had said, or tried to interview him, at which he became almost 'angry', and remarked, 'I know when I am speaking to you that it is your business to communicate to the world what I say, and I act accordingly. I do not care if you published every word I said to you, but when you hear things from that dunderhead the Crown Prince you should know better.' [Whereupon Russell retorted], 'Do I understand I have your Excellency's permission to publish your opinion of the Crown Prince?'

This remark, or question, was not fortunate,

> ... but I confess it was rather hard to be told that a most offensive *communiqué* was unauthorised, and yet to be unable to get a line of official contradiction from him who was alone able to give it. I have said enough of our interview. It was closed by Count Bismarck exclaiming, 'My minutes are precious. I have given you more time than I give to ministers or even crowned heads themselves.' 'I came to your Excellency, by your directions, here to-day, and I have not sought to detain you a moment more than you were good enough to speak to me!' And so I made my bow and retired.

Russell had done well to persevere with this formidable man and his boldness was to lead to complete vindication. *The Times* backed him to the hilt, reaffirming their total trust in his integrity and included in an article by Thomas Chenery an extract from a German newspaper which clearly exonerated Russell.

In a letter to his daughter, Russell suggested that Bismarck acted out of pique: it seemed that the King had told the Crown Prince more than he had told his Chancellor about the famous interview and this was Bismarck's way of hitting out at the Crown Prince, for whom he seems to have had scant regard. Ironically, Bismarck was to say years later: 'The English Correspondent at Headquarters, Russell, was himself as a rule better informed than I concerning events and intentions, and a necessary source for my information.'

Towards the end of September it became apparent that the Germans were intending to bombard Paris. Russell wrote to Morris and Delane that,

> ...after much reflection I have come to the decision that I cannot, with regard to my own feelings on the subject and to your interests, remain here to chronicle a

bombardment of Paris, a city of two million of men, women and children... If the forts only are attacked that is not a horror for one's old age to remember.

Delane replied as follows:

Let me beg of you for your own fame as well as for our sakes not to think of giving up to anyone else your place with the Prussian Army. You have acquired by much desert and by much hard work and exposure a great social position, such as many men would consider cheaply purchased by the labour of a life, and you will forfeit it altogether if you do not see this business through to the end.

Towards the end of October, Russell was complaining that 'my spirits are becoming dull to a degree, and I cannot rouse myself. Others are affected as well as myself. Even the sick and wounded seem inclined to give up the struggle, and, judging from the increasing number of funerals, they often do so altogether.' Apart from a few minor engagements in the environs of Paris and a marked deterioration in the weather, the only news of any interest was that Metz had finally surrendered.

Such a tremendous catastrophe! A crushing blow for France—a crowning glory for Germany! The continuation of the contest now seems hopeless, for Prince Frederick Charles will be free to march with three-fourths of his Army to break up the bands gathering behind the Loire, and to strengthen the investing force round Paris.

Russell's diary gives an interesting glimpse of the Prussian opinion of the British: '*Au fond*, there is a sort of patronising sentiment in Junkerdom towards England. She is considered as a kind of offshoot of the Germanic race, who have also, through her, founded the American colonies.' Russell had his own feelings about the Prussian character: 'He is, in the abstract, a man one cannot love; but he is a man we must respect, even were it only on the grounds of his immense respectability of character.'

On 30th November, to no-one's surprise as it had been rumoured for weeks, the French made a valiant effort to break the siege. Through a fatal lack of communication between Gambetta on the outside and the French government on the inside, 'The Great Sortie' failed. With it went all hope of breaking the German stranglehold on the city. Russell was frustrated in his attempts to see the fighting and this seems to have been a constant problem for him during the siege. He explained the difficulties:

On the days of sorties, one has to rush off in a hurry without any idea of where the fighting is, and get hustled along with columns of horse, foot, and artillery in the narrow roads, till the sentries on the rear of the line bring you up there in some excitement; but it is soon over, and difficult to reach. And I cannot leave, for there might be a great affair, a tremendous action, at any moment.

Throughout December and well into January the stalemate continued. Everyone longed for peace. Disturbed by Prussia's apparent desire to crush the French completely, foreign sympathy was now firmly with the French. Paris was starving. Having eaten all the horses in the early days of the siege, the Parisians had gravitated to dogs and cats. They had eaten all the animals in the zoo, including two elephants. Now it was the turn of the rats.

When the bombardment finally began after Christmas, it proved to be a failure from the Prussian point of view. In the three weeks of its duration only 97 people were killed and 279 wounded. Russell's only real reference to it appears in his diary on 9th January: 'Paris burning in three distinct quarters... It was a calm, frosty night—moon shining, stars bright—lights in the windows of Versailles—noise of laughter and tinkling glasses. What a contrast to the tortured city beyond!'

On 18th January King William of Prussia was created Emperor of Germany in the palace of Louis XIV of France: a personal triumph for Bismarck who had now achieved

A French cartoonist's view of the shortage of food during the siege: 'The queue for Rat's Meat.'

his ultimate goal—the unification of Germany. Russell was invited and although his diary records the ironies of the ceremony, his account in *The Times* was handled with precision.

Roll, drums! Stand to your arms, Guard of Honour! It is 12 o'clock. The boom of a gun far away rolls above the voices in the Court hailing the Emperor King. Then there is a hush of expectation, and then rich and sonorous rise the massive

The interior of Fort Issy which lay to the south west of Paris and was
heavily bombarded during the siege. Here it is shown in the possession
of the Prussians after the capitulation.

strains of the chorale chanted by the men of regimental bands assembled in a
choir, as the King, bearing his helmet in his hand, and dressed in full uniform as a
German General, stalked slowly up the long gallery, and bowing to the clergy in
front of the temporary altar opposite him, halted and dressed himself right and
front, and then twirling his heavy white moustache with his disengaged hand,
surveyed the scene at each side of him.

Five days later he had a stroke of luck such as the dreams of correspondents are made
of. He met an agitated friend in the street who said he had just seen Jules Favre, the
French foreign minister, passing by in a carriage.

This was news, indeed. I said not a word to a soul—hurried off to the Chancellerie
and Les Ombrages—had the news confirmed—saw him with my own eyes—sent
off a telegram—and London next day read in the *Times* that Jules Favre was in
Versailles, and the negotiations for capitulation had commenced.' This was a
great coup for Russell (the only one of the war for *The Times*). It went a long way
towards restoring his morale and that of Mowbray Morris: 'You have achieved a
great success... We have beaten everybody. I make you my compliments and
thank you heartily.' Russell was able to follow up this coup with exclusive details
of the terms of capitulation. Morris was again quick to congratulate him: 'Some
people think we are not doing so badly, and that barring two or three defeats at
the hands of the D.N. [*Daily News*], we have maintained our old supremacy.
There is a general consent about the superiority of an old hand who goes by the
name of "Little Billie."

Paris finally capitulated on 29th January and the preliminaries to peace were signed on
the same day. Four days later Russell drove to the Pont de Neuilly and 'witnessed the
extraordinary spectacle, never to be forgotten, of the French passing into Paris through
the Prussian Guards'. Russell was well aware that all those who had been in the city
during the siege must be near starvation, so he filled his carriage with bread, meat and

vegetables and drove straight to the British Embassy to distribute it to his famished countrymen. On the 11th February he moved into Paris from Versailles where:

> ...the storm was rising fast, and the revolution of the Commune might be seen in the tumultuous meetings of armed men, the placards on the walls, the rage of contending parties, and the wild theories mingled with unbounded invective and abuse of the authorities, which formed the staple of speeches and newspaper articles.

On 1st March, although the French had protested bitterly against this further humiliation, 30,000 victorious German troops made a ceremonial entry into Paris. Determined to be first with the details, Russell had laid on a special train to Calais that afternoon. But Paris was seething with anger, directed towards anyone and everyone alike. After seeing the German Emperor join his soldiers and march into Paris, Russell bolted for the station. But he had been seen in the company of the hated Prussians and with cries of 'Prussian spy' and 'Down with him! kill him!' he found himself caught in the streets of Paris like a rat in a trap. He kept his wits about him and eventually broke free to reach the station and finally Calais. Having handed over his despatch, he returned to Paris. He remained in the stricken city during the Commune, watching the ensuing events with horror.

In the Spring of 1871, Russell returned to London and to his work at the *Army and Navy Gazette*. Professionally, he had suffered setbacks: his despatches had constantly reached *The Times* as stale news, outstripped by those of rival correspondents who used the telegraph extensively or devised cunning ways of getting their news back quickly. As a neutral reporting someone else's war, he had done his utmost to remain impartial and, although he had great respect and admiration for the Prussians, the impression was that his sympathies were with the French. The Prussians, however, awarded him the Iron Cross, the Crown Prince insisting that he pin it on with his own hand. However, Russell's last experience of a major war had been generally rather an unhappy one.

Prussian artillery marching up the Champs Elysées during the triumphal entry into Paris on 1st March 1871.

Journeys with the Prince of Wales

Russell's reporting of the marriage of the Prince and Princess of Wales in 1863 led to a friendship between him and the royal couple. Russell's life was enriched by this association in many ways, although his feelings for the Prince were often confused and contradictory; he was shocked by the scandalous behaviour of many of the Prince's friends and sometimes irritated by the jokes and sallies made against him by the Prince himself. He was often invited to dine at the Prince's London home, Marlborough House, and was a frequent member of the Prince's shooting parties at Sandringham and in Scotland.

In 1869 the Prince and Princess of Wales undertook a royal tour of Egypt and the Near East. Russell was asked to join them at Cairo. He travelled across Europe in mid-January with his friend the Duke of Sutherland, who was also a friend of the Prince. The Duke, one of the richest men in England, travelled in style and they clattered across Europe in special trains, munching their way through splendid banquets ordered in advance by telegram. As a friend of Garibaldi, the Duke was received at Brindisi with a good deal of Italian pomp and circumstance. Next he and Russell were put on a ship bound for Alexandria. From there they were transported by another special train to Cairo which Russell had first visited on his way to India in 1858: 'No city in the world contains such a heterogeneous flow of various races and rascalities.'

> There is a peculiar sound in the air, coming in through the jalousies of the open window. It announces the East at once—an Oriental people, without cares about

> Members of the party which accompanied the Prince and Princess of Wales on their second trip to Egypt in 1860. Russell is standing behind the Princess's chair with the Prince on his left. The Duke of Sutherland is seated on the floor on the right.

The flotilla of boats which carried the royal party on their sightseeing tour down the Nile in February 1869.

sewage or rates for the Victorian Main Drain. It is the shrill whistle of the innumerable buzzards—a quavering, not unmusical note, repeated for the live-long day on all sides, as they flap over house-top and garden... To my mind there is one great drawback to the pleasure with which the eye would otherwise rest on such an animated scene as every thoroughfare in Cairo affords to the stranger. It is that the population have such a limited allowance of eyes among them. I doubt if there is a good sound pair to be found among every three persons—men, women and children. Aged and young, it is all the same. The prevalence of ophthalmia, produced perhaps, humanly speaking, by dust, dirt, and flies, is most destructive to the comeliness of the race; but somehow or other, the women of the better class of lower order are, as far as one can judge, free from the worst ravages of this plague, and gaze on the stranger with a fair share of the organs of vision above their masked cheeks. The eyes afflicted by the disease are surrounded by bleared lids, and are either half-closed or diminished in size, so that the pupil, dull and whitened with opaque spots, is like that of a half-boiled fish.

The Duke's party then set off down the Nile to see the Grand Barrage which had been built across the great river—thus irrigating thousands of acres of previously barren land. This trip was followed by another to see the work in progress on the Suez Canal. Although there was much work still to be done, the canal was opened to traffic in November of that year.

A week later the Prince and Princess of Wales arrived in Cairo. After a succession of state engagements, the combined parties steamed down the Nile in a flotilla, which was said to be carrying: 'a supply of 3,000 bottles of champagne, 20,000 bottles of soda-water, 4,000 bottles of claret; and so on as to sherry, and ale, and liqueurs of all sorts.'

They stopped at many of the sights along the way. After a visit to see the wall paintings at Beni Hassan, Russell observed that the paintings had been defaced by the names of passing tourists. Horrified, he watched as one of the crew of their flotilla chipped away the nose of a mighty statue as a souvenir. He had the foresight to make this appeal:

Can nothing be done by the civilized nations of the world together to preserve Karnak and Luxor? All nations have a common interest in the preservation of

The approach to Philae. Photograph by Francis Frith, 1857.

these magnificent monuments. They are in great danger. The Nile menaces them every year, and it would need very little to cause the fall of many a glorious pillar which a very little outlay could render safe.

Of their visit to Luxor he wrote:

It is in the idea of 'what must have been' that much of the impression produced by these ruins is based. They are the only works of human hands I know of which produce the effect of awe. The immense antiquity of what we see affects us only in relation to that fact. Any stone at our feet is older by countless ages. But our fellow-men hewed these blocks and built them up, and drew those figures and cut those emblems in the nonage of the world. There is a god-like grandeur in the labours of these poor, nameless multitudes. Time has cast over them the shadow of eternity. What lies before us seems superhuman, but only because no human creature now can wield the power to which these owe their erection.

In the shade cast by the colonnade of the Great Hall, the party ate their lunch seated on carpets spread out among the ruins.

The effect of the streaks of sunshine which fell through the rifted walls and colossal columns on groups of Egyptians, Arabs, Turks, Arnaouts, and guides, gathered about the horses and donkeys in the Great Hall, and on the various coated, booted, hatted, and knickerbockered Europeans, was very picturesque.

A similar excursion was made to the island of Philae, justly celebrated for its Roman temples built to the goddess Isis. When the Aswan High Dam was completed in 1970, the island was flooded for eleven months of the year, leaving only the tips of the highest building protruding from the Nile waters. Now these magnificent temples have been painstakingly moved, stone by stone, and re-erected on a larger adjacent island. Russell's nineteenth-century warning, and plea for action, has been answered in part.

At Aswan, the Duke of Sutherland was scheduled to turn back for England. Russell accompanied him as far as Cairo where they arrived on 1st March. As Russell was to rejoin the Prince and Princess when they continued their journey to Greece, Constantinople and the Crimea, he had time on his hands. So he decided to use it profitably by making a solo trip to Palestine.

He was horrified by the city of Jerusalem and indignant over the *laissez-faire* attitude of the Turks who had retained the guardianship of the Holy Places as a result of the Crimean War. Although the Turkish officials strutted about the streets 'polished and superb', they did little to maintain either the city or its sacred monuments, let alone restore them. After visiting Bethlehem, Jaffa and the Mount of Olives, he arrived in Cairo in time to greet the Prince and Princess on their return from their Nile trip. Having completed a further round of splendid entertainments in Cairo, the Prince and his royal entourage boarded the *Ariadne* in Alexandria and sailed for Constantinople. The *Ariadne* arrived off the Golden Horn on 1st April and was met by the state caique of the Sultan, 'the most lovely of floating creations, with fourteen caiquejees in silk shirts, followed by three grand caiques.'

Russell was far more impressed by the Turks in their own country than he had been in Palestine. 'The "sick man", to the outward eye, has shaken off all signs of the incurable disease from which he was supposed to be suffering so dreadfully, and today the Turk could put 800,000 men into the field.' After a ten-day visit packed with festivities of great magnificence, the royal tourists departed for a very different venue, the battlefields of the Crimea, which the Prince had long cherished a wish to see for himself. When they first sighted Sebastopol, Russell noted:

> The effect of Sebastopol on strangers in its present state is to surprise them. The town is so much smaller than they expected it to be... It is difficult to understand how the genius of an engineer [Todleben] and the bravery of an army could have cast a wall so strong around those ruined heaps, that the legions and fleets of two great Powers and two potent auxiliaries were held at bay for eleven long months and more.

With Russell describing in vivid detail the events connected with each famous location, they toured the whole area which was still, some fourteen years later, desolated by the war. The gate of the cemetery on Cathcart's Hill was closed 'but the Princess ascended the steps and entered the enclosure, and there, in company with her husband, she walked slowly through the noiseless street, reading the names inscribed on the stones, and stopping now and then to pick a flower or a weed from the side of the grave of one whose friends she knew.' They visited the British headquarters:

> Perhaps there is no spot on the plateau so familiar to English readers... On that humble abode the hopes and fears of the empire were at one time concentrated... To me the spot was full of interest, and the sight of it recalled the long dark nights, when candleless, I sat in my tent looking at the bright lights in the windows, and listening to the rolling of musketry which came up the ravine, and sounded close at hand... Every important landmark was carefully examined by the company.

To Russell it must have been intensely interesting to go over the ground with their Russian hosts, who described each event as it had appeared to them. The whole company then returned overland to Yalta where they were luxuriously entertained at the imperial palace of Livadia:

> To pass from the bleak plateau of Sebastopol, its graves, and its sad if glorious memories, to the refined elegance of Livadia, and find high officers of Court in grande tenue, waiting for us, Imperial liveries, brilliant rooms, and a banquet set out with rich plate, fruit, and flowers, was startling.

The pilgrimage over, the royal party left the Crimea for a brief visit to Greece and then home to England after an absence of seven months.

Six years later Russell was again asked to accompany the Prince of Wales on a state visit, this time to India. His inclusion in the party, however, caused a good deal of resentment in Fleet Street: he was to act as special correspondent for *The Times* and to travel with the royal party, thus giving him and his newspaper a decided advantage over all its rivals. After much negotiation and manoeuvring, Russell was given the cosmetic title of 'Secretary to the Prince of Wales'. Years later he gave a hilarious account of the whole affair in a letter to a friend:

Dizzy was consulted, and he suggested that I should be attached to the suite as 'précis writer' and act as such, and added, poor man, that he was sure it would be 'considered as a great compliment by the Press'! He was even undeceived. There was a howl, which shook the India Office and Marlborough House, from Fleet Street and Shoe Lane and dear 'Bottley Beer', as the Bombay Parsees called him (Sir Bartle Frere) quailed before the storm. It was arranged that I was to be styled 'Honorary Private Secretary to H.R.H. the Prince of Wales' (without salary) but with diplomatic uniform, etc. And the whole of the great metropolitan Press, with one very remarkable exception, fell into violent convulsions every night and produced the results in the morning. Then the mighty ones kowtowed to Moses, Jacob, and Israel generally, and it was suggested that I might prepare copy for the organs of the Jehad, but I told Sir Bottley it could not be done no how, and he retired to secret places and wept bitterly. Finally it was arranged that I was not to address the editor of the *Times*, or the *Times*, from the *Serapis* at all during the voyage, but if someone on board thought proper to send a letter on shore it would be surprising if the *Times* now and then was not 'favoured with an interesting communication respecting the Prince of Wales's journey to India,' etc., etc., etc.

The anger of J.T.D. was lava-like, and lavish, shared no doubt with J. Walter. The former wrote to Sir Bartle Frere a letter which made him skip like a man kangaroo for several hours and glare at me menacingly through his glasses for days. He said: 'We have provided the foremost member of the staff of the first

An early photo of the Suez Canal, built by the French engineer Ferdinand de Lesseps and opened in 1869. The second of the ships anchored alongside the docks at Port Said is H.M.S. Serapis.

Left: William Russell. A caricature by Ape (Carlo Pellegrini). *Right:*
Ismail Pasha, Khedive of Egypt, with his eldest son Tewfik.

journal of the world with the salary of an ambassador (£300 a month) to furnish a
trustworthy narrative of this memorable visit of the Heir to the Throne to the
subjects of the Queen, and you yield to the jealousy and clamour of those, our
rivals as they claim to be, who exercise no influence on the opinion of the
intelligent public,' etc., etc.—something of the sort.

On a national scale there had also been considerable controversy over the advisability
of the Prince going to India at all. Disraeli and others, including Sir Bartle Frere—who
was to be responsible for the administration of the tour—felt that a visit by the heir to
the throne would be tangible evidence of the Queen's, and the government's, close
involvement with that part of the British Empire. Queen Victoria did not share this
view and only agreed to the trip under duress and on condition that she should
personally supervise all the arrangements; a condition which did not simplify the
drawing up of the complicated plans one bit.

Finally, all the problems were resolved and the Prince set off with his chosen suite,
not accompanied by the Princess, as the tour was to last for eight months. Russell met
up with the party at Brindisi and sailed south for Egypt on 16th October 1875, in a
flotilla led by the royal yacht the *Serapis*.

A stop was made at Athens which Russell called 'the newest city out of the United
States'. The Prince was royally entertained by the King and Queen of Greece and
presented their majesties with a strange mixture of gifts: 'a steam-launch, an Alderney
bull and cow, a ram and sheep, and a few fine specimens of the British pig.'

On 23rd October, the *Serapis* arrived at Port Said, the town which had sprung out of the desert since the building of the Suez Canal.

> It is the most curious spot on the face of the globe. On the strip of land between Lake Menzaleh and the sea there is pitched, tent-like on the loose sand, which rises over the shoes where asphalte or planking has not been deposited, a city of wooden houses, laid in perfect parallelograms, and furnished with shops and magazines, where every article of European luxury can be had. Outside, on the same belt of sand, in a condition akin to savagery, there is a settlement of Arabs. The commerce of one quarter of the world passes by the city, but few traders land, and none remain there.

Passing through the canal as far as Ismailia, they were met by the Khedive and transferred to a special train to Cairo. The Khedive, Ismail Pasha, although his country teetered on the brink of financial disaster, proved a charming and lavish host. Russell described him as a man who spoke French, Turkish and Arabic with ease. 'His powers of calculation are extraordinary, his conception rapid, his memory acute, and his love of work inexhaustible. He has a fair fund of anecdote, and appreciates a joke most thoroughly, for all his Turkish gravity.'

After suitable festivities, including a firework display among the Pyramids (of which Russell obviously disapproved), the Prince's party rejoined the *Serapis* at Suez and set sail for the Red Sea. Although Russell was lucky enough to have a cabin on the cooler, port, side of the ship, the voyage proved to be insufferably hot.

After a short official stop in Aden, the *Serapis* and her attendant flock steamed on through the Indian Ocean, arriving at Bombay on 8th November after a week at sea. Russell remarked drily: 'The morning was very bright and beautiful. A glorious sunrise promised one of those fine days which are somewhat too common in this part of the world, and the thermometer marked 80° with a persistency which led the observer to

The arrival of the Prince of Wales in Bombay on 8th November 1875.

think that the instrument must have received a permanent injury.' It must have taken a considerable effort for those on board to don their various resplendent uniforms in preparation for the official reception and subsequent procession through the 'fiery furnace of the streets'. For six miles the line of carriages passed through 'animated banks of human beings', dancing lights, magnesium flares and other 'melodramatic effects' until they arrived, satiated with spectacle at Government House. This was to be the pattern of the weeks to come.

Russell was now on familiar ground again and gives an affectionate description of various servants assigned to him:

> Once more in a tent, with black faces all around one! People and trees and sur-roundings all different—mango-trees and mango-birds, the gold mohur-tree, cocoa-nut and toddy-trees...the wheeling kites overhead—higher still, the soaring vultures—the cry of the great woodpecker, and the chattering of the familiar minah—a new land, but a glance revealed that you were in India, and you felt it too. There is the Head-quarters' barber, in a great red Mahratta turban, waiting outside—a handsome smooth-faced fellow who makes his English go a long way, and who is a master in his art, though his fingers are deadly cold, and he is for his trade overfond of garlic. Him be sure, you will never lose sight of as long as you are in India. There is the bheestie with his water-skin ready to fill your tub. There is the syce with your horse outside, if you are minded for a morning ride. There is the sweeper hovering in the distance, the khelassies or tent-pitchers awaiting orders, the khitmutgar with a cup of coffee, and the Bombay 'boy'—in my case one Jivan—a slight, quiet, demure-looking man of forty or so—who has already taken possession of my property—boxes, bags, clothes, money and all—to the intense astonishment of Maclachlan, who would have resisted his assumptions by force, but that I told him it was the custom of the country. These and others. Each tent is a centre of existence to seven or eight of the people called 'Natives', to whom you are for the time being lord and master.

The day following their arrival in India was the Prince of Wales's birthday, and also marked the first of the official receptions, or durbars, for the Indian maharajahs and their suites.

> The heat even at 8 a.m. was quite sufficient to warn us that we were in India, and yet the Prince was obliged to wear a uniform of European cloth, laden with lace and buttoned up to the throat, and to stand and sit for hours, going through the same kind of labour with each of the Rajas whom he received, who after a time must have appeared very much like the same people who had just left the room and were coming back again—figures lighted up with jewels, followed by crowds in white robes and gay headdresses.

Russell's official account of the royal tour was obliged to mention them all, but his description of one in particular stands out:

> All eyes were dazzled when Maharaja Syajee Rao, the little boy whom the Government of India installed as the Gaekwar of Baroda, stood at the threshold of the door—a crystallised rainbow. He is a small, delicately-framed lad for his twelve years and more, with a bright pleasant face. He was weighted, head, neck, chest, arms, fingers, ankles, with such a sight and wonder of vast diamonds, emeralds, rubies, and pearls, as would be worth the loot of many a rich town. It is useless to give the estimate I heard of their value, and the little gentleman has more at home.

It was this splendid child who, only six months previously, had been 'running about the streets adorned with the most limited wardrobe' (in the words of the Prince of Wales), the previous Gaekwar having been deposed and detained after an attempt to poison the

Left: Maharajah Syajee Rao, the Gaekwar of Baroda, who attended the magnificent Durbar given for the Maharajahs and their suites. *Right:* Sir Bartle Frere for whom Russell had a great liking and respect while disapproving of many of Frere's views on colonialism.

English Resident the year before. The boy was the adopted son of the widow of the previous Gaekwar's brother.

Every detail of Indian etiquette had to be observed, bewildering and complex though it was. The official carpet laid out for these receptions was of great significance: the Prince of Wales would receive certain of his guests at the edge of it and others in the middle. One of those he met in the middle was Sir Salar Jung, the Prime Minister of Hyderabad, who was representing his sovereign prince, the Nizam, a mere child, who had declined to make the journey to Bombay. The Prince of Wales described the Prime Minister in a letter to a friend as 'fit for the most enlightened society in Europe... His wonderful ease of manner and conversation, with that wonderful Eastern dignity, made a great impression on me'.

Reception followed reception, with the Prince making official return visits to those whom he had received. Sir Bartle organised various excursions for the Prince during his stay in Bombay, one of them being to Baroda, where he toured the city mounted on an elephant of 'extraordinary size':

> ...on his back was a howdah of surpassing splendour, which shone like burnished gold in the morning sun, and which was either made of gold or of silver gilt. It was covered with a golden canopy. This exquisitely finished carriage, reported to have cost four lakhs of rupees, was placed on cloth of gold and velvet cushions, fastened over the embroidered covering that almost concealed the outline of the great elephant, which stood swaying his painted proboscis to and fro as if he kept

time to the music of the bands outside... His tusks had been sawn off to the length of three feet, and false tusks of greater diameter, also shortened, were wedged over them by bands of gold. His painted legs were encased in thick round coils of gold.

The royal party then watched various sporting contests, including an elephant fight, although Russell suspected that 'these sagacious creatures were...only making believe. They merely put on the gloves and had a few rounds. Certainly there was hard hitting and tremendous head-collisions; tusks rattled and clattered, proboscis met proboscis in intricate convolutions, the vast hulls shook under the strain of combat.' This Indian equivalent of the Roman arena was followed by a day's shooting and hunting with cheetahs: '...five or six cheetahs...surrounded by their attendants, were standing upright on cars drawn by oxen, their eyes hooded, lashing their lank sides with their tails, hissing and purring by turns like monster tabbies.'

On 25th November, the royal party left Bombay by sea, bound for Ceylon (now Sri Lanka) but pausing briefly at the old Portuguese settlement of Goa. After an amusing interlude when the Prince and his friends went fishing in the surf, wading in and out of the sea to the delight of the local fishermen, they continued their journey.

Russell had come to like and admire Sir Bartle Frere, but could not agree with his friend's conviction that the British had been sent by God to 'civilise and Christianize' the Indian people. As the ship sailed past the ruins of the Portuguese Empire of Goa, Russell pointed to the white chapels on the shore and asked Sir Bartle:

'What has become of their congregations?' These were the evidence of the work of Saint Francis Xavier. 'Yes,' said Sir Bartle, 'but, my dear friend, they were the work of a missionary of the Church of Rome.' And when I reminded him that the Hindu rule had endured for hundreds of years before the domination of Mohammedans and that the latter had lasted for some six or seven centuries while we had only been in evidence for a couple of centuries, he said: 'That is true. But

Kandy Lake, said by Russell in a diary entry to lend 'a charming repose and freshness to the scene which is mirrored in its waters'.

we are called by God to found His Kingdom here for ever.' And so collapsed the dialogue.

But the dialogue was taken up again when the two met in South Africa four years later.

The *Serapis* arrived in Colombo on 1st December where the Prince was received with great enthusiasm, although Russell commented that there were no women to be seen 'except some wretched old hags of the lower order' and a few eyes visible through the chinks in the doors and stockades of the houses. The following day a special train transported the whole party to Kandy, passing through some of the 'softest, and yet grandest, scenery in the world'. Russell described their first view of the city:

> In a deep ravine at one side of the plateau, or, more properly speaking, of the broad valley surrounded by hills, overlooking a still deeper depression, on which the town is situated, the Mahawelli Ganga River thunders in its rocky bed. The small lake by the side of which part of the city is built lends a charming repose and freshness to the scene which is mirrored in its waters. Wherever the eye is turned rise mountain tops, some bare masses of rock, others clothed with vegetation.

They were greeted by one of the most picturesque crowds ever seen:

> I doubt if ever anything so unmasculine, uncomely, and unbecoming was ever devised as the dress of the great Chiefs. There are various orders of Chiefs. The higher they are the more ridiculously elaborate is their attire. The dress of the upper ten thousand is an enormous stiffened white muslin petticoat, with gigot sleeves, nether garments puffed out as if they were strongly fortified by crinoline, the work of cunning seamstresses, made with exceeding art. On their heads elevated pincushions, like tinselled crowns, singularly unsuited to the climate or to dignity of appearance. The few women visible wore white muslin jackets and comboys, and displayed a considerable wealth of bangles, necklaces, and rings.

Throughout the royal tour, Russell's official account is enriched with titbits of historical, botanical, ornithological and anthropological information, which is astonishing in its range.

> I have never seen in any part of the world such an extraordinary exuberance and variety of growth. In addition to every tree and plant properly belonging to Ceylon, there are numbers of exotics, which have been imported, and which grow freely in the open air. Mr Mudd, the botanist attached to the Prince's establishment, went about in a subdued ecstasy, knife and book in hand, attended by a native gardener speaking English who seemed an excellent botanist. We entered through a magnificent avenue of the india-rubber-tree (*Ficus elastica*), and drove along sweeping avenues by the borders of the river, through a park-like expanse, which was one marvellous exhibition of the glories of the vegetable kingdom. Orchids in every variety; palms of stupendous size, thickness, and height; talipots, palmyras, date-palms, gigantic clumps of reeds, the coco demar, the traveller's tree, almost shut out the light in places, or were scattered over the green meadow in detached blocks, or concentrated into central masses, over which whirled thick clouds of flying foxes. Perhaps the most interesting and astonishing objects, where all was so new, were the jungle-rope creepers, and elephant-creepers of the *Bauhinia* class, which seem to seize the trees in giant folds, as if intent on their destruction, an object in which, it is said, indeed, these tremendous vegetable reptiles too often succeed.

Amid all this verdure, they were warned, lurked venomous spiders, ferocious ants, ticks, centipedes and a deadly snake referred to by Russell as the *Tic polonga*. As if these dangers were not enough, the real scourge seemed to be the leeches which did not even wait for them to venture off the beaten track, but

...came wriggling and jumping along the grass. They must smell one's blood. If you stood on the gravel-walk for a few moments you could see them making their way from all parts of the surrounding country towards you as a common centre of interest. Most horrible of all their properties, they can stand erect on their tails and look out for what is coming.

A special detour was made to see the Sacred Tooth of the Buddha in the Audience Hall at Kandy. Russell's reaction was irreverent:

The 'Dalada', as it is called, is a piece of bone or, as some say, ivory, with a suture up the side, nearly two inches long and one inch round, of irregular cylindrical shape, tapering towards the end, which is rounded. If the article ever was in Buddha's mouth, and if he had a complete set to match, he must have possessed a wonderful jaw, and a remarkable stomach, for it is easy to see that the tooth is not a human molar or incisor.

The Prince's passion for big-game shooting was to be given full rein as a trip into the hills had been arranged. Operating from a tented camp, the Prince and his party spent prolonged and frustrating hours plunging through the jungle in search of elephants which seemed reluctant to be killed. Not until it was almost dark did the Prince, 'streaming with perspiration, his clothes wet, and torn to shreds' succeed in felling one of the great beasts.

After all this excitement the party left Ceylon for the Indian mainland. There they left the *Serapis* at Tuticorn and journeyed north east by train through the mountainous scenery of the Nilgiris to the city of Madurai, which Russell found one of the most charming towns in Southern India. After a short stay the train clattered on to Trichinopoly, the town which had been the 'central point of the struggle between the French and English for the sovereignty of Southern India...an area suffused with memories of Clive'. Above the town hangs 'the vast pyramid—the Rock of Trichinopoly—crested with the Temple of Ganesa, whose festivals were attended by thousands of pilgrims. Not very long ago a panic occurred at one of these meetings, and before it could be allayed, upwards of 500 persons were precipitated down the sheer precipice over the granite steps, or trampled to death.'

On to Madras, where the Prince paraded about under a vast golden umbrella which distinguished him from the sea of faces to perfection. There had been many complaints during the tour that few of the thousands that flocked to see the heir to the throne went away knowing whether they had really laid eyes on him or not. No fewer than 126 different schools and colleges attended one of the receptions and Russell meticulously listed every one by name. A visit to the races was one of the highlights, full of conflicting images:

Many of the native spectators perched in trees; there were strange contrasts between the civilisation of European jockey-caps, jackets, breeches, boots and spurs, and the turn-out of native aspirants, or at least of one who rode a very losing race in a huge red turban, white petticoats, and parti-coloured robes; between the bustle of very small but fierce jockeys, who strode through the crowd of long-legged natives, and waved them aside as if they were so many rushes; and the calm of great Chiefs...who were there, attended by numerous familiars in all their bravery.

Russell was greatly impressed by the major event of the Madras week:

Men will never see any spectacle more strange—nay, awful—than the 'illumination of the surf.' Neither pen nor pencil can give any idea of it. It was exciting, grand, weird and beautiful. As if to render homage to the occasion, the wind rose in the course of the day, the surf was high—enormous curling breakers ran between the base-pillars of the pier. The moonlight revealed now and then dark

Left: Drawing of one of the native chiefs of Kandy, made by Sir Arthur Ellis, equerry to the Prince of Wales. *Right:* The Maharajah of Rewah whom Russell described as wearing '...a golden crown, exquisitely worked, blazing with gems.'

objects rising and falling on the billows, between the outer darkness of the horizon, against which the hulls and rigging of the *Serapis*, *Osborne*, and *Raleigh*, lighted up with lanterns, stood out in relief, and the breakers on the beach. These were massoulah boats and catamarans lying off in the rollers till the time came for setting fire to the lights, which were to burn in, and to illuminate the water. The buildings, transparencies, and triumphal arches, above which rose steeples, domes, and columns, brilliantly illuminated, formed the background along the beach. Southwards, where the rollers swept up to the roadway, rows of natives, facing seawards, with blazing torches and blue lights lighted up an ocean of white turbans. First there were fireworks. The *Osborne* and *Serapis*, emitting volumes of coloured flames, vied with each other in all kinds of pyrotechny. It seemed as if volcanoes were bursting up from the deep. In a grand discharge from the *Raleigh* there were 190 coloured rockets. Presently appeared from afar seawards many flames, dipping and rolling amid the waves, drifting landwards like fire-ships. These multiplied. Occasionally lights flashed right through the rollers from the other side. Suddenly the line of black massoulah boats and catamarans from the beach dashed into the surf like a squadron of cavalry. With the wildest yells they charged the serried ranks of the foam-crested breakers. Amid a sea now black as ink, now like glistening jet, now creaming in surf, the catamaran men contended with waves, which seemed to be mounds of flame. Sometimes they were swept off, and disappeared beneath the billows, or were seen swimming in the mad turmoil. There was an agonising suspense till they regained their craft, or, striking out with strong arms, were borne in on the surf, and landed safe on the beach. The massoulah boats, swept from stem to stern by the breakers, forced their way out over the rollers to the smoother sea, only to return, at full speed, and engage with wild emulation in still more animated contests.

Once more on board the *Serapis* they sailed up the east coast of India, arriving in Calcutta on 23rd December, to be met by the Viceroy who was surrounded by a sea of dignitaries and crowds of spectators. The following day was taken up with a prolonged Reception of the Indian Chiefs by the Prince at Government House. With his usual thoroughness and remarkable research Russell described each Maharajah's appearance, a summary of his past history, and how he was received by the Prince. Russell even listed what revenue each Chief received. He described the sirdars of the Maharajah of Rewah as 'animated nuggets, ambulatory mines of jewels—one especially, who wore a suit of chain-armour, arabesqued breast and back-pieces, jewelled plume, casque of gold, and enamelled gauntlets. Rewah...wore a golden crown, exquisitely worked, blazing with gems.' These immense receptions must have wearied all who took part in them and, as Russell expressed it, 'diamonds, emeralds, rubies, and pearls had begun to look very much of the same size and brightness.'

The twelve-day stay in Calcutta over, the royal party left for Benares where the sacred temples and ghats were visited:

The Golden Temple and the Sacred Pool (which is a foul pool covered with green scum, and emitting poisonous vapours of sulphuretted hydrogen), were duly inspected. These and the Great Temple of Ganesa, on ordinary occasions are thronged with priests, fakirs, pilgrims, devotees from all parts of India; but they

Vishnu Pud near the Burning Ghat at Benares (Varanasi), visited by the royal party in January. Photograph by Samuel Bourne, 1865.

Two hundred princes and chiefs greeting the Prince of Wales on his arrival in Agra. The principal hosts were the Maharajahs of Bikaner and Boondee.

were now carefully swept of 'the perilous stuff,' and there were only a few trusty Brahmins to exhibit the shrines, bulls, and holy places, under the guardianship of a strong body of police.

Lucknow was the next official stop. Once again Russell was surrounded by sights which he had last seen under very different circumstances, although the city had changed greatly in seventeen years. The Prince visited all the principal places involved in the Mutiny. He laid the foundation stone for a memorial to the native troops who had remained loyal to the British and who had died in the defence of the Residency. On an impulse, he asked to meet any of those who still survived. 'He would not allow them to be hurried by; he spoke to each one, ragged as he might be, squalid or unclean.' Russell was indignant at the 'stolid indifference' shown by the British for the religious feelings of the Indians, displayed in their treatment of some of the sacred buildings damaged during the Mutiny. 'If we ever lose India, it will be from "want of sympathy" ' was his prophetic remark, strong words indeed to find their way into the official account of the tour. A similar pilgrimage took place at Cawnpore where the Prince paid his respects at the memorial to those whose bodies had been thrown in the well.

On 11th January the Prince's entourage arrived in Delhi, where he reviewed 18,000 troops. Russell, who was bucked off his horse at the beginning of the proceedings, admitted to a somewhat 'dim appreciation of the march-past'. A ball in the palace of Selimghur followed and Russell remarked again on the inappropriate use of some of the historical buildings:

All the world has heard of the Dewan Khass, wherein stood the 'Peacock Throne'. 'If there is Paradise on earth it is this! it is this! it is this!' But ideas of Paradise cannot be altogether realised in a pavilion filled with men in uniforms and evening

The Dewan i am, or hall of private audience, at Agra. Russell rather disapproved of such buildings being used for frivolities like balls in honour of the Prince.

dress, women in ball dresses, military bands playing Offenbach and Strauss, and, above all, a ceiling of a distressing colour. Nevertheless, when the dancing was at its height, and the dancers were seen whirling in the arched spaces, between rows of snowy columns, the scene presented by the marble 'halls of dazzling light' was very brilliant.

Next on the agenda was Agra and of course the Taj Mahal, which the royal party visited at night when it was illuminated. Russell had seen it seventeen years earlier, on his return from convalescing in Simla, and he was just as moved by the experience on this occasion.

Ascending the terrace, the Prince walked over to the shelter of the dark gateway of the mosque. Gradually there grew out, in all its fair proportions and beauty, framed in the purple of the starry heavens, the marble 'Queen of Sorrow,' which has power to dim every eye... But the eye mastered every sense, and the loveliness of the Taj stole over the soul. In spite of blue lights, and lime lights, of lively dance music, of clank of spurs and sabres on the complaining marble, there was not a point which the peerless mausoleum could make which was for an instant marred or lost. Entering the tomb itself—the culminating glory—the party stood and gazed, almost trembling with admiration. Presently a clear, sustained note rose up into the vaulted roof of the tomb, and there found its counterpart, and the two commingled, swept upwards, and soared away, 'till naught remained 'twixt them and silence.' Again and again the notes soared, and the auditors stood breathless.

An excursion was made to Fatehpur Sikri, which Russell, quoting someone else in his diary, called a wilderness of stone, 'attesting the vigour of Imperial selfishness and the futility of human aspirations'.

Russell's account of a reception in the palace of the Maharajah of Gwalior furnishes an example of how some of the Indian princes lived at that time:

> The building is double-storied, and the wings and turrets are three- and five-storied...the first storey is Tuscan, second Italian Doric, and the third Corinthian order of architecture... Upwards of 300,000 leaves of gold were used to decorate the Reception-hall... The Grand Drawing-room, one of the finest saloons in the world, is hung with wonderful chandeliers, and decorated with enormous mirrors. The Prince's bedstead, washing service, and bath were of solid silver.

After the visit to Agra the royal party dispersed in several directions, the Prince and his companions going on a shooting expedition to the Terai, an undulating prairie extending for hundreds of miles which lay within the shadow of the Himalayas. It was covered in jungle, reeds and grasses, as tall as an elephant's howdah. This part of the tour had been arranged as a rest for the Prince after the strain of months of protocol and ceremony. Russell, for one, greeted with delight the simplicity of his snug, blue-lined tent, pitched among the vast tented camp close to dense jungle.

The nights were very cold, the wind coming directly from the Himalayas. Russell described their first awakening in camp: 'A concert of coughing, sneezing, chattering and shivering from the camp-followers around the tents awoke me this morning. The poor creatures from the south, with nothing but thin cotton robes to cover them, must have been miserable indeed. I believe we should all be more charitable if we lived in tents.'

Each day the shooting-parties set off on a fleet of elephants and spent all day out in the Terai, often returning to camps which had been moved to a new location in their absence. This must have been no easy matter when one considers the extent of the camp.

> The camp contains 2,500 persons...there are 119 elephants, 550 camels, 100 horses, 60 carts drawn by oxen, many goats and milch-cows, sheep, and perambulating materials for food. There are nearly 600 coolies, 60 tent-pitchers, 20 men to supply water, 20 men to clean, 20 messengers, 75 non-commissioned officers and men of 3rd Goorkhas and their band, 20 troopers 11th Bengal Cavalry, 16 of the 28th Native Infantry, a detachment of native camp police (it will be observed the Prince's person is guarded by natives exclusively), and there are odds and ends which add to the total, without counting mahouts and their families and camel-men, assembled round the Prince and his thirty or forty Europeans. Certainly I should feel rather proud of myself if I were a wild beast and knew all this.

The Terai teemed with game of every description: wild boar, tiger, black buck, leopard, bear and antelope, to say nothing of the great variety of game birds. The party shot at almost anything that moved, and the daily 'bag' could range from a kingfisher to a porcupine. However, the main objects of the expedition, tigers, although all about them, were remarkably elusive.

At midday 'tiffin' would be taken: this consisted of hot food cooked over special stoves by French cooks transported to the appointed place during the morning. Even blocks of ice were brought to cool the wine.

> In the evening, after dinner, great logs were heaped up in front of the mess-tent; chairs were brought, and before the huge camp-fire, burning brightly, the Prince and the company sat listening to the delightful anecdotes of Sir Henry Ramsay, who invests the land and the people and the chase with fresh interest. He told us of a certain village in his territory where the people were terribly troubled by a tiger; so they sent for the wise man...to charm the beast away with his drum and

songs. The tiger, however, came out and ate the wise man—whereupon the villagers arose and migrated. 'For,' said they, 'now that the tiger has eaten our sage, he will know all our secrets, and we shall have no chance of evading him.'

The band of the 3rd Goorkha Regiment has moved up with us. The strains of Verdi, Offenbach, Donizetti and Mozart mingle with the howls of wolves and jackals. It is clear moonlight; the stars are shining brightly; above us tower the Himalayas. Who knows what lies beyond these snows? Who can tell what the crowd who sit afar, with their cloaks thrown around their heads, are thinking of, as they gaze at the white-faced strangers laughing and chatting so merrily in front of the camp-fire?

On 19th February the shooting party set off for the border of Nepal where they were to be met by Sir Jung Bahadur, the Nepalese ruler, their host for the next two weeks. Russell had last seen him during the Mutiny when he had brought a troop of his Gurkhas to assist the British. Russell gives a remarkable description of the baggage train as it moved from one camp to another.

There were strings of camels... There were men carrying all the quaintnesses of an Indian camp, boxes, labelled 'Agra Ice Company', dependent from the ends of bamboos; men with hooded falcons; men with greyhounds; old women on ponies; young women wearing breeches; men with no clothes on their legs and voluminous folds of calico on their heads; Sepoys guarding camels or elephants, or nothing but themselves; wallahs, with boarspears; soda-water bottles ...cases with wine bottles, glistening in the sun, bearing the honoured names—'Lafitte,' 'Chateau Margaux,' and the like on their mendacious sides. Then a flock of goats and sheep, our milk and mutton. Thereafter, on an elephant, a red iron pillar, labelled 'Post Office', and animated creatures of the same department on his back.

'The Prince's first Tiger', which he shot in the Indian jungle. The Prince is seated on the wall with a gun. Russell, looking rather dishevelled, is to his right.

The following day, having met up with Sir Jung, the whole vast column crossed into Nepal. Success was immediate; the Prince shot six tigers on the first day, one of them a known man-eater. But there were rumours that the tigers were not quite 'game' and had been too easy to kill. Sir Jung, however, had organised a very different sport to stimulate the company, that of hunting wild elephants with domesticated ones. The leader of the wild herd was challenged and fought by a hand-picked domesticated elephant of great strength and ferocity. Sir Jung had two such on hand, Jung Pershaud and Bijli Pershaud.

Russell's account of 25th February opens with the words: 'Today there was such a hunt as it comes rarely in any man's lifetime to see or enjoy.' He continues: 'A herd of wild elephants, led by a tusker of enormous size, strength, and courage, who had engaged and beaten Sir Jung's best, was discovered in the forest some seven miles from camp. Sir Jung vowed they should be his.' The expedition set off on horseback, led by Sir Jung wearing a quaint jockey cap with gold-laced peak and a suit of hemp of English make. Scouts reported that the wild tusker had his herd in a narrow gorge up which the pursuing elephants and their mahouts were advancing. The royal party dismounted and waited with baited breath.

> Every eye was turned towards the glen. The stalls and boxes were filled, the theatre was ready, but the actors did not appear. Sir Jung became impatient, jumped on the back of one of the Nepalese, and with two men at the side of his 'mount', to steady him, was borne down the rocks, over the river-bed, and up the hill on the opposite side by his roadster, at a wonderful pace—certainly six miles an hour. He was lost to sight ere one could finish a comfortable laugh. In a quarter of an hour he appeared, urging his bounding biped on his mad career.

The wild tusker was making for a pass in which they had halted earlier.

> All that remained for it was to ride with all speed to the place we had left. The harder Sir Jung rode the better spirits every one was in and the better the horses went. How it was no one came to grief is not to be understood. The old halting place—a moraine—was reached, and all dismounted. Scouts were sent out, and it was proposed that lunch should be eaten. But, lo! Sir Jung interrupted the hasty meal. 'We are dead men if the elephants break down upon us. We must all get into trees...' The Prince, who laughed at the idea of a tree at first, was persuaded to yield.

The whole suite shinned up a fine banyan tree, perching precariously in its spreading branches. The elephants did not come and Sir Jung's face was a 'picture to see, and if looks could kill, the fugitive was a dead elephant'. The party dropped out of the tree and on to the horses and tore through the undergrowth until, on reaching the verge of the forest, their prey was seen in the tall grass:

> ...a huge brown back, borne along on invisible legs, reminding one very much of a half-submerged whale cleaving its way in a placid sea. The cheer that burst forth—a joyous English hunting 'Tally-ho!' 'Hark-forward!'—was such as was never heard before, and will probably never be heard again, in Nepalese jungle.

They pursued him until he turned at bay out in the open, exhausted but undefeated:

> ...suddenly uttering a shrill cry, he made a run at the horsemen who were circling before him. There was something so ludicrous in the gait and attitude of the charging elephant that every one, as he bent down on his saddle and rode literally for his life, burst out laughing—all except Sir Jung, who, with one eye over his shoulder, kept calling out, 'Look out, Prince! Take care, Prince!'

The next charge was directed at the Prince,

> ...who was shaking with laughter as he put his horse—a splendid Arab—to his top

speed. Fast as he went, the terrible proboscis was not many yards behind him for a second or two; but the pace was too great to last. The horses evidently had the pull in this ground and there was nothing to fear but a fall or stumble, and then —well—'nothing can save you!' Over and over again the bold attack and precipitate flight were repeated.

Eventually, the brave beast turned and made for a swamp. 'Nearer and nearer loomed the tall rushes, the waving reeds, the long feathery grass of the swamp. "He will escape, by Jove! Can nothing be done? Where are those wretched elephants?" This last remark referred to Sir Jung's tame fighting elephants. After a delay of nearly an hour, during which time the fugitive elephant (which Russell had aptly nicknamed Miserrimus) refreshed itself in the swampy water, Jung Pershaud arrived. He wasted no time but attacked Miserrimus, ramming him hard until his foe decided that retreat to the nearest patch of forest was the wisest course—with everyone hot on his heels.

'Horsemen in a forest have no chance of escaping an elephant. Sir Jung's anxiety was intense. "Don't go near him! Keep him in view, that is all!" It was marvellous to see how the elephant, resistless as fate, crashed along, only turning for the larger trees.' Russell, having 'skimmed gracefully along the ground' when his horse jumped a stream, had remounted and was amazed when he saw Sir Jung pull up outside the forest, shake his fist and start pouring a volley of invective on someone inside.

'He is abusing the elephant,' said Captain Grant. 'He is insulting his female relations, and calling him every name in the world!' And there, sure enough, standing against a tree, was Miserrimus listening intently to Sir Jung, as if he were taking notes for an action of defamation. There were only the four of us. Whether he thought we could finish the little lot off-hand, or that his feelings were roused to madness by a remark affecting the reputation of his deceased mother, I cannot say; but without sound or note of warning, like a house undermined by a flood, he plunged into the stream, and was at us in a moment. At this supreme moment Bigli Pershaud emerged from the covert a few yards away. Not so large as Jung Pershaud, but comparatively fresh, and of great courage. Miserrimus saw his new antagonist. He halted...set his fore legs a little apart, lowered his head and prepared for battle... Bigli came on at full speed, and the two met with what ought to have been concussion of brains and smashes of frontal bones. It was a terrific encounter.

This ramming continued until, finally,

...poor Miserrimus said, as plainly as elephant could say it, 'I give in!' There must be some elephant language as plain as any spoken words. He dropped his proboscis, as a vanquished knight lowers his sword-point, blew a feeble tootle of a trumpet, full of despondency—a cry for mercy—and stood screening his shame with his huge ears. Bigli accepted the surrender on the instant. He approached in a fondling sort of way, wound his proboscis round the captive's neck, and, I daresay, complimented him on his very handsome resistance.

It was not until the gallant animal had been made fast with ropes that it was discovered that he was totally blind in one eye. It was decided, with the approval of the Prince, to release him the next day. In Russell's words: 'So ended the elephant hunt, which was perhaps the "best day" in India.'

After this crescendo of activity, the remaining few days in the Terai passed routinely enough in general slaughter, although one tiger had the temerity to attack the Prince's elephant and was shot only in the nick of time. On 6th March the royal party left for Bombay, the *Serapis* and England:

'The Prince has travelled nearly 7,600 miles by land and 2,300 miles by sea, knows more Chiefs than all the Viceroys and Governors together, and has seen more of the country in the time than any living man.

The Zulu War

On Russell's memorial in the crypt of St Paul's Cathedral are listed the four major conflicts on which he reported, together with the Zulu War of 1879. In this case, however, he did not arrive in South Africa until the war was all but over and his task was not to report the day-to-day events, but to carry out his 'old-world sort of correspondence with reminiscences and a general view of affairs'—the words of the proprietor of the *Daily Telegraph* who had accepted Russell's offer to represent the paper after *The Times*, with correspondents already in the field, had declined it.

Until 1877, South Africa had been divided into four main areas: two British colonies (Cape Colony and Natal) and two Boer republics (the Orange Free State and the Transvaal). There was constant trouble on the border between the Transvaal and Zululand —which was part of Natal—and it was feared that the warlike Zulus, led by the warrior-king Cetewayo, would get out of hand. The Boers sought help from the British and in 1877 the British government annexed the Transvaal—a further step towards its ultimate aim of confederating South Africa.

The British High Commissioner, Sir Bartle Frere, was determined to settle the border problem between the Boers and the Zulus, by force if necessary; on his own initiative and after issuing an impossible ultimatum to Cetewayo, who did not reply, he ordered Lord Chelmsford to march into Zululand. The Zulus responded by carrying out a surprise attack on part of Lord Chelmsford's army at Isandhlwana: they killed and disembowelled over 1,500 soldiers and left the camp a smoking ruin. The stupefaction with which news of this disaster was received in England was only slightly alleviated by further news of the gallant defence of Rorke's Drift by a mere 110 men.

All this had taken place before Russell even left England on 30th May. He travelled out on the same ship as Sir Garnet Wolseley who was being sent by the British Government to take over command from Lord Chelmsford after the debacle of Isandhlwana. Russell passed his time on the voyage reading up on the government's policy in South

A panorama of Rorke's Drift with the rock of Isandhlwana clearly visible in the distance. The tiny mission post was defended by 110 men against repeated onslaughts by 4,000 Zulus.

A historic picture of the survivors of the famous company of the 24th
Regiment who defended Rorke's Drift. Eleven of them were awarded
the Victoria Cross.

Africa, and found himself at odds with much of it. An angry entry in his diary reads:

> The wonderful way in which Sir Bartle Frere is involved in the shedding of blood
> and cattle lifting excites my admiration. I observe we always punish others for our
> own faults... We are for ever talking of the peace and order which prevail under a
> Government which is for ever at war somewhere or other.

While Russell was still at sea another incident had taken place, which caused a considerable sensation abroad and some embarrassment to the British government. Napoleon III's son, the Prince Imperial, who had fled to England with his mother in 1870 and joined the Royal Artillery, was caught in the open while on a sketching trip with fellow officers and speared to death by Zulu tribesmen. In his old age Russell was to meet and become friends with the Prince's mother, the ex-Empress Eugénie, and visited her at her house in Hampshire.

On 28th June, Russell arrived in Durban, then travelled inland to Pietermaritzburg. Sir Garnet was furious as he had received no communication from Lord Chelmsford as to what he and the army were up to. Russell notes in his diary: 'Wolseley says it depends on Chelmsford's explanation whether he will put him under arrest for disobedience or not.'

Lord Chelmsford, however, now had the bit between his teeth and was bent on destroying Cetewayo and his warriors once and for all, thereby restoring British supremacy and repairing some of the damage done to his own career at Isandhlwana. In July he achieved both aims: a force of 3,000 men won a classic victory on the plain before Ulundi, Cetewayo's capital, although the king himself escaped.

With the war virtually over, Sir Garnet's tasks were to establish order and to capture Cetewayo. He set off up country, leaving behind a disconsolate Russell, whose lame leg was playing up. 'I ought to go to the war in an ambulance' he lamented. The army doctor he consulted turned out to be none other than Dr Ross from Simla, who had treated the same leg 21 years before.

While still unfit for the arduous journey north, Russell was just well enough to travel about within Natal, using his eyes and ears as he did so. He was amused to find a Kaffir woman gaoled for infidelity and remarked in his diary: 'How full our prisons would be chez nous!'

Among the many people that he met, he was particularly impressed by John Colenso, the Bishop of Natal. Colenso was a fluent Zulu speaker and had become the principal spokesman for the Zulu people, mediating on their behalf both with the Boers and the British. He and Russell found they had many views in common and the following comment in Russell's diary leaves no doubt about his regard for the man: 'What a grand nature in a noble presence. I believe a more straight, direct, truth-loving, justice-worshipping man never walked this earth or any other.'

Russell did not find himself nearly so in tune with the practitioners of his own government's policy. In a letter to the Duke of Cambridge, Commander-in-Chief of the British army, he was very outspoken: 'Sir Bartle has caused more man and woman killing and blood shedding in a few months if he be responsible for this war than Cetewayo did in all his reign, and the murders of the wounded prisoners are too horrible to think of. I'm glad I didn't see what I hear of for my pen would not have been stayed no matter what the result.' One can be sure that he would have been as good as his word: Russell was never afraid of expressing his views and was particularly courageous when defending the underdog.

By the beginning of August, Russell was able to undertake the trip north to join Wolseley and the army, and set off in a wagon with Dr Ross. On the way he received a letter from Wolseley which, from a man who had the reputation of despising journalists, was remarkably friendly: 'Our camp is dull without you, and the sooner you join it the better I shall be pleased. I am extremely sorry to hear from Brackenbury that you are still laid up with your leg, and as your health is of the first consequence I think you did wisely in not trusting yourself in a country where there are no roads.' He went on to say that the Zulus were slowly surrendering their arms.

Wolseley had come to respect Russell during the Crimean War, and the two men were to maintain a mutual affection and trust for one another in spite of a major disagreement in the months to come. The cause of this dissension was Russell's criticism of the conduct of the British soldiers in South Africa. A letter to Lawson of the *Daily Telegraph* illustrates his concern:

As to this Army, no words can express the shame which would fall upon us if we were to be engaged with any foreign army in serious warfare with such battalions. It would need years of careful weeding and training to make them fit for campaigning. The disorders on the line of march—whenever there are grog shops or canteens or any places to be broken into—are scandalous, and this place has been the scene of disgraceful orgies, which the officers seem to be unable to prevent and afraid to punish... I have, *entre nous*, some doubts of Wolseley's present settlement being permanent, but sufficient unto the day is the evil thereof. I am still less hopeful of any great results being achieved in the way of a South African Empire, or Dominion, or Confederation—'Empress of India and South Africa,' etc., etc. Niggerdom is too potent for us and we can't make it work for us.

Russell's pessimism was once again justified. By January 1881 the Boers were fighting the British from whom they had sought protection only eighteen months previously.

In September, Russell finally joined Sir Garnet and the army on the march. He wrote his daughter an amusing description of his new servant, Hughes:

He is a wonderful young man; he loses everything I have, and he is quite ignorant of his work, and yet I am glad to have him and pay a great price for his assistance. His first work was to take charge of my horse from Durban to Fort Pearson... He told me he could ride, and so off he set. When I joined the column a week later Hughes came to me all the colours of the rainbow from falls, and Biggs told me that every half-hour there was a cloud of dust on the road and he heard 'Dr Russell's servant off again!' Then he got fever and lost his memory—and so I lost my

Left: Ape caricature of John Colenso, the Bishop of Natal. *Right:* General Sir Garnet Wolseley, sent by the British Government to take over command of the army from Lord Chelmsford.

things. I have little left now, not being able to look after anything in my recent condition.

There seems to have been very little else which amused Russell at this time. He was obviously finding the long marches very tiring in his debilitated condition. The food was poor, and his three score years were beginning to tell. His state of mind was not improved by the news that the British Resident at Kabul had been murdered by Afghans.

What a dreadful blow to the Government! I fear it will be followed by worse. Well! If we will go empiring it all over the world we must expect such startling news and deeds. And we are talking of a Burmese War and a Maori War! Queen Victoria's reign has been an incessant record of bloodshed.

He wrote again to Lawson with further criticisms of the conduct of the army, and these were published in the *Daily Telegraph* on 21st November. He claimed that the British troops, while in the town of Heidelberg, stole chickens, ransacked houses, broke into stores and even took the church clock, and went on to accuse those in command:

For my own part, I think the military authorities have been culpably remiss and negligent in the discharge of their bounden obligation to maintain discipline and to protect the property and secure the peace of well-disposed loyal citizens. What the reasons or motives for their indifference may be I do not pretend to surmise, but I am sure they are pursuing a course which must lead to most serious consequences if they gloss over or pretend to ignore the excesses which in Natal and the Transvaal are covering the army with odium and disgrace.

This letter in the *Daily Telegraph* stung the Duke of Cambridge into writing to Wolseley requesting verification, or otherwise, of the charges. Wolseley denied them completely. Russell repeated the accusations in a letter to his editor, giving details of other towns in which the soldiers had run amok. He went on to say:

> I hold the very strongest notion that the annexation of the Transvaal was an in-curable and criminal blunder and that the course now pursued by my friend Sir Garnet is in direct opposition to the principles of liberty, justice, and sound policy.

Russell and Wolseley pursued their disagreement by letter long after Russell had returned to England. The letters were always courteous and friendly as in Wolseley's last word on the subject in June 1880:

> Your letter of the 9th inst. has at last found me here. Many thanks for it. 'Let the dead bury their dead.' Why should we two continue a paper warfare? Both have only one object, namely, the good of the State. Both being human are liable to error, and are influenced by passions at times in a manner which we regret after-wards. You stung me—I am sure most unintentionally—in the most susceptible point, and I endeavoured to hit out straight in return. There are many things connected with South Africa I shall endeavour to forget, and amongst them is the circumstance that you and I had ever had any difference of opinion regarding the soldiers there.

It will be remembered that Russell had made similar charges of misconduct by British troops at Kertch in 1855 during the Crimean War. He was deeply attached to the British army and it distressed him to see its soldiers behaving badly. In South Africa it is possible that, in poor health and lacking the energy to check his sources, he relied too much on the not unbiased accounts of his informants.

During Russell's time in South Africa he suffered yet another serious riding accident. Returning from the successful conclusion of the campaign against the Basuto chief Sekukini, he was riding ahead of the column. An interview he gave to the *Strand Magazine* in 1892 tells the story of what followed:

> I rode six miles from the camp over a sprint, reaching a road which led down a steep hill to a ford. The threatening sky told me to look out for a Cape storm. They rush down upon you with scarcely a warning. I knew the river at the bottom of the road would swell rapidly, so I urged my horse forward down the hill. I got into the middle of the ford just as the storm burst on us in all its fury. A flash of lightning struck the water, my horse reared violently, lost his footing, threw me over his shoulder, and I fell under him. My right leg was caught by the stirrup: my left leg was under the horse's shoulder; his neck lay over my chest, preventing me from rising. There was I on my back, with my head just up, supporting myself with my right hand on the bottom of the river, and with my left jogging the reins to make the poor beast rise—the water slowly rising with the pouring torrents—I was drowning. I could feel the water getting higher and higher—it reached my neck, my chin—when, with almost a dying effort, as my horse struggled up a little, I made an attempt to move my leg, but down he went again. However, the strap of my spur gave way—my right leg was liberated—I was able to raise myself on it and to pull at the horse's head. My horse got up; I managed to lean on him, and he just carried me to the bank. I tried to get on his back, and down he went again, so with my leg doubled under me I put one hand on his shoulder, and so I crawled on to the house of an old Scotch farmer named Gray. He put me into bed, and rubbed me with 'Cape smoke,' and I found that I had not only lost my helmet, note-books and despatches, but that my leg was useless, with a chance of being lame for the remainder of my days.
>
> In the morning the headquarters staff rode across the ford, amongst them Lord Wolseley. He called at the farm: Gray told him of my plight and he came to my

The capture of Cetewayo, who had escaped after the Battle of Ulundi.
He is shown here being brought into Sir Garnet Wolseley's camp.

side. 'I thought my last day had come, and that my body would never be found,' I
said to him.

'My dear fellow,' was his characteristic reply, 'I would never have left the
country until I had found you, and I would have given you a jolly good burial!'

His diary has the terse words: 'Lamed for life' which proved to be true. There was now
no alternative but to return to England. He left Pretoria on 23rd December and after
an appalling journey in the sweltering heat, savaged by mosquitoes and in constant
pain, he arrived at Cape Town on 6th January.

He stayed with Sir Bartle Frere and had this to say of 'the dear old codger': 'He has
as much real nobility of governing about him as any one I ever met but he is also
bigoted in his belief that he can do no wrong, very angry with Gladstone and not well
with Wolseley.'

As if matters had not gone badly enough for Russell during his time in South Africa,
he received the news, while still in Cape Town, that Delane had died. This was a body
blow. He wrote a miserable letter to Delane's sister:

The pain I feel now is incurable... I have been very near meeting the oldest, most
valued, kindest and best of friends in the land to which he has gone, and I feel
that we shall not be long separated. It is now more than thirty years since he
began the friendship which on his side was marked by the greatest kindness, and
on my side, I know, by affection and gratitude, and now I feel the last link in the
chain which bound me with and to the past is gone. I can write no more.

The Zulu War was Russell's last campaign, although he only narrowly missed the battle
of Tel-el-Kebir in Egypt in 1882. He was in Alexandria at the time, but was unable to
obtain permission to accompany the army—once again under the command of Wolseley.
'What a sight to have beheld, our army moving out this night to bivouac in the desert.
Alas! Why was I not with them? This is my last chance perhaps. My very last.'

In 1883 he fell in love with an Italian countess, Antoinette Malvezzi, almost half his
age: he married her three months later. It was to prove a perfect match. He spent his
last years growing fat and contented, with a wife who took the greatest care of him and
gave him the affection he had always craved. She also managed to bring some order out
of the chaos of his finances. They travelled a good deal, making several trips to Chile
and Egypt.

In 1895 Russell received the news that he was to be knighted. 'Not before time' was
the opinion of many of his friends. It was felt that this clear recognition of his services
to his country was long overdue. He continued to run the *Army and Navy Gazette* until
1903 when he was over eighty years old.

Sir 'Billy' Russell in old age.

Sir 'Billy' Russell died on 10th February 1907, at the age of eighty-seven. *The Times* devoted two and a half columns to his obituary saying, among other things:

To all who knew him he was the cheeriest, brightest, most likeable of companions... All newspaper work is of its nature ephemeral. Mr Russell, however, could have said truly that he had accomplished a feat unparalleled in the annals of journalism, that he had written newspaper articles which would be remembered as long as Englishmen interest themselves in the records of English valour, English heroism, English disasters and English victories.

A line from the obituary in the *Manchester Guardian* makes a fitting epitaph: 'He was an entirely honourable and patriotic journalist.'

Bibliography

Atkins, John Black *The Life of Sir William Howard Russell* John Murray, 1911

Bentley, Nicholas *Russell's Despatches from the Crimea, 1854-56* Andre Deutsch, 1966

Blake, R.L.V. Ffrench *The Crimean War* Leo Cooper, 1971

Churchill, Winston Spencer *A History of the English-Speaking Peoples* Cassell, 1956

Clifford, Henry *Letters and Sketches from the Crimea* Michael Joseph, 1956

Compton, Piers *Colonel's Lady and Camp-Follower* Robert Hale, 1970

Cook, Sir Edward *Delane of the Times* Constable, 1915

Dasent, Arthur Irwin *John Thaddeus Delane* John Murray, 1908

Furneaux, Rupert *The First War Correspondent* Cassell, 1944

Furneaux, Rupert *News of War* Max Parrish, 1964

Gernsheim, Helmut and Alison *Roger Fenton: Photographer of the Crimean War* Secker & Warburg, 1954

Grey, Elizabeth *The Noise of Drums & Trumpets* Longman, 1971

Hankinson, Alan *Man of Wars* Heinemann, 1982

Harris, John *The Indian Mutiny* Granada Publishing, 1973

Hibbert, Christopher *The Destruction of Lord Raglan* Longman, 1961

Hibbert, Christopher *Edward VII* Allen Lane, 1978

Hibbert, Christopher *The Great Mutiny* Allen Lane, 1978

The History of the Times Volumes 1 & 2. The Office of The Times, 1935 and 1939.

Horne, Alistair *The Fall of Paris* Macmillan, 1965

James, Lawrence *Crimea 1854-56: the war with Russian from contemporary photographs* Hayes Kennedy, 1981

Johnson, Curt and McLaughlin, Mark *Battles of the American Civil War* Roxby Press, 1977

Kinglake, A.W. *The Invasion of the Crimea* William Blackwood, 1863-87

Knightley, Philip *The First Casualty* Quartet, 1978

Mason, Philip *A Matter of Honour* Jonathan Cape, 1974

Morris, James *Heaven's Command: An Imperial Progress* Faber & Faber, 1973

Palmer, Alan W. *Bismarck* Weidenfeld & Nicolson, 1976

Russell, William Howard *The British Expedition to the Crimea* G. Routledge, 1858

Russell, William Howard *My Diary in India* Routledge, Warne & Routledge, 1860

Russell, William Howard *My Diary North and South* Bradbury & Evans, 1863

Russell, William Howard *A Diary in the East During the Tour of the Prince and Princess of Wales* Routledge, 1869

Russell, William Howard *My Diary During the Last Great War* Routledge, 1874

Russell, William Howard *The Great War with Russia* Routledge, 1895

Russell, William Howard *The Prince of Wales' Tour* Sampson Low, Marston, Searle & Rivington, 1882

Taylor, A.J.P. *How Wars Begin* Hamish Hamilton, 1979

Wilkinson-Latham, Robert *From Our Special Correspondent* Hodder & Stoughton, 1979

Woodham-Smith, Cecil *The Reason Why* Constable, 1953

Woodham-Smith, Cecil *Florence Nightingale* Fontana, 1964

Woodham-Smith, Cecil *Queen Victoria* Hamish Hamilton, 1972

Index